It's Your Hour

A Guide to Queer-Affirmative Psychotherapy

By Michael Bettinger, Ph.D., MFT

alyson books
los angeles | new york

MANUFACTURED IN THE UNITED STATES OF AMERICA.

THIS TRADE PAPERBACK ORIGINAL IS PUBLISHED BY ALYSON PUBLICATIONS,
P.O. BOX 4371, LOS ANGELES, CALIFORNIA 90078-4371.
DISTRIBUTION IN THE UNITED KINGDOM BY
TURNAROUND PUBLISHER SERVICES LTD.,
UNIT 3, OLYMPIA TRADING ESTATE, COBURG ROAD, WOOD GREEN,
LONDON N22 6TZ ENGLAND.

FIRST EDITION: AUGUST 2001

01 02 03 04 05 a 10 9 8 7 6 5 4 3 2 1

ISBN 1-55583-534-1

LIBRARY OF CONGRESS CATALOGING-IN-PUBLICATION DATA
  BETTINGER, MICHAEL.
    IT'S YOUR HOUR : A GUIDE TO QUEER-AFFIRMATIVE PSYCHOTHERAPY /
  BY MICHAEL BETTINGER—1ST ED.
    ISBN 1-55583-534-1
    1. GAYS—MENTAL HEALTH. 2. BISEXUALS—MENTAL HEALTH.
  3. PSYCHOTHERAPY. 4. GAYS—COUNSELING OF. 5. BISEXUALS—COUNSELING OF.
  6. TRANSSEXUALS—COUNSELING OF. I. TITLE.
  RC451.4.G39 B48 2001
  616.89'14'08664—DC21   2001022574

COVER DESIGN BY MATT SAMS.

For Bob

Contents

Appendices

Resources

Acknowledgments

My process in the actual writing of this book was mostly a solitary one. With the exceptions noted below, I wrote this book without discussing its content with colleagues or friends. This book is a product of my 30 years of work as a psychotherapist. But I would not be the psychotherapist I am today without the help of numerous people, some of whom I wish to acknowledge here.

First, I would like to thank all my clients, past and present, for having taught me the true meaning of queer-affirmative psychotherapy and for making this book possible.

Most psychotherapists have a clinical consultant, usually a more experienced psychotherapist with whom they discuss cases and get perspective. Psychotherapists learn from and are shaped by their consultants. During the past 20 years, I have had two clinical consultants who have had a profound effect on shaping who I am. One is Eva Wald Leveton, MS, with whom I consulted for most of the 1980s. The other is Alan Leveton, MD, with whom I have consulted from 1989 to the present. I want to acknowledge their help and support through the years. The values I learned from them are reflected throughout this book.

In addition to my consultants, I would like to acknowledge all those individuals who were my personal psychotherapist at one time or another. They too have helped me to be able to write this book. I would especially like to mention Marilyn Geist, MA, my present individual psychotherapist. She has listened attentively and nonjudgmentally and has thoughtfully responded when I have talked about the various parts of my life, including the writing of this book. She has provided me a place where I can be totally open and integrated. And that is important to me.

There are two colleagues who read portions of this manuscript and gave valuable feedback. One is Orren Z. Perlman, MD, who helped with the chapter on psychopharmacology. The other is

Marcia Perlstein, MA, who read the manuscript and gave me both feedback and support. She provided many of the stories about lesbians in therapy.

I would also like to acknowledge the help of my editor at Alyson, Scott Brassart, for his help in organizing the book and for his editing. I am a better writer today because of what I have learned from him.

The biggest thank-you of all is for my life partner, Bob Goldstein. For the past 15 years, he has been the steadiest force in my life. He consistently gave me an anchor when I felt overwhelmed by this project. He has put up with all my moods, which can vary considerably.

I wish to acknowledge these people and say thank you.

Preface

Sixteen years ago, when *The Lavender Couch: A Consumer's Guide to Psychotherapy for Lesbians and Gay Men* was published, I was chagrined. Marny Hall had written the book I wanted to write. It was now done. I would have to think about another book.

Many years later, in February 1998, I was asked to write a chapter on mental health and finding a therapist for a book to be published by the Gay Men's Health Crisis of New York City. In the course of writing that chapter, I interviewed Marny Hall. As a result of that interview and the discussions that followed, I was asked to write an updated version of *The Lavender Couch*. I leapt at the opportunity.

I am a passionate person. I am passionate about being a gay man and passionate about my profession, psychotherapy. I believe in both. I also believe in truth. I believe truth is both freedom and power. I am also aware that many people believe things that are not true, either about homosexuality or about psychotherapy. My passion drives me to do things that correct these misconceptions. Writing this book is a part of that mission.

There was a time when I myself believed many things that are not true about both gayness and psychotherapy. For instance, I believed homosexuality was a mental illness. In the 1950s, I was a precocious youngster. I went to the library and looked up homosexuality. And all the material I found said it was a mental illness, a sin, or a crime. There was nothing even remotely positive about homosexuality in the books I read.

I also believed that psychotherapy, or "going to a psychiatrist," was shameful, something to be kept secret and not discussed. "Mental illness" was a failure. When my older brother, as an adolescent, was depressed and had suicidal thoughts, he was sent to a psychiatrist. I was told by my mother to keep this a secret, to not discuss it with anyone, inside or outside our family.

Thus, it was quite difficult for me to admit to myself as a young adult that I was a gay man, that I was terribly unhappy, and that I needed professional help to find my way out of unhappiness. For several years, I dealt with my homosexual feelings alone. I wanted to talk about them but could not. There was no friend or family member I could safely approach. And I knew from my older brother's experience that to admit I needed psychiatric help would brand me as an emotional failure.

Finally, it became too much. My life was on hold and I was going nowhere. I gathered the courage to ask my older brother (who by this time was a physician doing his internship) for the name of a psychiatrist who might help me. He did not ask why I wanted to see a psychiatrist, nor did I volunteer any information. He gave me the name of a mental health clinic where one of his friends had been seeing a psychotherapist. I was relieved that he did not ask me for more information.

I called and made an appointment. I did not know what, if anything, to ask. I had hoped to see a male clinician for reasons I could not at the time understand. And when I was assigned to a female clinician, I did not say anything. I did not know anything about her as a person or as a psychotherapist. I did not know that different psychotherapists practice differently. I did not know that most psychotherapists were not psychiatrists. I had no understanding of the process of psychotherapy or the wide range of choices I could have made. I simply accepted what was offered.

I told her why I was seeking help, and she said that I should see her two times each week, letting me know what the fee would be. I accepted her recommendations, no questions asked. At the second session, she asked me to lie on the couch and talk to her without being able to see her. I went along because I did not know any better.

In the third session, I tried to say the word *homosexual* for the first time. The word would not come out. Three times I opened my mouth to say the word, and three times I could not. On the fourth attempt, I succeeded. And from there I began to discuss my interest in members of my own sex.

In writing this book, I hope to make it easier for others to travel the path I walked so long ago.

When I began writing, I quickly realized that updating *The Lavender Couch* meant writing a new book. Much has changed in psychotherapy since the early 1980s. The field has evolved and is continuing to evolve. Also evolving are the methods of paying for psychotherapy. This has a huge impact on the therapy process, especially in regard to the issue of confidentiality. And, I wanted to talk about psychotherapy as I see it.

The community has also changed. When *The Lavender Couch* was written, it was appropriate to refer to the community as the gay community or the lesbian and gay community. Today, such descriptions are inadequate. As I will discuss later, I have chosen to use the word *queer* instead of *gay* or some other combination of words.

Similarly, lavender is no longer the color associated with the community; the rainbow is. And very few psychotherapists have client lie on couches anymore. So *The Lavender Couch* is no longer an appropriate title for this book. Since much of this book is about enabling you as the consumer of mental health services, *It's Your Hour: A Guide to Queer-Affirmative Psychotherapy* is a more appropriate title for the 21st-century version of this book.

That said, I hope this book helps you in some way.

Part One
The What and Why of Psychotherapy?

CHAPTER 1
PSYCHOTHERAPY AND BEING QUEER

At the beginning of the 21st century, psychotherapy remains a controversial subject. It is warmly regarded or even passionately embraced by those who see it as a legitimate tool for helping people with severe emotional problems and for helping people in general lead happier lives. Others reject psychotherapy, claiming it does not work, and that there is no scientific evidence that it does any good. They say it is a waste of time, money, and effort, and its practitioners are either naive do-gooders or scam artists interested in either in controlling the client or separating the client from his or her money. Still others fear that psychotherapy is a form of brainwashing.

A great number of people know very little about psychotherapy. They either do not care about it, or they never think about how it might help them. They do not know what happens in psychotherapy, and consequently, the entire concept is foreign to them.

I am a psychotherapist, so as you might expect, I am a proponent of psychotherapy and its many benefits. I have written this book to assist people who are queer, as I am, and who wish to know more about psychotherapy. In the course of this book, I hope to begin or to broaden your understanding of what psychotherapy is and how it operates, so you can use it to your advantage.

Psychotherapy is a tool you can use to live a happier life.

It is one of many tools, and it may or may not be a good tool for you. If it is, it makes sense to keep it handy in your toolbox. You might not always need to use it, but the tool will be there when you do.

The ultimate goal of psychotherapy, happiness, can mean different things to different people. Almost everyone knows what they feel like when they are happy, and no two people need the same things to achieve happiness. There are, however, some common aspects of happiness that can be addressed in psychotherapy. Among those elements is a feeling of mastery and control of one's life. If you feel empowered, able to see and create options and to shed toxic relationships, happiness often follows. Psychotherapy can help you become so empowered.

Psychotherapy is a conversation, or series of conversations, between two or more people. One or more of those individuals is a psychotherapist, and the other(s) are the client(s) or patient(s).

In the most basic of configurations, that is all there is to psychotherapy: a conversation between two or sometimes more people. Some psychotherapists use items in their work, perhaps toys or art supplies. But most of the time, psychotherapy is two people sitting and talking. Nothing more.

What is special about psychotherapy is that the conversations are almost always focused on an aspect or aspects of the client's life. The conversations relate to the thoughts, feelings, ideas, intuition, behavior, and experiences the client is having, and to the people with whom the client is interacting. These conversations are focused, especially in the beginning of the psychotherapy process. After all, there are specific reasons why a person is coming to the psychotherapist. The psychotherapist and the client have a conversation about those reasons and attempt to figure out how best to proceed. Sometimes the psychotherapist and the client decide to have only that one conversation. Quite often, though, they decide to make further appointments. In a small number of situations, the conversations go on for years. They continue for as long as the client thinks it makes sense to continue.

Psychotherapy can be especially helpful if you happen to be queer. It's not easy being queer, being part of one of the few groups that large parts of our society feel it is acceptable to legally and socially discriminate against. This discrimination has an impact on our happiness. Thus, as a group, we have unique issues with which to deal. Every other identifiable group can make the same statement, but the impact of being queer is different from that of gender, race, ethnicity, or other groupings. Good psychotherapy can help a queer person deal with this unique impact.

This is especially important because until about 30 years ago, it was downright dangerous for a queer person to go to a psychotherapist. Many queer people were harmed by the "treatment" they received from psychotherapists. The mental health profession and many of its practitioners were clueless about what it meant to be queer, and made unhappy queer people unhappier. But queer activists worked hard to educate mental health professionals, and the situation today is almost completely reversed. Yet intense homophobia still exists among some mental health professionals. With knowledge and caution, the dangers posed by these psychotherapists can be avoided, and the potential rewards can be greatly increased. So, while it is generally safe and helpful to use the services of psychotherapists, dangerous practitioners do still exist. If you follow the information in this book, you will be able to tell the difference between psychotherapists who can help you, and those who will cause you problems, particularly if you happen to be queer.

Perhaps your biggest question, as you read this book, is whether you should involve yourself in psychotherapy at all. Unfortunately, there are relatively few situations in which it is clear that you should or should not be in psychotherapy. The answer depends on what you want.

If you decide to investigate psychotherapy, the next question to ask is what form of psychotherapy will be most helpful to you. While all forms of psychotherapy are essentially conversations between the two or more people, what is talked about will be quite different depending on the psychotherapist with whom you are talking. The more you understand about yourself, who you are, and what you need, the easier it is to figure out what kind of psychotherapist you should see.

Then comes the question of how best to negotiate the world of psychotherapy. This book will help you navigate the psychotherapy maze. And it is well that you should have a guide. The psycho-therapy sector of the mental health industry is complicated and specialized.

I must also warn you, psychotherapy is vastly overhyped. Claims are made that are either not true or cleverly worded dis-tortions. There are people who, for their own reasons, intention-ally oversell psychotherapy, making claims that cannot be justi-fied. There are also psychotherapists who make claims based on their own ignorance of what is possible. The truth of the matter is that psychotherapy can be a helpful tool, but it is not a miracle drug that will instantly cure you of whatever ails you.

Furthermore, psychotherapy is not what most people expect. It does not do for most people what they hope for or imagine it can do before they begin. It does not perform miracles. It does not change someone into a different person. It does not change a per-son's basic personality. It does, however, have an impact on how a person lives his or her life, and thus it often helps that person to live a happier life. If you live to be 100 years old, and if you involve yourself in psychotherapy for parts of your life, you will probably be able to say that you were the same person before and after psychotherapy, but you were able to lead a happier life after psychotherapy.

The Book and the Author

The first goal of this book is to give you an understanding of what psychotherapy is and the diverse perspectives that exist within the field in order to help you to choose a psychotherapist whose perspective is best suited to you and your needs. There are at least 450 recognized approaches to psychotherapy. Many approaches are similar, differing only in minor details. But others are radically different. After reading this book, along with some understanding of your own nature, you should be able to find a psychotherapist well- suited to your needs.

The second goal is to help you to understand how the field of psychotherapy operates—the nuts and bolts, so to speak. The book addresses many practical questions that might arise, such as the ins and outs of using medical insurance to pay for psychotherapy.

Because there are so many different approaches to psychotherapy, I feel it is helpful to explain who I am and what my biases are. I am a queer man and have been a psychotherapist for over 30 years. I was born in 1945 and became a psychotherapist in 1971, just after the modern gay rights movement began. A year later, I joined one of the early gay rights organizations, the Gay Activists Alliance in New York City, not only to fight for gay rights but also because that organization suited my generally rambunctious nature. Through my activities in the GAA, I actively challenged the cultural and political system that oppressed queer people, as well as the outdated ideas and oppressive nature of traditional psychotherapy.

Since 1981, I have maintained a full-time private practice in San Francisco, usually having 20–25 conversations a week with my clients, most of whom are gay or bisexual men. I also meet with a small number of lesbians as well as heterosexual men and women.

When someone asks what is my "theoretical orientation," I say I am an eclectic psychotherapist. This is a concept explained more fully in chapter 6. For now, I will say briefly that it means I do not subscribe fully to any one theoretical orientation of psychotherapy. I am not a Freudian, though I do agree with many of Freud's ideas. I am not a behaviorist, though I do at times use behavioral modification techniques with my clients. I have chosen to learn about many different approaches to psychotherapy, philosophy, and life in general, and to use from each of these approaches ideas or techniques that I believe will help my clients.

In working with my clients, I use a *growth model* as opposed to a *medical model*, concepts that will be more fully explained in chapter 5. Growth model psychotherapists believe each client is our equal. Clients hire us for our time and expertise, not because we are better than or superior to them. Our clients believe we have knowledge and skills we can use in their behalf. Each time a client pays the bill in full, the relationship is even. At that point, our clients do not owe us anything more. If the client wants to continue to see the psychotherapist, and if the psychotherapist agrees, it is only then that the obligations continue.

While I have synthesized concepts and used tools and techniques from almost all the major schools of psychotherapy, I have been most influenced by the humanistic, family systems, and psychodynamic schools of psychotherapy, all of which will be explained more fully in chapter 6. My outlook on the world has been most shaped by humanism and its close cousin, existential philosophy. Very simply put, I am a child of the progressive and liberal school of Western civilization.

How I actually work with my clients is based mostly on family systems and psychodynamic theory. I have at times identified myself as a queer family therapist. In brief, I believe that to make changes in your life, you need to deal with three things: the impact of what has happened to you in the past, the natural impulses and forces inside of you, and the impact that people who are important to you are having on your life. Those three factors make change easy or difficult, depending on your story.

Now that I have attempted to define myself for you, I will undermine myself by saying I am a lot more than a humanistic, family systems, psychodynamic psychotherapist. I am also spiritually based—Western with a heavy dose of Eastern thrown in. Words are woefully inadequate to describe my spiritual approach, but words are all we have. I do not believe there is any one "answer." It is up to each of us to ask our own questions and find a way to exist that makes sense to us as individuals. This is the approach I use when working with clients.

When I am with clients, I have an active conversation. I am definitely not an "uh-huh" psychotherapist who keeps asking the client to say more without offering much feedback or input. I share my thoughts, feelings, and intuitions during the psychotherapy hour. The focus is always on the issue or issues the client brings to the hour, but it is a two-way conversation.

A bit more about myself: My love for learning has led me to many traditional and nontraditional sources. I attempt to take from each what seems relevant or important, and to integrate that material into a coherent view of the world. I have not developed a unique approach to psychotherapy for others to follow. I am not original, creative, or clever enough to do that. I am, however, good at synthesizing. I am intuitive by nature, and I trust my intuition and my feelings. So when someone asks why I accept certain ideas from one school of psychotherapy and not other ideas from that same school, I cannot always explain my reasons. But I know from experience that the ideas I have accepted help me work effectively with my clients.

This approach to psychotherapy requires a tolerance for ambiguity on the part of both the psychotherapist and the client. And it is not the psychotherapy traditionally depicted by Hollywood, where the patient does almost all the talking and the nearly silent psychotherapist occasionally says something of great and profound importance.

Like most psychotherapists, I have found a professional approach to psychotherapy that suits my personality. Throughout this book, you will see my bias toward involvement in long-term noncognitive psychotherapy. (Long-term does not necessarily mean with the same practitioner.) As a client, it behooves you to find a psychotherapist well-suited to working with your unique personality. *There is no one right way for psychotherapy.* There is no approach to psychotherapy that has been proven to be significantly more effective for most people. Everyone is unique and needs to figure out what is right for him or herself.

There is truth and value to almost all the kinds of psychotherapy that exist. All forms of therapy have been shown to work successfully with some people some of the time. The best form of psychotherapy is the one that is most effective for you. And the one that will be most effective for you is the one best suited to your nature and needs as they exist in the present.

In this book, I will tell the stories of many people who have been in psychotherapy. These stories are real. However, a major tenet of psychotherapy is confidentiality. Thus, all identifying information has been changed to ensure anonymity. Since I work with relatively few lesbians, I have relied on colleagues for illustrative stories of lesbian women in psychotherapy. All identifying information about these women has also been changed.

Terminology

The other issue I need to address before proceeding is terminology. There are three terms that require explanation at this time.

The most controversial is my use of the word *queer* to describe people who are lesbian, gay, bisexual, or transgender. Lesbian, gay, bisexual, and transgender are very specific terms, and many people will not self-identify with any of them, or even as queer. Queer, in fact, was once considered derogatory, even though it is now embraced, especially by younger people, as a positive and inclusive term that describes more than what we do in the bedroom. I choose to use queer in a similar fashion as an inclusive term of affection that identifies us as different in many ways, yet distinct as a culture.

Many individuals outside the queer community are fearful of using the term queer, worrying they will be misunderstood. Queer is our word for ourselves, and others tread lightly before using it. This will probably remain true for many years. To those offended by the term queer, I deeply apologize, and I hope my use of the word will not prevent you from otherwise deriving some benefit from this book.

I have also chosen to call a person who seeks mental health services a *client* rather than a *patient*. Modern psychotherapy and mental health services began as part of the medical profession, so the users of these services were originally called patients. But *patient* is not the right term for people in psychotherapy. Patients come to the doctor to be treated and hopefully cured. The doctor is supposed to do something to or for the patient to make him or her well. Patients are passive participants in the process.

Clients, however, are customers, consumers, shoppers. The right term for those involved in psychotherapy is client. Clients are active participants. Clients are people in need of services, and shoppers looking for people to provide those services. (Later in the book, there will be a fuller examination of the relationship between psychotherapy and the medical profession and why major parts of psychotherapy have moved away from the medical profession.)

The third area where terminology needs to be discussed is pronouns. Historically, the pronoun *he* was used and meant to include both men and women. During the 1960s, women began to point out the inequality of this. For people reading this book, there is a further complication. Many people who consider themselves transgender use the pronoun that best describes their psychological, not physical, makeup. So a biological female might use masculine pronouns and a biological male might use feminine pronouns. Most of the time in this book, male and female pronouns will be used together. If one is left out, it is for a specific purpose that should be obvious from the context. In some instances, out of respect for the preference of the person being discussed, this book will use whatever pronoun the individual prefers. Thus, if the story is about a female-to-male transsexual who regularly uses the pronoun *he* as a personal descriptor, *he* is the pronoun that will be used. The most respectful thing a person or psychotherapist can do when talking to or working with a transsexual is to use the pronoun the person prefers to be addressed by.

Chapter 2
What is Psychotherapy?

At the very heart, psychotherapy is a conversation or an ongoing series of conversations between two or more people about issues in the life of the client or clients. For dramatic purposes, psychotherapy has been made mysterious by writers and filmmakers. In these scenarios, the client, while talking to a psychotherapist, comes to a realization—he hates his mother; she was sexually molested by an uncle—and the problems that brought the client to the therapist instantaneously disappear. This may make for good entertainment, but it does not present an accurate picture of what psychotherapy is or how it can help someone.

People go to a psychotherapist because they want to change something in their life, and want help with that change. The psychotherapist has studied human development, feelings, and behaviors, and has been taught to listen carefully and to understand what a client is saying. The psychotherapist works with the client to help the client. Most of this takes place in the office of the psychotherapist, and the client pays for the psychotherapist's time.

The goal of psychotherapy from the perspective of the psychotherapist is widely misunderstood. The psychotherapist's goal is to help the client grow as a person, so when the process is completed (and this can be after one or many meetings), the client is a better functioning person. It is not to "shrink" the client, mentally or in any other way. There is no mysterious process after which the client emerges as a happier person. The goal is not to make the client into someone he or she is not. The goal is to make the client a better version of his or her authentic self.

To better understand what psychotherapy is, I suggest comparing it to music lessons. Music lessons, by the way, are another tool that some people use to build a happy life for themselves. Each week, you pay someone for their time, usually an hour or two. Each week, the two of you focus on either learning something new, or unlearning bad habits you learned long ago. You go back each week because you want to get better at playing music (or at being happy), and it seems to you that music lessons (or psychotherapy) will help you. It seems worth the time, financial cost, and effort you have to put into it between meetings.

Your music teacher (or your psychotherapist) gets to know you quite well. In perhaps a less direct way, you get to know him or her quite well too. After a long enough time, the music teacher (or the psychotherapist) gets to see you in all your moods and begins to understand how those moods affect you and the work the two of you are trying to accomplish together. If you keep going back, setting aside your time and money week after week, it is probably because you are getting something out of it.

One huge difference between taking music lessons and being in psychotherapy is that most people are proud of taking music lessons. The same is not true for psychotherapy. The two processes are similar, but the reactions we have to them are usually quite different—as is also the case with how we perceive others will see our participation in each process. In chapter 3 I will talk more about shame related to psychotherapy and how to deal with it.

Psychotherapy and the Talking Cure

The most common notion about psychotherapy is that it is some sort of "talking cure," in which someone who is not feeling well mentally or emotionally goes to a psychiatrist and talks about what ails them. The person is supposed to talk about his or her childhood, and out of that talking comes a cure. While there is a small element of truth in this, it only partially explains what psychotherapy is. It does not clarify much more than just saying psychotherapy is a tool that people can use to lead a happy life. That the person undergoing psychotherapy primarily talks is true, but change does not usually result from merely talking. Rather, change occurs as a result of the conversation. The client gets ideas from talking about what he or she needs to do to clear away the clutter from his or her life and feel less stuck. In a lesser way, just talking helps, such as when a person needs someone with whom they can be themselves and not have to hide anything. For some people, one small part of leading a happy life is being able to be known just as they are.

Psychotherapy and Healing

We have all been injured in life. No one has had the perfect life. The question is not whether we have been damaged but how we deal with the damage. Some of us have been massively injured. Our persons and our bodies have been violated. We have been subjected to abuse: physical, mental, or emotional. For others, the damage has been much less. But there is no escape from the damage. An automobile provides a good analogy: It is impossible to own and drive the same car for years without picking up a few dings and dents. If nothing else, normal wear and tear takes its toll. And if a car has been in an accident, it might need massive repair. At the very least, cars—and people—can use some maintenance.

One of the beauties of psychotherapy is that the process itself, talking to someone about what has happened in your life, is healing. You have probably experienced this with friends. You tell a friend about something terrible that happened, and you feel less overwhelmed by the experience. You are healed a little by telling the story. Telling the story to a psychotherapist helps in the same way.

Psychotherapy and Being Witnessed

Another reason people seek the help of a psychotherapist is that they want and need someone to witness their lives. Many people want someone to know them as they are. They feel they cannot tell friends or family members the details of their lives for any number of reasons. That usually means there is not a single person in this world who really knows them, no one who knows *all* the facts, *all* the feelings, *all* the desires. For some, a priest in the privacy of a confessional booth serves this purpose. Others get this from a 12-step program. Still others rely on a friend or confidante. And some choose to see a psychotherapist.

Unfortunately, the same priest may not be available to hear your confession all the time, and not being Catholic eliminates that possibility anyway. Twelve-step programs are limited by the way they are set up. Friends are not always available; they have their own lives and problems, and they may not be good listeners, or they may get upset if they hear how much pain you are in. They may want to give you advice that you do not want or need. A psychotherapist can fill the gap. You can be reasonably assured that if you select your psychotherapist wisely, he or she will be there on a regular basis to witness your life in a manner well-suited to your needs.

Psychotherapy and Slowing Down

The reason for some people to be in psychotherapy is to slow down and look at their lives. We live in a busy society that gets busier all the time. Despite claims that technology will free time for all of us, the opposite has proved true. Instead, more is expected of us. People work more hours today than a generation ago. Very few people have a significant amount of free time. If you want to slow down occasionally and look at your life, time must be set aside for that purpose. For some people, psychotherapy fills this need. Once a week, for an hour, you can stop and take a look at how well or poorly you are doing in life.

The 17 C's of Psychotherapy.

There are 17 words starting with the letter C that can help you to understand what psychotherapy is. They are:

Counseling: Another word for psychotherapy—one that is less emotionally charged—is counseling. Some people prefer so say they are in counseling or talking a counselor, rather than that they are in psychotherapy.

Client: A person seeking the services of a psychotherapist is known as a client. At one time, that same person would have been called a patient. In some mental health settings, the person is still referred to as the patient. But increasingly, the consumer of psychotherapy services is referred to as a client.

Clinician: A clinician is the provider of psychotherapy services. It is the person the client is seeing. A clinician is usually a psychiatrist, psychologist, clinical social worker, marriage and family therapist, pastoral counselor, drug or alcohol counselor, crisis counselor, or peer counselor. There are other types of clinicians, but these are the most common.

Consumer: This is an alternative way of looking at the client. Rather than thinking of yourself as a client (or patient), it is possible to view yourself as a consumer of mental health services. As a consumer, you shop for and buy mental health services. This is essentially the same as when you are a consumer of other services, such as legal, financial, or cleaning services.

Consultant: This is an alternative way of understanding the role of the clinician. A mental health consultant is knowledgeable in human development, thinking, feeling, behavior, interactions, and the range of human functioning. You hire a consultant to utilize their knowledge, experience, and skills. A mental health consultant works closely with you to help you understand your issues and choices, and to help you develop and implement a plan for dealing with these issues and choices.

Consciousness: One of the primary goals of psychotherapy is to help people be more conscious of various aspects of their lives—or in simpler terms, to be able to say what is going on in their life. Some forms of psychotherapy emphasize being conscious of inner feelings or thought processes; other forms emphasize being conscious of how we behave. Still other forms of psychotherapy emphasize consciousness about something else. But almost all emphasize being more conscious of your life in some way.

Control: The subject of how much control of our lives we can actually have is hotly debated by the different branches of psychotherapy. But in just about every case, the client and the clinician work together to help the client be more conscious of his or her life so that he or she can exert greater control over aspects of that life.

Change: The goal of psychotherapy is usually change. The person, couple, family, or group who comes to psychotherapy wants to change in some way, usually how they feel, think, act, react, or interact. More than any other reason, the belief that something needs to change is why people seek help through psychotherapy.

Connection: The most common change people seek through psychotherapy is greater connection either with themselves (their bodies and feelings) or with others (partners, friends, and family).

Conversational: Psychotherapy, at its heart, is a conversation or series of conversations. If someone from Mars could peek in on a psychotherapy session with a powerful telescope, all they would see most of the time are two people sitting in chairs, looking at and talking to each other. Occasionally, there will be more than two people there. Occasionally, someone might be standing or sitting on the floor. Occasionally, the people are not looking at each other, or not talking, or they are doing other things. Some of the change people seek will happen just because a conversation took place. The person who tells a psychotherapist a long-held secret will probably feel different by merely telling someone. Conversations alone can change a person. At other times, what is talked about will lead the client into doing something outside of the therapy hour that produces change. That action can be concrete, such as deciding in psychotherapy to go to an AA meeting rather than a bar. Or the action can be subtle, like learning to think before speaking.

Candid: The conversations a client has with a clinician are often about difficult to discuss matters, topics the client rarely or never discusses with others. The client is usually more truthful in psychotherapy, more open and straightforward. Issues are addressed in a blunt, candid manner. This results in the client feeling genuine, feeling real.

Confidentiality: One of the hallmarks of psychotherapy is confidentiality. A psychotherapist is forbidden from talking to others about what has been said by a client. There are a few rare exceptions to this, and those will be discussed in chapter 13. But almost always the psychotherapist is ethically forbidden from talking about what is said in the therapy hour. The client, however, is free to say whatever he or she wants. It is the psychotherapist that is bound by silence. The client should feel confident that friends, relatives, coworkers, or others will not hear stories about what the client said to the psychotherapist. The purpose of this is to give the client a sense of safety so that whatever needs to be said in therapy can be said without fear of others finding out.

Consistent: An important aspect of psychotherapy is consistency. Psychotherapy is ongoing, with both the client and the psychotherapist setting aside the agreed-upon time(s). Both show up, ready to do the work of psychotherapy. The psychotherapist is bound by the ethics of the profession to be available on a consistent basis to the client to whom the psychotherapist has made this commitment.

Continuity: There is a continuity to the conversations. While many issues may be discussed, they are usually connected in a way that is understandable to the client and the psychotherapist.

Caring: For psychotherapy to be effective, the client needs to feel the psychotherapist is in his or her corner, that the psychotherapist cares what happens to the client.

Cognizance: It is essential to the success of psychotherapy that the psychotherapist be cognizant or knowledgeable about many areas of life. The psychotherapist must be cognizant of human nature and the process people go through in order to change. The psychotherapist should be cognizant about what is normal or abnormal behavior, which may be quite different from what people generally believe. The psychotherapist should also be cognizant about what is actually healthy and unhealthy, which also may be quite different from what the general public believes, and which in addition varies from person to person. Basically, the psychotherapist should be an expert in human development, behavior, interactions, and relationships.

Competence: While a psychotherapist may be caring, cognizant, and consistent, and while the psychotherapist may hold information confidential, one more essential criteria must be met. The psychotherapist must be competent to provide the psychotherapeutic services a particular individual needs. Competence includes all of the aforementioned characteristics. In addition, the psychotherapist must have a personality suited to sitting and talking with people, the psychotherapist must be able to recognize when they lack the knowledge needed to work with a particular client, and the psychotherapist must know his or her self well enough to recognize when he or she is not emotionally suited to working with a particular individual.

In short, psychotherapy or *counseling* involves *clients*, also known as *consumers*, seeking the services of *clinicians*, also thought of as *consultants*, to have *candid, confidential conversations* to bring about *change*, often meaning greater *connection* through greater *conscious control* over the clients' lives. They meet *consistently* in order to have a *continuous* conversation, with the clinician providing *caring, cognizance,* and *competence.*

Richard

Richard sought psychotherapy because he was unhappy. He grew up in what appeared to be the ideal Southern California middle class family. What the neighbors did not see, though, was his father getting drunk and falling asleep every night in front of the television, leaving his mother to vent her anger at Richard and his sister. When Richard played make-believe and acted out his fantasies of Hollywood movie stars and European nobility, his mother criticized him mercilessly. When he entered into psychotherapy, Richard was already aware that having a drunk for a father and a shrew for mother had left him with a lot of damage—and even more he did not fully recognize

Richard began psychotherapy while in his 20s. Off and on for years, he visited the same therapist, who got to know him quite well. Sometimes they met weekly; other times, every other week. Occasionally, there were years between appointments. Most of the time their meetings were for individual psychotherapy, but for a couple of years Richard was in group therapy with the same psychotherapist.

The subject of the conversations was always Richard: what worked in his life, what did not, and why. Sometimes his therapy focused on pressures coming from inside his own head, other times on pressures from without. At times, the conversations were about what was happening in his life at that moment; other times they focused on events that had occurred many years earlier.

At one point, the psychotherapist facilitated a six-hour meeting held over two days between Richard and his parents. To help the parents feel more comfortable, a second psychotherapist, who had never met Richard or his parents, was asked to co-facilitate the session. For the first time, Richard was able to tell his parents how he felt about his father's drinking and his mother's anger.

Psychotherapy is where Richard learned to understand and to be honest with himself, to see how *he* got in the way of his having a happy life and how he could change himself and his life. It was a place where, once every week or so, he could stop whatever he was doing and focus on himself and what he needed to do to get the most happiness and contentment he could out of life. Psychotherapy was a place for Richard to learn how to grow.

Chapter 3
Psychotherapy:
Who is That For?

Many people believe that psychotherapy is only for those who are "mentally ill"—those who are severely depressed, extremely anxious, disoriented, psychotic, or who experience hallucinations or delusions. While these are people who might benefit from psychotherapy, they are only a small percentage of the individuals actually involved in psychotherapy. Modern psychotherapy serves a much wider range of people. Almost anyone can benefit, whether they are mentally ill or not. Even high-functioning people with few signs of serious emotional problems can benefit from psychotherapy. Underlying this is an important understanding: Psychotherapy tends to change your life, rather than changing who you are.

To possibly benefit from psychotherapy, you must fulfill the following three requirements. First, you must be human. Second, you must exhibit some human weaknesses or frailties. And third, you must want to use psychotherapy as a means of dealing with these weaknesses or frailties.

Clearly, almost everyone can benefit from psychotherapy. And that is the point. Psychotherapy is not just for individuals with severe emotional problems. The most important factor in deciding if you should be in psychotherapy is the third one, the desire to use psychotherapy as a means of helping yourself deal with the ways you undermine yourself. Psychotherapy does not work on anyone who does not want to be in psychotherapy. Courts that sentence unwilling defendants to counseling are wasting everyone's time. Only when you want to use the tool of psychotherapy to improve your life can it possibly work.

The common notion that psychotherapy is for people who are mentally ill has a basis in reality. Someone with significant emotional or mental problems is definitely a candidate for psychotherapy. If you are severely depressed and cannot get out of bed, go to work, or generally function as an adult needs to function, you are a candidate for psychotherapy. The same is true if you are acting inappropriately. Perhaps you are physically abusing your life partner or even yourself in some way. If so, psychotherapy might help.

But one of the least understood things about psychotherapy is who can benefit the most from it. The average person, when asked who would benefit most from psychotherapy, would probably describe someone whose life is a mess. In fact, though, psychotherapy is the most helpful to people who least need the help, when they least need the help.

If you are generally a high-functioning person and have most of the basic issues of your life together, you are likely to receive greater benefits from psychotherapy than someone whose life is a mess. So, the happier you are with your life, the more likely it is that psychotherapy will help you have an even happier life.

The same is true for timing. When you least need psychotherapy is when you are likely to receive the greatest benefit from it. If your life is in crisis, it is more difficult to benefit from psychotherapy than when your life is calm. If you have just broken up with your partner, are having trouble with your job, and are drinking too much, you may well have a need to sit and talk with someone about what is going on, but it is very difficult to contemplate and evaluate your life when there are so many issues to deal with. Furthermore, when a person is in crisis, they are likely to want quick changes, and in general, psychotherapy does not provide quick changes. Nevertheless, many and perhaps most people begin psychotherapy while in crisis. Crisis can be an effective jump start for change, and the person in crisis can form a strong therapeutic alliance that he or she can use to work on issues beyond the crisis. Still, it is far more effective to begin psychotherapy *before* a crisis occurs.

To state that virtually anyone can benefit from psychotherapy may seem like an attempt to hype psychotherapy, but there is truth in the statement. Here are some reasons why:

1) In life, there is pain and suffering. Pain and suffering are experienced by everyone and damage us in significant ways. None of us escape. This idea has roots in both Eastern and Western philosophy and religion. The best we can hope for is to manage the inevitable pain we experience in a way that makes sense. Psychotherapy is one way of trying to manage the pain.

2) All of us can stand improvement. We may need humility to admit our shortcomings, but it is true that every one of us can stand improvement, regardless of how well we are doing. Even the most together people mess up their lives at least occasionally. Psychotherapy can help us not to mess up our lives—or at least lessen the impact of messing up.

3) We all have different resources, abilities, and experiences. Some people have advantages. That's the way it is. However, each of us can only use what we have or what we can get. What matters is not how well we are doing in comparison with others but how well we are doing with what we have. The question that needs to be asked is this: "Are we using the resources and advantages we have in a way that permits us to have a happier life, or are we undermining ourselves?"

4) We can change. We do not have to make the same mistakes over and over. We may not be able to change everything or even many things, but we can change some things, and many of those changes will be important. We can all do a better job of going through life.

5) We are the only ones who can make the changes. No one can do it for us. It is our life, and each of us does things differently than anyone else. People can help us in the process, but ultimately it is up to each of us as individuals—and to no one else—to make the changes.

WHO SHOULD NOT BE IN PSYCHOTHERAPY

Psychotherapy is not right for everyone. Many do not benefit from it. It is difficult to know in advance who will not benefit from psychotherapy, but certain groups of people *tend* to get little from it.

The majority of those who do not benefit from psychotherapy are people who do not want to be in psychotherapy in the first place. The reason for an individual's lack of desire to be involved in psychotherapy does not matter. If he or she does not want to be there, it will not work. The least productive sessions I have had as a psychotherapist are with people who do not want to be in psychotherapy but come because someone else mandates or pressures them to be there. These individuals say they do not know what to talk about, and when suggestions are made, they rarely pick up on them. Generally, these people are wasting their time and money, besides boring their psychotherapist.

To be effective, psychotherapy requires a desire on the part of the client to use the process to change. Change requires a lot of hard work. Usually, a person must challenge him or her self to grow more self-aware and then be willing to use that self-awareness to live a happier life. People who do not want to be involved in psychotherapy do not make the effort needed.

Typically these people come to psychotherapy only at the urging of a friend or family member or by court order. Unless that person has a sudden awakening and wants to take responsibility for his or her life and actions, the process is a waste.

Another group of people who do not benefit from psychotherapy are those without a conscience—individuals who really cannot tell right from wrong. In the world of psychology, they are typically diagnosed as having an antisocial personality disorder. While our prisons are filled with such people, the majority of them are our neighbors, family members, and friends. They like to believe that the rules of society do not apply to them, and they are always looking for ways to get something to which they are not entitled.

Experience has shown that such people rarely benefit from psychotherapy. They not only do not understand the nature of their problem, they rarely will admit to themselves or anyone else that there even *is* a problem. They see problems elsewhere but not in themselves. The best kind of psychological intervention for such people is *not* individual psychotherapy. They will tend to tell the psychotherapist what they believe the psychotherapist wants to hear. For some, a special form of group psychotherapy occasionally helps. But in the majority of the cases, these individuals respond best to a structured program that teaches them right from wrong.

A third group of people who benefit little from psychotherapy consists of individuals who have a significant problem with acting out and are not prepared or willing to change their behavior. Acting out means they are engaging in behavior that to most everyone else appears clearly self-destructive. That behavior could be excessive drinking, drugging, gambling, eating, sex, or any other compulsive activity. Therapy in these cases can be a place where the person eases their guilt about the behavior and receives some warmth and nurturing. Unfortunately, this nurturing and easing of guilt can make it easier to continue acting out. Many psychotherapists say that if a person is acting out, they should not be seen in psychotherapy.

Interestingly, it has been found that some people once deemed unable to respond to psychotherapy actually can benefit from it. This group includes people who are not innately introspective—people who, for whatever reason, have a hard time looking inward at what they are thinking, feeling, sensing, and experiencing, and then talking about that. The ability to be introspective is necessary for psychotherapy, since that is what usually occurs in therapy. Experience has shown that people who are not innately introspective can learn to be. Thus, people who in the 1950s would have been rejected by psychotherapy clinics due to a lack of being introspective are now welcomed as prospective clients who initially need to be taught how to look inward.

Resistance to Psychotherapy

Many people struggle to avoid psychotherapy. It is seen as the last alternative. They will try everything else they can think of, and if nothing else works, they will go to a psychotherapist. They will endure the pain and suffering for as long as they possibly can rather than go to a psychotherapist to discuss the problems. The reasons for this are many.

DENIAL

Denial is the refusal to admit the truth or reality of a situation. The simplest way to resist the idea of psychotherapy is to deny there is a problem. While it might be obvious to everyone else that something is wrong, human beings have a strong capacity to interpret facts in a way that allows them to believe what they want or need to believe.

This is not always a bad thing. Denial helps individuals to cope with difficult times. A person in a concentration camp during World War II, where people were disappearing or dying every day, might have easily become so overwhelmed by the truth of the situation that he or she might not have been able to function in a way that allowed him or her to survive. This person might have told him or herself that the people who disappeared had been transferred to another camp. Such denial might have enabled some in the camps to survive long enough to be liberated by the Allied forces.

When it comes to psychological problems, denial is a double-edged sword. If you are a young child living with a highly abusive family, denial might help you survive. You might deny that your parents are acting in a way that shows they do not love you, or that your father or mother is an out-of-control alcoholic, because you might believe that acknowledging such facts would cause social service workers to break up your family, and that is too scary for you to deal with. So you deny the truth and make up stories to explain away everything that is happening. Or you develop a selective memory, "forgetting" about all the bad things.

While denial sometimes helps people get through situations from which they cannot escape, it also causes problems. It permits bad situations to continue, and it prevents people from truthfully confronting problems.

Often, couples come to therapy and one member of the couple sees problems while the other does not. One, in effect, brings the other into therapy, while the other is still in denial.

Joan and Priscilla

Joan and Priscilla, a lesbian couple, are a prime example of the situation described above. Priscilla is a pharmacist, and Joan is a carpenter. Priscilla realized there was not sufficient intimacy in their relationship. Joan resisted both Priscilla's notion and the idea of going to couples therapy. In this case, the class issue was important. Joan, from her perspective as a blue-collar carpenter, felt Priscilla was overreacting. Finally, when Priscilla began an affair with another professional, Joan's denial broke down and she was willing to come into therapy. The nature of the therapy was to make sure that Joan was not made into the "problem" of the relationship and that Priscilla took responsibility for her part in the trouble the couple was having. Priscilla resisted, blaming everything on Joan and denying any part in problems they were having as a couple.

They ended up living separately for a while and then started to date each other again. This enabled them to reconnect in a real way. Joan learned to acknowledge there were problems and to communicate her concerns. She especially wanted Priscilla to know that she felt disrespected and put down by her. In communicating this, Joan became able to stop withholding affection and intimacy. Priscilla then found she did not need to have an affair to get the physical and emotional contact she wanted. Priscilla was able to let go of the affair because now she was getting what had been lacking in her primary relationship. Joan came to feel more respected by Priscilla, and eventually she moved back in.

Both had issues involving denial. Initially, Joan denied there were problems. It took Priscilla's affair to break through Joan's denial. Priscilla, in turn, denied her role in the problems the couple was having. It took the couple's breakup to set her straight. When she came to truly understand her disrespect for Joan and its role in their problems, they were able to progress and reestablish their relationship.

David

David is a 48-year-old bisexual man who used denial to avoid looking at his life and addressing the problems he'd had for many years. Denial began early for David. He was repeatedly sexually molested as a child by older brothers, twins who forced him to "service" them. This began when he was 6, and he had felt he could never could tell anyone. So he made believe it was not happening, trying hard to forget after each molestation. There was no one at home to talk with. His mother was an alcoholic and his father was absent. Later, he too became alcoholic.

As an adult, he continued to deny the existence of problems in his life. He saw himself as a happy-go-lucky guy who liked to work, drink, and have lots of sex with both men and women, including his long-term boyfriend. He spent hours in adult bookstores having sex with other men, "servicing" them and then "forgetting" about what had just happened and the problems his actions were causing.

Going to a therapist was difficult. He broke through his denial long enough to finally admit that he had problems and needed help. He called his managed care insurance company, who referred him to me. I received a call from his insurance company asking if I would see him. After I said yes, the insurance company sent me some papers, and I expected to hear from him within a day or two, which would have been normal. For six months, I did not get a phone call from him.

When he finally did call, I asked about the delay. He said that after he called the insurance company he forgot about the referral and went about his life. His therapy, which only lasted six sessions, focused on his way of denying to himself what was going on in his life. He said in the second session that he went to adult bookstores on a regular basis, but he had no idea how often. I asked him to keep a log of the time he spent at adult bookstores, and he was shocked to see the results. Several weeks after the therapy began, he told me that he and his partner were moving to another city, and he thought that would solve his problems. I never saw or heard from him again.

FEAR AND SHAME

The second reason people avoid psychotherapy is fear. Fear is a powerful emotion, perhaps our most basic one. People resist psychotherapy because they fear what will happen if they go. They fear that loathsome, shameful truths about themselves will come out. At the core of this fear is shame.

Shame arises when a person consciously feels guilty about something he or she has done, or about a personal shortcoming that he or she believes is self-characterizing. People fear the shame they will experience when they tell the psychotherapist about what they have done or what they believe about who they are. Shame prevents them from being honest and open to themselves and others. This makes going to psychotherapy difficult.

Two things are drilled into all of us from the time we are young. One is that a clear right and a clear wrong exist for most situations. There is very little room for gray. You are either in compliance with what society asks of you, or you are not. And if you are not, you are guilty and should feel ashamed. Your guilt extends not only to what you have done but also to who you are: You are a bad person. One of my clients would say over and over how he believed he was a "bad fag." He could not do anything right, or so he believed. His shame was compounded by working in the computer industry, where things either work or do not work. He believed the same was true for himself.

The second thing we are taught is that we *should* be ashamed of doing something wrong or having something wrong with us. We are taught that we should feel guilty for having problems. We learn to reproach ourselves for having problems. We feel personally responsible in a harsh, critical way.

We live in a society that supports feeling shame. "Shame on you" is one of the primary responses to a child who has violated some rule. Children are taught that not only is it bad to violate rules but also they are bad people for doing whatever it is they did. The children *should* feel ashamed. Further, if they did whatever they did because of feelings inside of them, then those feelings are also bad. Or so they are taught. Given this, it is easy to see how having sexual and romantic feelings for members of one's own sex can make a person feel guilty and ashamed.

The same type of shame also occurs in response to physical illnesses. The woman who has had a mastectomy may feel ashamed of her body or even of herself for getting breast cancer. The same is true for people with HIV and AIDS.

As for emotional problems, we are taught to be even more

ashamed. We are taught that such problems indicate a *character defect*, and that if only we stopped being lazy, we could concentrate on the problem and fix it. We are told by others, and eventually come to believe, that we are weak and the problem is our fault. And then shame takes root. This encourages us to procrastinate in seeking help, and to hide the fact that we have a problem from family members and friends, leaving us isolated, holding in a secret, and filled with shame.

When a person can learn to accept who he or she is in a non-judgmental way, he or she can then ask for help. Acceptance, especially when it come to problems, is an acknowledgment that something is wrong and needs to be addressed. Acceptance helps lessen shame and can get people into a psychotherapy office where they can learn to deal with their problems in a rational and non-judgmental manner.

Coincidently, one of the first great gains most people get from psychotherapy is a lessening of the shame they experience about whatever it is that brought them to psychotherapy. They learn to accept who they are. This does not mean they learn to like who they are but to accept themselves. They also learn they can talk to others about who they are without feeling overwhelming shame.

If this is all someone gets from psychotherapy, it is often enough. The lessening of shame is accompanied by a decrease in the intense emotional pain that accompanies shame. Without the pain, many people can either learn to live with what it is they were ashamed of, or more likely, become able to deal with the problem in an open, unashamed way.

Sally

Sally is a good example of someone who overcame feelings of shame and social pressure. A court reporter, Sally had openly lived as a lesbian and a feminist for a number of years. Still, she wondered if she might be bisexual and therefore wanted to re-explore relationships with men. She was not sure if this was the right move, though, and needed to be able to comfortably reidentify as a lesbian if her foray into bisexuality did not work out. She was afraid that if she ended up identifying once again as a lesbian, the more rigidly queer women in her social circle would not accept her. She cited how several women she knew had been shunned after experimenting with bisexuality.

She did not feel she could share these thoughts with her lesbian friends. She felt shame about wanting to do this exploration, and was afraid her friends would view it as a betrayal. Her shame prevented her from exploring relationships with men as well as talking with a psychotherapist about her dilemma.

Later, after talking through her conflicts in therapy, she decided to explore her interest in men. What she learned, or relearned, from this experience were the many things she did not like about straight men. She returned to the lesbian community and began a long-term relationship with a woman. Sally credits therapy as being instrumental in helping her explore what she needed to explore, calling it a safe place where she was able to let go of her shame.

Artie

Artie provides another good example. Artie grew up in an Irish-Catholic family, and although he thought he had rejected the church's teachings, he could not stop himself from feeling shame about his life.

Artie had felt shame as a child because he was feminine, and he did not have friends until he was in high school. As an adult, he was ashamed that he was gay and liked to be the bottom during sex. He was ashamed of his body. He was ashamed that he was judgmental of others. He was ashamed that he was HIV-positive and still not interested in safer sex. In short, he was ashamed of anything that indicated he was not a perfect human being. And he drowned his shame in alcohol and drugs.

Artie's shame prevented him from calling a psychotherapist. He could not believe a psychotherapist would want to work with him. He felt he was a terrible human being. When he finally realized he was slowly killing himself with alcohol and drugs, he felt so desperate that he finally called a psychotherapist. It took all his courage to make the call. He was surprised when, after the first session, the therapist said he wanted to work with him. He could not fathom that. His shame ran too deep.

FAMILY LOYALTY

Many families believe they should not air their dirty laundry in pubic. In those families there is a strong rule stating that no one is to bring disgrace on the family by talking to nonfamily members about family problems. The only possible exception would be talking to a religious leader. And since most psychotherapists are not religious leaders, it follows that there is no permission to visit one. Problems in the family are supposed to stay in the family.

There are two powerful dynamics at work here. One is that family loyalty is actually a subsection of shame. All members of a family will be embarrassed—shamed—by having it known that a family member is queer or depressed or has a drinking problem. Loyalty to the family says the individual should keep that information to him or herself.

The second dynamic is trust—or lack thereof. Inherent in the family loyalty argument against talking to others is the belief that others cannot be trusted. This distrust extends to members of the mental health profession, who are believed to hold both their interests and those of society above the interests of the individual and the family from which the individual comes. Psychotherapists, it is thought, will use the information in ways that will hurt the person or other members of the family. No one except a family member can be trusted. Thus, many people in need resist talking to a psychotherapist because they do not want to break a family rule that they have come to believe in themselves.

Lucy

Family loyalty made it difficult for Lucy, a lesbian in her 30s, to enter therapy and begin to talk about her issues. The oldest of three children—she had two younger brothers—Lucy had been beaten and hospitalized as a child. Her mother beat each of the children at different times. When the beatings were severe and a child needed medical attention, Lucy's mother would swear the other two children to secrecy, saying she would not call an ambulance unless each child agreed to swear the injury was an accident. (This was many years ago, before medical workers were taught to look for signs of child abuse.)

Lucy's mother inculcated the notion of family loyalty, and consequently Lucy was afraid to talk about anything that had happened. As an adult she continued to be afraid to talk about her childhood. This made psychotherapy threatening. Her mother's old warning, Lucy found, extended to the present. Lucy found it difficult to talk to her therapist about not only her past but her present.

Lucy believed that if she talked about family secrets in therapy she would somehow hurt her mother. Though she had been out of her mother's house for years and had spent much of her adult life trying to recover from her childhood wounds, she still felt a need to protect her mother. She eventually became able to talk in therapy about her childhood, but she continued to have trust issues and difficulty with intimacy.

Leonard

As with Lucy, loyalty to the family of origin made it difficult for Leonard to see a therapist for the first time. From the time he was young, he was told that no one outside the family could be trusted. Though he did not realize it consciously until much later, he also learned by experience that no one in the family could be trusted either. Thus, he had no one with whom to discuss his problems.

Leonard was an all-American boy type in high school, and he married his high school sweetheart soon after graduation. For 20 years they lived together, raising their daughter. Leonard and his wife developed a bond that more closely resembled a mother-and-son relationship than a husband-and-wife relationship. He was, however, able to be a good father and quite loyal to the family he had created.

Sex between Leonard and his wife disappeared soon after the birth of their daughter, and neither discussed why or what could be done. Leonard replaced sex with his wife with sex with men. He became adept at finding men in situations similar to his own—men who were loyally married to women but wanted to have sex with men. His self-identity confused him; he did not think of himself as heterosexual or bisexual because he felt little physical attraction to women, but he did not consider himself gay because he was married and had a daughter.

For years he was unhappy. He thought of going to see a psychotherapist, but remembered the stories his mother had told him of his Northern European heritage. The stories involved the lives of his ancestors in a small village overrun by invading armies, destroying the village and killing numerous inhabitants. The moral of the story was clear to Leonard: Outsiders cannot be trusted. Leonard learned his lessons well. He could not talk to outsiders. Unfortunately for Leonard, he could not talk to family members either.

As he neared 40, Leonard spent more and more time escaping from his life. His drinking increased to the point where he was concerned, and he spent much of his time away from home with other married men he had met. But he was frustrated by the limitations of those relationships.

What changed things for Leonard was an unrelated event. He was sexually harassed by a male supervisor. Leonard rejected the man's advances, but the overtures did not stop. Eventually, Leonard reported the man to the Human Resources department. Concerned for Leonard's well-being, Human Resources strongly suggested that he seek counseling. He was subsequently referred to me.

The issue with the supervisor was quickly resolved, but Leonard then found himself in a situation both intriguing and repelling. For the first time, he was able to talk about his life, but each time he did, he felt the old admonishments against talking outside the family come back.

Leonard began and stopped psychotherapy numerous times over the next five years. He moved out of the house he shared with his wife when he started therapy. As soon as he was settled in his new accommodations, he stopped therapy. He later moved back in with his wife and began therapy again. He ended therapy after he moved out again and initiated divorce proceedings. Several more times he started and stopped. Each time he began therapy, he did so because of an overwhelming need to talk about his life. Each time he stopped, it was because of an equally overwhelming sense that he was not supposed to talk about himself or his family.

INDEPENDENCE

Another reason people resist going to see a psychotherapist is the misguided belief that they can and should figure things out for themselves. Quite often, under the veneer of independence is a fear of becoming dependent on the psychotherapist. Other times, a person who has been staunchly independent in his or her life may not recognize a need to depend on others occasionally. When that need is denied for a long time, the desire grows. So many people who resist psychotherapy actually do so because they fear their natural, normal dependent side.

While individuals who have resisted psychotherapy because they considered themselves independent may have taken a great step by admitting there is a problem, there still remains an element of denial to overcome. They still deny the facts that show they have been unable to work out solutions to their problems on their own.

Dorothy

Dorothy, a woman in her 30s who grew up in the Midwest, is a good example of someone who resisted going to therapy because she considered herself independent. She lost her father in her early teens and went through 10 years of intense therapy following that. Dorothy had a distant mother who did not know how to talk with her about her feelings of loss. Indeed, Dorothy came to realize her mother was struggling just to survive and that talking about feelings was alien to the woman.

Dorothy relocated to the West Coast in her late 20s. She knew she was not finished with the work she wanted to do in therapy, yet she felt independent and wanted to create her own new life. She certainly hoped she would not need a therapist again. When she finally called a therapist, she made it clear she wanted a consultant. The therapist found that Dorothy needed to feel as if she were calling the shots in therapy and seeing her therapist/consultant only in a casual way.

Dorothy asked to have conversations every other week to avoid the feeling of dependence that more frequent meetings would have likely caused. Her therapist responded that every other week might be a good idea, but then asked Dorothy to come every week for the first month to give the therapy process some momentum. Meeting weekly, at least in the beginning, would help Dorothy understand what she might be able to get from therapy.

At the end of the first month, the therapist asked Dorothy if she wanted to schedule meetings every other week. The therapist's willingness to allow Dorothy to set the schedule allowed Dorothy to feel interdependent, as opposed to dependent or independent. Dorothy was able to feel comfortable about how she used the services of her therapist and asked to continue meeting on a weekly basis. Her therapist, paying homage to Dorothy's need for independence, told Dorothy she would agree to see her every week. At the end of each month, though, the therapist made sure to ask Dorothy if she wanted to continue on a weekly basis or switch to meeting every other week.

Warren

Being independent made it difficult for Warren to call a psychotherapist as well. Warren had learned in early childhood to not depend on anyone else. His family was moderately dysfunctional. His passive mother allowed his blustery father to rule the house. Warren tried both to please his father and hide from him but found he could not do either successfully. He soon realized he could not rely on either of his parents.

Warren became independent, and by age 35 he had given up on dating and trying to find a relationship. Instead, he went back to school and secured the credentials he needed to become an independent professional. He set himself up in business and worked as a sole proprietor for the next 15 years. He occasionally went out to bars but invariably went home alone and masturbated to porno tapes for several hours.

A combination of getting older and discovering the world of cybersex changed things for Warren. He realized he was lonely. The Internet provided a way for him to meet men safely without much personal risk. But it was still hard to let someone in. Curiously, all the men who caught his interest lived in faraway cities. And all the men with whom he corresponded seemed to want a more limited relationship than Warren believed he now wanted. Still, even this low level of dating opened an old yearning, and he found himself at times eager for connection and at other times quite upset. He tried to deal with these feelings by himself, but the situation grew worse.

Only after all the years of loneliness and suffering did Warren admit that he could not work things out by himself. His need for connection finally overcame his need for independence, and he asked a close friend in therapy for the name and phone number of a psychotherapist. Warren then began the process of recognizing that his independence had served him well—sometimes too well.

SUFFERING IS GOOD FOR THE SOUL

Some people resist going to therapy because they believe suffering is good for them. Suffering occurs when a person endures pain or distress over a period of time. In Western society, suffering is not considered to be wholly a bad thing. We are taught that a certain amount of suffering is good for our soul, that suffering gives us humility. Suffering is our reminder that we are not all-powerful beings.

Consequently, Western (and many Eastern) people have intentionally sought ways of suffering. In the Middle Ages, monks in Europe lashed themselves with whips to cause suffering and to make themselves more holy. All Western religions have prohibitions against certain actions. Some of these prohibitions are there not because the actions are inherently bad but because God wants us to be humble. Thus, we are asked to do (or not do) certain things—compliance with which causes us to suffer.

There are strong non-religious beliefs, too, that suffering is healthy. Suffering that cannot be avoided builds character; for example, someone who is suffering with AIDS learns what is truly important in life. But suffering for suffering's sake can be taken to an unhealthy extreme.

Unhealthy suffering is generally based in personal guilt and shame. For instance, if you believe that you have violated God's commandments by being queer or by physically loving a person of the same sex, you have committed a sin, and one way to expiate the sin is through suffering. Going to a psychotherapist might mean losing your sense of suffering, leaving you feeling unpunished for a sin for which you think you need to be punished. Therefore, not going to a psychotherapist, suffering with whatever problems you have, is from this perspective good for the soul.

Marcy

Marcy provides a good example of someone who suffered "for her own good." Marcy's childhood was sacrificed to help with the care of her sisters and brothers. She learned to endure the loss of play in childhood in order to do the right thing, as she understood it from her parents. And the right thing was to be the third parent in the family.

Marcy is still work-oriented, and she describes herself as a workaholic. She has difficulty letting go of work, and she has a need to always be in control and needed. She does not know how to play; she cannot go on vacation without being productive. She still carries the message that if she is not suffering, then what she is doing is not worthwhile. Suffering gives her self-worth and self-respect. Anything that lessens her suffering also lessens her positive self-regard. Consequently, she avoided therapy for many years. It was only when the suffering became unbearable that she sought help. She now understands the pressure she is under and has vowed to let go of some of it.

THE EXPENSE

One of the most common reasons for avoiding psychotherapy is the expense. Usually, that cost is money, but occasionally the use of time also factors in.

The money issue is almost always a red herring, something someone says when the real reason for avoiding psychotherapy is something else. (Chapter 11 talks about the ways to pay for psycho-therapy.) In major urban areas, low-cost psychotherapy is almost always available. Of course, low-cost psychotherapy usually comes with strings attached. You might be forced to see someone who is in training as a psychotherapist, or you might need to go to a public clinic. But psychotherapy *is* generally available, even for those on limited budgets.

Debra and Karen

A good example is provided by Debra and Karen, a high-income couple. One worked in advertising, the other in high technology. Both were raised to have stiff upper lips, to never tell anyone what was going on and to never show signs of weakness. They both resented the idea of paying for the couples therapy they needed. This resentment had stopped them from seeking help sooner and continued as long as they were in therapy.

Debra and Karen's relationship had become a battle, a power struggle; everything had to be negotiated, from use of the bathroom to doing the dishes. They did not know how to resolve their issues. Finally, they got scared when two of their friends split up. They did not want that to be their fate, so they contracted for three months of weekly therapy. They rolled up their sleeves, stopped complaining about the expense, and started to do the work of therapy. Eventually, they decreased the frequency of their sessions— but only after beginning to connect with each other in a deeper way than ever before.

The corner was turned on the expense issue when Debra and Karen came in one day and requested the names of therapists who might be able to see each of them individually. That way they each could build on the work they had already done in couples therapy. Each woman, after understanding what part she had played in the power struggle and the resultant lack of intimacy, soon started individual therapy. Fear, plus the success of the work they were doing in couples counseling, enabled Debra and Karen to overcome the expense issue.

Luke

For Luke, cost was also a factor. He had been diagnosed as HIV-positive less than a year earlier and subsequently found himself feeling isolated and losing weight. The weight loss did not bother him, since he had weighed over 300 pounds in his teens. However, he felt he needed to get back on his path and "be happy again."

Luke's income was almost $70,000 a year, and his medical insurance covered one third of the cost of his therapy. But he said he needed a psychotherapist who would see him on a sliding scale.

He cited student loan debt, which required him to pay $1,000 a month, and the high cost of living to support his request. When told in the second session that he would be required to pay the amount not covered by his medical insurance, he changed his mind about psychotherapy. He said he just could not afford psychotherapy and would need to find less expensive alternatives. Sadly, to my knowledge, his depression remains untreated.

MAGICAL THINKING

We all engage in magical thinking of some kind. A child who avoids stepping on cracks in the sidewalk exhibits a degree of magical thinking. Similarly, a person in pain might resist dealing with issues in psychotherapy because they believe someone will get hurt if the client talks about that person in therapy. Talking about someone in psychotherapy makes some people feel as if they are being disloyal and causing harm to come to the person they are discussing. It is as if the spoken word has the power to hurt someone who is not in the psychotherapy session. While this sounds far-fetched, it is actually a common reason for avoiding psychotherapy.

Therapists stress that what is said in the office is confidential, but some individuals must get past their magical belief that talking about someone can harm that person before the individual can accept psychotherapy as a viable option.

OVERCOMING RESISTANCE TO PSYCHOTHERAPY

How to overcome resistance to psychotherapy depends on the source of the resistance.

Denial is generally the most difficult resistance to overcome, because the person in denial truly believes there is not a problem. Fortunately, denial is never foolproof. Usually, there are doubts in a person's mind, thoughts that *maybe* everything is not well. Taking a personal inventory of your life might help you see how you are doing. How many jobs have you had? How many relationships have you had? Have you ever had a problem with alcohol or drugs? Do you have many friends? Is your life balanced between work and play? The questions are myriad. In the end, what is important are the answers.

When the resistance is fear, courage is needed. We have all, at times, been able to do things we were afraid to do. If you are avoiding psychotherapy out of fear, ask yourself how you managed to overcome your fears at other times and apply that method to your fear of psychotherapy.

There are other exercises you can do to overcome your fear of seeing a psychotherapist. Perhaps the best is to think of someone with whom you have had a good experience when you talked about your life. That could be a parent, sibling, aunt, uncle, teacher, friend, religious leader, or a stranger sitting next to you on a plane ride. Remember how it felt to be able to say what you wanted and have it heard and understood.

If you cannot remember such an experience, imagine a person with a big heart. Imagine someone who is loving, accepting, non-judgmental, and who really cares about you. Then imagine that person is a professional psychotherapist.

Another good exercise is to imagine that you have already gone to therapy and your problem is now solved. You spent time and energy working at it, and you now can sit back and enjoy the fruits of your labor. You realize that the anticipation of what therapy would be was worse than the actual experience. You feel relieved.

If none of the above is helpful, please remember this: You can shop around for a therapist. You do not have to settle for the first one you meet. Later in the book you will read much about how to find and evaluate therapists. But for now, keep in mind that if the therapy is not working for you at any time, you have the right to stop and to go elsewhere. You are never a prisoner to a particular therapist. You can and should find a therapist whose personal and professional style is comforting to you. And that might not be the first therapist you meet.

One final thought on resistance to psychotherapy: It is all about procrastination. Resisting psychotherapy is putting off something you feel you should be doing. Like other things you procrastinate about, one way to get started is by doing a little at a time.

Perhaps you can go to a lecture given by one or more psycho-therapists. (Psychotherapists are always giving public lectures about one thing or another.) Maybe ask a question or two at the end of the lecture to see how the various therapists respond. Try to imagine yourself in a series of conversations with that person. After that, you might be ready to take the next step.

Chapter 4
Why a Queer Person Might Want to See a Psychotherapist

Years ago, a queer person often went to a psychotherapist to try to change his or her sexual orientation. Today, however, queer-affirmative therapists rarely see people who want to change sexual orientation. The presenting problems of queer people mirror those of the general psychotherapy population, with some additional issues unique to queer people such as coming out. Though there are numerous reasons why a queer person might want to see a psychotherapist, three general categories cover why most people engage the services of a psychotherapist.

The most commonly understood reason to see a psychotherapist includes experiencing debilitating symptoms such as severe anxiety, panic attacks, depression, or sexual dysfunction. Or you may be experiencing more severe problems such as bipolar disorder, psychosis, or other states in which you become disconnected from reality. This is the generally understood category of reasons for someone to seek "professional help." It is this type of reason for seeing a psychotherapist—that something is wrong with your mind—that causes the most shame.

A second and slightly less shameful reason a queer person might see a psychotherapist is to discuss problems he or she is having with normal life-cycle events such identity formation, coming out, relationships, career issues, aging, life-threatening illness, or death and grieving. These can be stressful, and some people feel they benefit at these times from talking with another person. Often the talk is to help clarify what is going on in the client's life and what the client wants and needs to do. This might involve talking individually with a counselor, couples counseling, family therapy, or even sessions with a counselor and the client's friends.

The third reason a queer person might see a psychotherapist is fairly simple and increasingly more common: The client wants someone with whom he or she can regularly discuss what is going on in his or her life. It is not that there is a big problem or that the person is facing a life-cycle issue. In fact, he or she may be high-functioning and fairly happy. But for reasons that make sense to the individual, he or she wants to engage the services of psychotherapist.

While this is perhaps the least shameful reason for seeing a psychotherapist, it is often denigrated as "paying for friendship." Many people believe this is what friends are for, and there is truth to that assertion. However, in our fast-paced world, very few of us have a friend who is willing to consistently take an hour or more out of his or her weekly schedule to sit and listen to someone talk about life issues. Our friends have busy lives too. Furthermore, some individuals are terrific friends but terrible listeners. Such a person may divert the conversation to what is going on in their life, or they may respond to trivial aspects of what you are saying, or they may not pay attention at all.

Nowadays, psychotherapists are more frequently taking on the role of "listener." The profession began with psychotherapists treating people with serious symptoms and later broadened to assisting people through difficult times. Although the first two roles continue to encompass the majority of work for psychotherapists, the profession has now further evolved to the point where increasing numbers of people are paying psychotherapists to be listeners, witnesses, and advice givers. The remainder of this chapter is designed to help you understand when seeing a psychotherapist might be appropriate.

Serious Symptoms

Most people believe serious symptoms are the reason someone should see a mental health professional. Very often, the person experiencing such symptoms is labeled "mentally ill." Serious symptoms can take many forms, but four important ones are depression, anxiety, psychosis, and substance abuse. Chapter 14, on diagnosis, offers a more complete discussion.

DEPRESSION

Depression is a common reason people seek help from psychotherapists. Depression occurs when you feel sad, blue, irritable, or down in the dumps. You may find yourself tearful or crying and not know why. When depression becomes severe, it is hard to feel anything at all. You wind up feeling numb. Depression often causes problems with eating and sleeping—too much or not enough of either or both. Other signs of depression include difficulties with work, friendships, relationships, sexuality, or life in general. Thoughts about suicide and death are common.

Within the mental health field, there is great disagreement over the cause(s) of depression. Some practitioners insist depression is caused by events, usually losses, in the life of the client, and that it often represents repressed anger. Others assert the causes of depression are genetic or biological. Many professionals believe depression is actually the result of a number of different conditions. The cause of depression is an ongoing debate among mental health professionals, with no side able to come up with a totally convincing argument. In all probability, depression is caused by a number of different factors, either singly or in conjunction.

More relevant than the cause of depression is its treatment. There are three approaches to treating depression, and often they are combined. The three approaches are psychotherapy, antidepressant medication, and an activity program.

Psychotherapy is effective in helping to relieve feelings of depression. Talking to a psychotherapist seems to help depressed clients become more functional. Each school of psychotherapy claims its treatment for depression is the preferred method. This is particularly true of cognitive psychotherapists. Cognitive psychotherapy, discussed more fully in chapter 6, focuses on what the depressed client is thinking and tries to work with the client to substitute other thought patterns that are believed to not lead to depression. The biggest proponents of cognitive psychotherapy for depression are, of course, cognitive therapists. Their public relations effort has been so effective that in some circles it is almost a mantra that the treatment for depression is cognitive psychotherapy.

While cognitive psychotherapy does help with depression, many other schools of psychotherapy are also effective. The psychodynamic school and its subsection, the psychoanalytic school, are both just as adamant in believing their treatment methods to be the best. Psychoanalytic treatment involves the client delving into his or her past in order to uncover hidden conflicts. Psychoanalytic psychotherapists believe that depression is related to unconscious and unresolved conflicts, and that bringing those conflicts into consciousness enables the client to face them and become less depressed.

Other psychotherapists believe that both the causes and cures of depression are genetic and biological, and that depression should be treated with psychoactive medication. Beginning in the 1950s with the discovery of the tricyclic class of antidepressants (see chapter 15 for a fuller explanation of antidepressant medications), various medications have been shown to be effective in relieving the symptoms of depression. Antidepressants comprise arguably the most prescribed class of all medications. Millions of Americans take antidepressants daily.

Increasing one's level of activity has also been shown to relieve symptoms of depression. If you are so depressed that you cannot get out of bed, then getting out of bed and walking around your bedroom would be an increase in activity likely to help with your depression. If you are less depressed, perhaps you are able go to work but then come home and vegetate. In that case, going to a gym and involving yourself in an exercise program is one activity often suggested.

Kevin

Kevin is a good example. Kevin was a workaholic, employed as an assistant manager by a chain of appliance stores. Kevin wanted more than anything to be a success. He had felt like a failure for most of his life. The youngest child in a large family, he was ignored by his parents and raised primarily by his older sisters. Kevin's father was also a workaholic, rarely seen by the family.

Life was not too bad for Kevin until a new manager was hired at his store. The new manager was intent on making his store the most profitable in the entire chain. Kevin and all the other employees were hounded to do a better job in less time. New responsibilities were added to Kevin's workload. As the Christmas sales season approached, the workload increased even more. Kevin looked forward to January. In January, however, the store manager let the employees know there would not be a letup. One day, the manager screamed at Kevin for not doing a job correctly. Kevin went home, feeling overwhelmed, tired, and confused. He went to bed and could not get up for work the next day, and for the next two weeks he called in sick.

Kevin was referred to psychotherapy, where he was diagnosed as having a major depression. (See chapter 14 for an explanation of major depression.) He was immediately referred to a psychiatrist, who prescribed both antidepressant medication and medicine to help him sleep. Kevin's improvement, however, was minimal. He sat at home staring at the television and relied on his sisters to bring him food, clean his house, do his laundry, and drive him to psychotherapy. They even helped Kevin to fill out papers claiming his depression was a work-related disability covered under workers' compensation law. Still, he was not getting better.

Kevin's sisters arranged for him to take part in a creative arts program for adults with emotional disabilities. Each day a van picked him up at his home and took him to the program, where he painted, sculpted, and created collages. In therapy, he learned of his need to please people, especially older men he saw as father figures. He came to realize he had vastly overextended himself, far beyond anything reasonable. For all his manager asked him to do, he tried to do more. He wanted his manager's approval.

Slowly, Kevin was able to become functional again. He began to ask his sisters to do less for him, and this was difficult for them to accept. Standing up to his sisters was his first major accomplishment. After standing up to them, Kevin found he could do even more for himself.

After two years on disability, Kevin took an office job with a travel company. Within a year, he was manager of the office, and a year after that, he became a part owner of the company. He learned that he could work hard but had limits he had to respect.

ANXIETY

Anxiety disorders are common and all related in some way to fear. Anxiety may take the form of a generalized anxiety disorder, a panic disorder, or various phobias. Obsessive and compulsive symptoms can also be related to fear. (See chapter 14 for a fuller explanation.)

Common signs of anxiety are tension in the body and/or shakiness, jumpiness, or jitteriness that is either fairly continuous or manifests itself in particular situations. Other signs include physical changes such as sweating, a fast heartbeat, clammy hands, dry mouth, and dizziness. An anxious person might find him or herself apprehensive and worrying about what might happen.

All of us feel anxious at times, and that anxiety can help us through difficult or dangerous situations. Some people, however, feel anxious either regularly or constantly. Anxiety gets in the way of their having a happy life.

For anxiety, as with depression, different schools of psychotherapy each believe their approach to treatment is best. The behavioral school of psychotherapy (explained more fully in chapter 6) is vocal in insisting that anxiety be treated with their methods of stress reduction, progressive relaxation, and conditioning. Behaviorists do not care how a client became anxious. Their focus is on the symptoms. They believe you cannot be anxious and relaxed at the same time. So if you can learn to relax using certain techniques, you can use those techniques when you begin to feel anxious, thus eliminating the problem.

Psychoactive medications, particularly antianxiety and sedative medications, are often prescribed for anxiety. Antianxiety medications work quickly, usually in less than an hour, and sometimes as quickly as 15 minutes. Often the person taking such medications will become somewhat sleepy (many antianxiety medications are also prescribed as treatments for insomnia, whether the insomnia is the result of anxiety, depression, or some other cause). Unlike antidepressant medications, which need to be taken daily, antianxiety medications can be taken as needed. The danger with most antianxiety medications is that they are habit-forming.

If you are experiencing anxiety, psychotherapy is one way of dealing with it. The school of psychotherapy you choose should depend on you and how you wish to be treated. Medication is available either with or without accompanying psychotherapy.

Josh

A good example of someone suffering from anxiety is Josh, disabled by his anxiety since he was a young boy. Both of his parents were fear-based, envisioning disasters around every corner. His father worked for the same employer for his entire career, valuing the security he had over the potential for making more money elsewhere. His mother was unable to say good-bye to Josh when he went to school without listing all the things he should watch out for. As a result, Josh was always anxious; he saw danger everywhere. He had few friends until college, where he was away from his parents and able to see life differently.

After college, Josh met a man who was 10 years his senior and successful in his career. This man asked Josh to be his lover and to move into the home he owned. Josh jumped at the opportunity. He did not love the man, but he did love the security the man offered. For 10 years, the relationship worked for the both of them.

Over time, however, Josh grew more and more distant from his partner. Since he did not love the man, he felt like a fraud. Josh had a number of affairs and worried that his partner would find out and throw him out on the street. Josh was consuming large quantities of Ativan, an antianxiety medication, just to get through the day. He felt he could not go on. He wanted to leave his partner but was afraid to do so. Finally, he sought psychotherapy.

Psychotherapy helped Josh understand his "perfection complex." Unless everything was absolutely perfect, he worried. This need for perfection, he realized, made him emotionally vulnerable. Since virtually nothing in life is perfect, Josh was always scared.

With the help of his therapist, Josh was able to start taking risks. In his case, that meant not doing things perfectly. He moved into an apartment, although not the perfect apartment he had been looking for. And he took a new job, a job he had previously rejected because it was not the perfect job. Josh remains an anxious person, but he has reduced his need for antianxiety medication by 90%. He believes he will always be an anxious person, but he can live with this level of anxiety, as opposed to the disabling anxiety he previously experienced.

PSYCHOSIS

Psychosis is the most serious mental health symptom an individual can develop. Psychosis means a person has lost connection with reality and is experiencing hallucinations (either visual or, more commonly, auditory), delusions (of power, persecution, religiosity, or something else), or impaired thinking. Psychosis can be intermittent, as often happens in people with bipolar disorders, or it can be persistent, as often happens with people who are schizophrenic. A person suffering from psychosis becomes much less functional during the psychotic periods and often cannot take care of him or herself.

Of all the people who can benefit from psychotherapy, psychotics are the most in need. Unfortunately, the field of mental health can do less for them than others. Both psychotherapy and medication are used for the treatment of psychotic conditions.

Though there are considerable differences of opinion regarding the safety and effectiveness of psychoactive medications used to treat depression and anxiety, there is little controversy over the use of such medications to treat psychosis. This is because, with few exceptions, psychotherapy by itself is not effective for people who experience psychotic symptoms.

The medications used to treat psychosis are powerful drugs and have serious side effects, but the alternative is continuation of the psychotic symptoms. Psychotherapy, coupled with medication, can be an effective treatment for those who experience psychotic symptoms only at particular times, such as individuals who are bipolar. The drugs relieve some of the symptoms, and psychotherapy is effective in helping the individual to cope. Family psychotherapy is often used to help prevent stressful situations, which sometimes exacerbate the psychotic symptoms.

Sam

Sam was 50 before he was diagnosed as bipolar. A crisis in his personal life caused him to have a manic episode, during which he became psychotic. For an entire month, he wrote down ideas that he thought made great sense. When the manic episode finally ended, he went into a depression. As he emerged from the depression, he looked back at his notes and saw they were nothing but gibberish. Although friends had told him this during the episode, he had been certain that what he was writing was important information. He realized he needed to do something, so he began psychotherapy.

One of Sam's first revelations in psychotherapy was that he'd had milder episodes of psychosis several times before, each during a manic episode. He also realized that long periods of depression had always followed his earlier psychotic manic episodes. He further recognized that the length of time between these episodes had been steadily decreasing.

Sam agonized over whether he should take medication for his bipolar condition, finally deciding to do so. He had resisted because he was afraid the medication would inhibit his creativity. By talking about his concerns in psychotherapy, however, he realized he was not being creative during the psychotic periods, and if he went into psychosis more and more often, he would not be creative at all.

After several months on medication to control his psychotic manic episodes, Sam found himself still in a deep depression, deeper than ever before. At that point, he agreed to begin taking antidepressant medication as well. So Sam, who had avoided both psychotherapy and medication for years, fearing they would take away his creativity, now saw that without both he would actually be less creative. Psychotherapy and medication were not what Sam wanted, but he came to the conclusion that the alternative was worse.

SUBSTANCE ABUSE

An issue that brings many people into psychotherapy is the abuse of alcohol and/or drugs. Substance abuse is widespread in the queer community. Bars are still the most common public meeting places for queer people. Alcohol and drugs are readily available and often used to enhance sexual activity.

The most commonly abused substance in the queer community is alcohol. Methamphetamine—also known as speed, crystal, Crissy, and Tina—is widely used among gay men. But many, many other drugs are also problematic for the queer community. Some substances such as sedatives and painkillers are legal and easily obtained with a prescription. Others such as cocaine and ecstasy are illegal. All are mood-altering and have the potential for abuse

In the broadest terms, substance abuse is a maladaptive pattern of substance use that results in distress and/or difficulty functioning in important areas of one's life such as work, school, relationships, or family.

Substance abuse indicates that something is wrong and needs attention. Substance abuse and emotional problems go together. The substances are often used to treat an already existing problem such as depression. This is known as self-medication. Conversely, the overuse of substances may cause problems such as depression. Regardless of which came first, both must be treated.

Determining if you are a substance abuser can be tricky. It is a judgment call that individuals must ultimately make for themselves. However, numerous questionnaires found in books and on the Internet that can be useful in helping you to determine if you are a substance abuser.

Treatment of substance abuse is controversial. Some people believe that only 12-step programs are effective, as described in greater detail in chapter 17. Yet there are alcoholics who stay sober without a 12-step program. (The same is rarely true for methamphetamine abusers.) My own belief is that psychotherapy combined with a 12-step program gives a person the greatest chance of success in dealing with substance abuse. In this way, emotional issues as well as substance abuse issues may be addressed.

Gwen

Gwen is a good example of someone whose concerns about substance abuse brought her into psychotherapy. Her story begins in 1979 when she was preparing to retire. For a long time she had felt lonely as the only lesbian at her place of employment. Although she had been in a lesbian relationship for 20 years, she had remained in the closet and always brought male friends to work-related social functions.

Gwen had been looking forward to retirement because she thought that finally she would come out when her livelihood was no longer an issue. Her lover, however, was adamant about not coming out, and during the first therapy session Gwen talked mostly about that. But right at the end of the hour, she mentioned she was also concerned that she was drinking too much, both at work-related social events and at home. During her second session she made drinking the focus of the conversation. Gwen's therapist asked her to track her drinking for a week, listing every drink she took. Gwen followed through with her therapist's request and was surprised by the results she tabulated. The following week her therapist asked her to experiment with not drinking at all. Gwen was not able to manage that.

When Gwen found herself unable to stop drinking for a week, her therapist asked her to go to a gay/lesbian AA meeting, just to check it out. Gwen went—and is still going. She developed a circle of lesbian friends who introduced her to others in the queer senior community. She continued her therapy for another two years, concentrating on depression and low self-esteem and using AA to remain sober. She came to realize her drinking had prevented her from dealing with the other problems in her life.

Fifteen years later Gwen's partner died. Her AA and queer senior friends put together a memorial service and helped her through the aftermath. She returned to therapy for grief work and to complete her coming-out process.

LIFE AND LIFE-CYCLE ISSUES FOR QUEER PEOPLE

It's difficult to be queer in a nonqueer world. Our culture is highly antagonistic toward anyone who demonstrates tendencies toward being queer. Queer people are devalued and at times hated and reviled. Some people who have access to the media repeatedly make wild assertions, such as that queers are mentally ill psychopathic child molesters. That's difficult for us to hear, especially during our formative years. Right-wing fund-raising literature mailed to millions of American homes has continually called queer people the greatest existing threat to the family. It is virtually impossible for queer people to escape this barrage of hate, even in the 21st century. We come to understand that we are the people our parents, teachers, and religious leaders warned us about. This heavy burden takes its toll on our well-being, both individually and collectively.

As queer people we must negotiate all the challenges other people face, in addition to the unique challenges of being queer. To be queer in a nonqueer world means to face a series of challenges and to deal with those challenges reasonably well in order to achieve a degree of happiness.

IDENTITY ISSUES

Perhaps the first and most important life-cycle issue queer people face is one of identity. Every one of us must ask, "Who am I?" From a young age, we usually know that we are not like most other people, but because being queer is almost never discussed except in a negative, antagonistic manner, we have little idea of who we are. We seem to know we do not fit into the mold that was prepared for us, but finding ourselves is another matter.

Mental health professionals generally agree that a positive self-identity is essential for a happy life. You cannot have a healthy self-image without being able to accept who you are. Step 1 is admitting to yourself that you are a queer person. Step 2 is having a positive regard for yourself. If you do not like who you are, you cannot be happy. If you feel that you are flawed, broken, or sick, having a positive regard for yourself is impossible.

Identity is a fluid concept. While the core of us stays the same throughout our lives, there are many parts of our identity that change. One woman thought she was bisexual when she was young and later identified as a lesbian. Another woman identified as a lesbian until later in life when she began to see herself as bisexual.

Identity issues for queer people are compounded by messages telling us we are not who we are. As young people, many of us were told that we were merely going through a phase and that our attraction to members of our own sex would change in time. It is always confusing to be told you are not who you think and feel you are.

While all lesbians, gay men, bisexuals, and people who are transgendered may identify as queer, especially in the sense of being different from the mainstream, that does not mean we are all alike or that our identity issues are all alike. We are the same in that our identity is different and still unaccepted. But we all have different issues to work out regarding our self-identities.

Lesbians

The identity messages lesbians receive are almost universally negative. Lesbians face a double challenge in that our society is both antiwoman and antiqueer. To have a healthy self-image as a lesbian, a woman must reject the societal notion that she is flawed because she is a woman and even further flawed because she is a lesbian. Being a lesbian is a nontraditional role for a woman, and until recently there have been few positive lesbian role models. Consequently, lesbians often face major challenges in generating a healthy self-image.

Gay men

The identity issue for gay men is compounded by the basic societal message that gay men are fools, voluntarily throwing away their birthright as a heterosexual male to superiority and dominance over women and the planet. Gay men are treated with contempt. To be gay is to be a sissy or a faggot, a less-than-human creature.

Buddy

Buddy was adopted as an infant by a family deeply committed to a fundamentalist Christian faith. His parents also adopted a daughter. They tried hard to provide a warm home and Christian family life for their children. Unfortunately, neither parent understood how to talk with or listen to their children. They provided for their children and thought that was enough.

Buddy was different from the children he grew up around in three important ways: (1) He (and his sister) were adopted, (2) he (and his sister) were ethnically different from their adoptive parents and virtually everyone else in the town where they lived, and (3) he was attracted to men instead of women.

Life became difficult for Buddy during his freshman year in a Christian college. He went to the student counseling service and told the counselor why he was depressed and having difficulty studying. This was the first time he had ever told anyone about his attraction to men. The counselor told him that being attracted to men did not mean he was gay and that there was a way out. Buddy was told to fight his urges through prayer and acceptance of Jesus into his heart. Buddy believed his counselor and became involved in a Christian community created to help people with similar desires to accept Jesus and not act on their sexual feelings.

This left Buddy quite confused about who he was for more than 10 years. Eventually, he left the Christian community and accepted an office job, not because he wanted the job, but because he had no idea *what* he wanted. He became involved in a relationship with a woman. He did not want this relationship, but was unable to end it. He told no one of his feelings for men.

Finally, Buddy entered psychotherapy, which helped him sort through his trio of identity issues: being gay, being part of a racial minority, and being adopted. He slowly came to understand who he was, and with that knowledge he had more confidence to make changes in his life.

Bisexuals

A bisexual person has sexual and romantic feelings for members of both sexes. Some people who are bisexual have an approximately equal attraction to both sexes, while others favor one sex but still have feelings for the other. While the argument can be made that almost everyone is bisexual, because almost everyone has had at least some passing attraction to members of both sexes, bisexual people are those who identify themselves as having *significant* feelings of attraction to members of both sexes.

Bisexuals have to deal with the fact that their identity has generally been rejected by everyone. Heterosexuals say they are homosexual. And homosexuals call them fence-sitters who want the perks of being both heterosexual and homosexual. Until recently, bisexuals have had little support and few role models.

Bisexuals face challenges other queer people usually do not. If a bisexual person acknowledges to him or herself that he or she bisexual, and if that person also wants to be in a monogamous relationship, he or she will have to acknowledge and accept that a part of him or herself will be unexpressed in some significant way. Friends, family, and acquaintances may get confused if they see the bisexual person in a long-term relationship with either a man or a woman, and assume the person is heterosexual, lesbian, or gay. Thus, bisexuals have to work hard to hold on to their self-identity.

Greg

Greg is a good example of a bisexual struggling with his identity. Greg was born to a middle-class family who loved him. But his family, like most families, knew little about bisexuality and could not prepare him for his future.

Growing up, Greg was the leader of his group of friends, not only in the normal teenage activities but also in introducing them to sex, both heterosexual and homosexual. Greg loved sex with both women and men.

For many years, Greg viewed himself as heterosexual. He married, fathered three children, and had an enjoyable family life. He also occasionally went to gay bars and went home with younger men, but that did not conflict with his identity as a heterosexual. One of these young men, however, mugged him one night, and he was severely injured. As a result of the mugging, Greg changed. He was tense, on guard, had trouble sleeping, and experienced flashbacks to the mugging.

The emotional fallout from the mugging caused Greg to start psychotherapy. He sought a queer psychotherapist because he knew he wanted to deal with the question of his self-identity. Because of his desire to be with men, he had begun to believe he was gay. His world was black-and-white. He was either gay or straight. Though he knew that some people were bisexual, he curiously never thought of himself as bisexual.

In psychotherapy he talked about these issues. He was surprised when I told him that he appeared to be bisexual. He thought of himself as either gay or straight. When he was predominantly having sex with his wife, he thought of himself as straight. Later, when he was predominantly having sex with men, he thought of himself as gay. But he never completely stopped having sex with either men or women, and he could not see a future for himself that did not include sex with both men and women. Psychotherapy allowed him to self-identify as bisexual, and accepting that identity greatly reduced the stress in his life. He now knew his place in the world, and the quirky side of his personality began to feel proud of his little-understood sexual orientation.

Transgender

A transgendered individual faces perhaps the greatest challenge of any queer person in developing a positive self-image. As little support as there often is for lesbians, gays, and bisexuals, virtually *none* exists for people who are transgendered. Furthermore,transgender is the most misunderstood of all queer identities, because it encompasses a variety of self-identities, including transsexuals, cross-dressers, and those who otherwise do not identify with the roles society has assigned their biological gender. Transgendered individuals must first acknowledge their transgender identity and then figure out where within that broad rubric they belong.

Transsexuals

Transsexuals are people who do not identify either emotionally or psychologically with their biological sex. Biological males who identify as female are known as male to female, or MTF. Biological females who identify as male are known as female to male, or FTM. Transsexuals often find that identifying with the gender of their emotions and psychology becomes extremely difficult in a world that wants to identify them solely by their biological sex. Though transsexuals usually ask to be addressed with pronouns consistent with their emotional and psychological sex, many people rudely and inappropriately address them using pronouns of their biological gender.

The traditional mental health diagnosis for transsexuals is Gender Identity Disorder. There are theories—most are biologically based—as to what causes someone to be transsexual, but none of those theories have been validated through research.

Cross-Dressers

Cross-dressers were once known as transvestites, but because of the negative sexual fetish association with the word *transvestite*, the terminology has changed. Cross-dressers have a strong identification with their biological sex but feel more comfortable wearing the clothes and adopting the mannerisms of the opposite sex. Most cross-dressers are heterosexual men who dress in female attire, though gay men, heterosexual woman, lesbians, and bisexuals sometimes cross-dress as well.

Gender Blenders, Gender Benders

A large number of individuals are neither transsexuals nor cross-dressers but nevertheless strongly identify with *some* of the cultural mannerisms, clothes, or activities associated with the opposite sex. Such people are known as gender blenders or gender benders. They are sometimes identified as androgynous because they exhibit both masculine and feminine traits. Identifying them simply as androgynous, though, misses the idea that they show a deep-seated affinity for aspects of both biological sexes.

Sasha

Sasha, who was given the name Alice at birth, provides a good example of the struggle for self-identity transgendered persons experience. His birth announcements said "It's a Girl!" because from all outward appearances he was female. As a child he was dressed in girls' clothing and expected to act feminine. From the time he was 4 or 5, however, he wanted to dress and act as a boy.

As a child, Sasha kept wanting to take off his dress and run around in his underwear. His parents were not too upset over this behavior when he was very young, but as he grew older, they resisted and wanted him to wear dresses. Minor battles often occurred over what he was to wear.

Sasha's father—whom Sasha later learned had wanted a son—unknowingly became his ally. When Sasha was growing up, he liked to hang out with his father and help with projects around the house. The oldest child in the family, he bonded with his father while being taught how to fix things with his hands. Sasha and his father came to share many warm memories of those years.

Sasha was popular among young girls who were his play companions. He led them on adventures, and all willingly followed his directions. This lasted until puberty when Sasha suddenly became quite shy. He was not interested in dating boys and retreated into the safety of home, becoming mother's helper around the house. In high school Sasha only dated a few times.

After graduation from high school, Sasha's world opened up. He joined the Air Force and received technical training in telecommunications. After his stint in the Air Force, he went to college and then to work for the phone company. Sasha's coworkers were almost always male, and he liked that. His coworkers jokingly called him "one of the boys," not knowing the profound truth of their jokes.

Sasha first heard the word *transsexual* while in college. He tried to understand it, but the concept was confusing. He thought he knew what it felt like to be a man, but he was not sure if he was transsexual. Later, he decided he was a lesbian since his primary sexual and romantic attraction was to women. He considered himself a "butch dyke," but that never felt entirely right.

In his first relationship, he and his partner would role-play with Sasha playing a man and his partner playing a woman. Both found this easy to do; it fit them. But for Sasha, it became more than role-playing. When he was in that role—and he was in that role almost all the time—he felt a peace that he had never known before. There was something *right* about playing the role of a man. During this time, he began to hear the word *transgender* and to wonder if it applied to him.

Sasha began to use the Internet to communicate with people who considered themselves transgendered, and he found he had a lot in common with them. For many years, he had dressed only in men's clothes, but now his identity was changing. He allowed himself to not merely *play the role* of a man, but to *actually be* a man. And with that, another level of peace descended upon Sasha.

Eventually, Sasha started going to transgender gatherings. He also began to take hormones, which radically changed his body. His voice deepened, he grew facial hair, and his body began to look more masculine. He talked to his partner about having breast reduction surgery, and that idea proved difficult for his partner. While Sasha's partner was happy with Sasha being a butch dyke and dressing like a man, the partner loved women. As Sasha's body became more and more masculine, the partner felt more and more distant from Sasha.

These physical changes also caused trouble for Sasha with his family. Although he did not see them often, they did talk regularly on the phone. His family could not help but notice that his voice had grown much deeper. He fended off their questions with stories of allergies and a long cold, but after a number of months and the family's insistence that he seek medical help for this problem, Sasha decided to tell them about the hormones and his plans for breast reduction surgery.

Neither his family nor his partner took this very well. He and his partner eventually split up, and his family thought he had gone mad. While they did not fully reject him, he had trouble talking with them since they were either distant and sad or vehemently expressed their concern about the choices he was making.

Sasha did find help in the transgender community, especially among other FTM transsexuals. He chose a male psychotherapist to help him through the process because he wanted to learn, from a man, more about what it meant to actually be a man. Now, most of the world believes on meeting Sasha that he is a man. And Sasha likes it that way. His driver's license, his checkbook, and personal identification have his adopted masculine name on them. He remains attracted to women but finds there are relatively few women, queer or otherwise, who accept him and want to be with him as a man. But the price is one he is willing to pay to be comfortable with himself.

Mitch

Mitch's path to a transgender identity differs from Sasha's. Mitch was born a biological male, and was raised by his mother and an aunt. His father was a gay man who'd had a short-term relationship with his mother. Mitch did not have any contact with his father until he was an adult.

As a child Mitch was shy and had few friends. He spent most of his time at home with his mother and aunt, whom he enjoyed helping, especially with "feminine" tasks such as sewing and crafts. But puberty came early for Mitch, and by the time he was 11, he had to shave his dark beard daily. Mitch's striking combination of a masculine look and a feminine nature was a source of confusion, both to him and those around him, but most people ignored him, and he tended to keep to himself.

As an adult Mitch moved to the city where his father lived and established a relationship with him. This facilitated Mitch's coming out as a gay man. But he was never comfortable calling himself gay, because he felt like a woman. He kept that secret inside, telling no one, including his father.

Mitch had seen listings for meetings of MTF support groups, but for years he could not bring himself to attend one. He did, however, read whatever books and articles on transsexuality he could find. After much hesitation, he finally dropped in on a support group. As difficult as it had been for him to attend the first time, he felt comfortable in the group and returned for several more meetings.

The support group helped Mitch become more comfortable with his identity as a transsexual. Virtually all the group members were taking female hormones, and many were considering surgical operations to make their bodies appear more feminine. Many also dressed and presented themselves to the world as women. Mitch discussed in therapy whether to take hormones and/or undergo various operations, including sex reassignment surgery, but he decided to take a different path. Although he disliked his chubby, hairy body as a man, he doubted that taking female hormones would greatly improve his appearance. And he was afraid that he would later regret having any body-altering surgery done.

Mitch decided to present himself to the world as a male. But when he was at home or among friends, he dressed as a woman and asked to be addressed as Marcia. Since the shadow of his beard appeared within several hours of shaving, he knew he was quite unattractive as a woman by conventional standards. But he felt good enough about who he was to endure the confused and often hostile looks he received when he occasionally went out in public dressed as a woman.

The most difficult challenge for Mitch/Marcia now is finding men who want to date him. He feels "in between"—that he is not attractive to most gay men because of his unusual feminine nature and that he is not attractive to men who like transsexuals because he will not take hormones or undergo body-changing operations. This is his greatest source of unhappiness.

Mitch is still in his 20s and expects his identity will change over time, but he is more curious than concerned about where he'll end up. For now, he is Mitch at work and Marcia when socializing.

Other Identity Issues

There are other groups within the queer community where the issue of identity is particularly complicated. In these communities, there is another identity beyond queer that society devalues. The person must make peace with that identity in order to have a positive self-image.

Later in this book, there is information about choosing a therapist. If you are a member of an ethnic minority, transgendered, or kinky, read those pages with the understanding that everything said about whether a therapist is queer-affirmative also applies to your special need. Many therapists who are clear as to what it means to be lesbian, gay, or bisexual are still woefully ignorant regarding what it means to be a member of an ethnic minority, transgendered, or kinky.

Ethnicity

The most common of these dual identity problems is when a person is queer and also a member of a racial, religious, or ethnic minority. A person growing up in one of these communities experiences rejection from society at large, and consequently looks to his or her racial, religious, or ethnic community for support and understanding. Unfortunately, most of these communities are hostile to their queer members. Similarly, when these individuals seek comfort in the queer community, they are sometimes shunned because of their race, religion, or ethnicity. As such, queer minorities often find themselves doubly discriminated against. The fact that most psychotherapists are not members of racial, religious, or ethnic minorities complicates matters further.

Luis

A good example of a "double minority" is Luis, the youngest child of parents who emigrated from Central America to the United States before he was born. His father died when he was a teenager. He began therapy, stating, "Sometimes I think I am going crazy." He was about to turn 30 and was depressed. His primary care physician had prescribed antidepressants, but he stopped taking them because they caused sexual difficulties. He was getting drunk several times a week, felt anxious most of the time, had lost interest in things that used to be pleasurable, and was staying home from work, often with hangovers.

At the urging of his supervisor, he called his managed care insurance company and asked for a referral to a Spanish-surnamed psychotherapist who was gay or gay-affirmative. He was surprised to find out that his managed care insurance company had not one therapist with Spanish surname or even one listed as bilingual in Spanish and English. The insurance company did, however, have several psychotherapists who listed "gay and lesbian issues" as a clinical specialty. Luis asked to see one of those therapists.

For Luis, going to a therapist was difficult. At the last minute, he canceled his first appointment. He did, however, ask for another appointment, which he kept. In the first visit, he talked about wanting to kill himself, of riding his bicycle in front of a bus hoping that it would hit him and he would die. He also said he was not out to his family or at work, only to a few friends. When he socialized, it was always at a gay bar that catered to Hispanic men and their admirers.

Luis did not stay in therapy long, but he did stay long enough for the therapist to give Luis a copy of a chapter from a book describing the issues faced by Latino gay men. This proved helpful for Luis. It helped him to understand the actions of a distant cousin who was rejected after he came out to the family 10 years earlier. The cousin disappeared after that, and had not been heard from since. Luis was frightened he would experience the same rejection.

Several months later, Luis called the therapist and gave an update. He had come out to a sister, who reacted by telling him how disgusted she was with the news and that he should not tell anyone else in the family. That changed things for Luis. He began to see his family with different eyes. He came to understand that while his family was Hispanic, they were not a typical Hispanic family in that they were much more rejecting of family members who were different. He came to see that his mother had many traits in common with Joan Crawford as portrayed in *Mommie Dearest*. This understanding enabled him to find peace with both his gay identity and his Hispanic identity. He realized the rejection he experienced was not because he was from a Hispanic family, but because he was from a particular Hispanic family.

Kink

Another subgroup within the queer community that faces a difficult identity challenge is those who identify as being into kink. These individuals have to grapple not only with being queer but also with belonging to yet another often despised minority.

The kink community is diverse. It includes those who are into leather, either as a fashion or as a fetish, those whose expressions of love and sexuality are sadomasochistic or fetishistic, members of the motorcycle/biker community, and others.

Within both the mainstream and queer community, kink is widely misunderstood. *The Diagnostic and Statistical Manual of Mental Disorders,* the bible of psychological diagnosis, lists many kinky sex practices as indicative of a mental disorder. The leaders of various queer pride celebrations have refused to allow speakers or organizations from the kink community to participate in their celebrations and festivals, fearing negative reactions from both the queer and mainstream communities.

Members of the kink community tend to strongly identify with the masculine part of their personality. Everyone's personality has both masculine and feminine parts. The masculine part represents those traits we associate with maleness—power, hierarchy, control, dominance and submission, physical achievement, putting aside one's feelings to accomplish tasks. The feminine part represents traits associated with femaleness—nurturing, negotiation, compromise, equality, relationships, behavior consistent with feelings. Some members of the kink community identify strongly with both the masculine and feminine parts of their personality, but most will identify more strongly with the masculine side.

The difficulty members of the kink community have in finding an affirmative psychotherapist is similar to the problem all queer people had in the past. For the most part, the mental health community does not understand the nature of human sexuality when related to kinky sex. As mentioned earlier, *The Diagnostic and Statistical Manual of Mental Disorders* lists many kinky sex practices as indicative of a mental disorder, just as it used to list homosexuality as a mental disorder. In most situations, however, involvement in kinky sex is no more indicative of severe emotional problems than merely being queer. While there are certainly people within the queer and kinky communities who are deeply troubled, the majority of those who are queer and/or kinky are simply expressing their love for another person in a way that mainstream society does not understand and therefore vilifies.

A problem for those who identify as kinky is that many psychotherapists, whether they are in the mainstream or queer community, hold negative prejudices concerning kinky sex and romance. They do not understand that being kinky involves the same identity issues as being queer.

Because kinky sex and romance are misunderstood by our society, and because all of us grow up exposed to those prejudices, those who are involved in kink need to find a way to accept themselves and to rid themselves of negative societal prejudices. Psychotherapy with a kink and queer affirmative psychotherapist can be a big help.

Eric

Eric is a good example of the obstacles faced by members of the kink community. A 41-year-old masculine-appearing man, Eric had difficulty accepting his identity as queer and a devotee of kink. He was in long-term therapy with a psychotherapist who no longer felt able to help Eric with his sexual-identity issues and suggested that Eric briefly see another therapist.

Eric's parents were highly sexual and kinky with each other. As a child, Eric found bondage restraints tied to the legs of his parents' bed. His parents did not discuss their sexuality, but they did not hide the evidence either. Despite this, Eric was a virgin until he was 31 years old. Needless to say, coming out was difficult for Eric.

In addition, Eric had trouble maintaining erections and had never experienced anal sex. He wanted to be able to penetrate another man, but every time he tried, he lost his erection. This did not happen during oral sex. He also wanted to explore his kinky sex fantasies, which involved dominating other men.

Through therapy Eric learned that he was disconnected from both his body and his queer kinky identity. He was unable to look at himself in a mirror unless he was wearing clothes. From the time he was a teenager, he masturbated by laying face down on the bed and rubbing his penis against the mattress. He never let his hand touch his penis while masturbating.

Eric's first two therapy homework assignments were to look in the mirror while naked and to touch his penis while masturbating. His third assignment was to combine the previous assignments. In addition small doses of Viagra prescribed by his psychiatrist helped Eric maintain his erection during attempts at anal sex.

Eric then took a job with a media company that produced gay male pornography featuring masculine men engaging in kinky sex. He took the job to be around the actors, who were comfortable with their kink proclivities. After several weeks of working for this company and after 14 psychotherapy sessions focusing on his identity issues as a queer kink devotee, Eric felt he had achieved what he had wanted to achieve. He felt more comfortable with himself and his identity, and decided at that point to take what he had learned back to his former long-term therapist and continue the work they had been doing for several years—but with greater acceptance of himself as a queer, kinky man.

COMING OUT

Coming out is a special time in the life of a queer person. It is a marker, a rite of passage. It is the time when someone declares to him or herself and to others who he or she is. Coming out to yourself is covered in the previous section on identity formation. Telling others is a different matter, though.

While coming out may have a starting point, it is a process that never ends, and it always involves risking loss of love or respect. A good psychotherapist values your right to be in charge of your coming-out process: whom you come out to and when. Your therapist can help you think through your unique process of coming out and can also guide you to resources such as coming-out support groups. If you are coming out, seeing a psychotherapist who also happens to be queer is a good idea, since he or she will have been through his or her own coming-out process and can share that experience with you in a helpful way.

Alicia

Alicia never thought much about her sexuality while growing up. She went to high school and married soon after graduating. She had two children and what she thought was a happy life. Then her husband asked for a divorce. After splitting up, she and her husband jointly raised the children, who spent time in both homes. Alicia saw her role as being a mother, and little more.

As her children got older, Alicia had more time on her hands. She became friends with another woman in a similar situation. They grew close, and one day Alicia and the other woman made love. This was the first time Alicia had ever had a sexual encounter with anyone besides her former husband. She could not believe the difference.

With her husband, Alicia had been indifferent to sex. If he wanted it, it was all right with her. Though she never enjoyed it or looked forward to it, she did not loathe it either. It was what it was: something to go through. But with her friend it was different. She felt alive and electric. She felt she had been touched in ways she never realized were possible. She felt this other woman understood her and had made love to her specifically.

Not surprisingly, Alicia became frightened and shut down after the encounter. Fortunately, Alicia's friend realized what had happened and recommended a female therapist she had seen years before when first coming out. Alicia agreed to meet with the therapist, who assessed Alicia's knowledge of human sexuality. Finding it to be limited, she referred Alicia to several books on sexuality. Like Alicia, the therapist was Catholic and therefore able to easily understand why Alicia had never remarried or had sex with another man as well as why making love to a woman was so disorienting for her. She directed Alicia to attend a church where 90% of congregation was lesbian, gay, bisexual, or transgendered.

After almost two years of psychotherapy, Alicia was ready to tell someone else about her lesbian feelings. She chose her former husband, with whom she had maintained a friendship. She was surprised that he did not think it was disgusting or reject her. It was more than a year before she could tell anyone else. Then, as if by magic, Alicia went from never having told anyone except her former husband to telling everyone she thought should know. She told her parents, siblings, and children. She told lifelong friends and coworkers. And she joined a social organization for slightly older lesbians.

For Alicia, the internal process of coming out was slow. But after it was complete, she was able to reenter the world as a different person. Alicia knew her coming-out story was not typical. But she also realized from her reading about other women's coming-out experiences that there is no typical story and everyone has to come out in his or her own way. The big surprise was when she told her son. He told her that he already knew and had a secret of his own. He was gay and had a boyfriend he wanted her to meet. A by-product of Alicia coming out to her son was his being able to come out to her. As a result, they have since had a closer relationship. Alicia's only regret is that she could not have come out sooner and made it easier for her son to come out to her.

AGING

Aging is a complicated issue that is difficult for anyone in our society to deal with. Queer people, unfortunately, encounter all the usual issues related to aging plus a few more. Psychotherapists can help queer people negotiate the emotional challenges aging brings on.

While the challenge of aging cannot be reduced to a single issue, one issue is overriding. That issue is loss—especially the loss of youth and the perks that go along with being young. Of course, there are perks that go along with being older, but those are often overlooked. It is the losses that stand out: decreased physical abilities, increased susceptibility to illness and injuries, loss of stamina, and more. Because of this, older people often find they have something in common—the losses resulting from living to an old age—and that often overrides any factors that may have previously separated them.

The losses due to aging are tremendous and, like all losses, need to be grieved. Hopefully, this will be active grieving. Active grieving makes it easier to accept the loss and move on. Inactive grieving, or no grieving at all, indicates a denial of the loss and makes matters worse. Grieving either takes time, or it never occurs.

The preceding is true for all men and women. For queer people, though, there are additional losses. Most women and queer men have been conditioned to place physical attractiveness on a high pedestal. Consequently, the loss of physical attractiveness that goes along with aging can become monumental. Being young and queer often correlates with being sexually and romantically attractive. With minor exceptions, the younger queer person has an easier time attracting others. The older queer person notices fewer and fewer people giving him or her sexual looks. This is particularly true for queer men, who often begin to feel invisible in the gay community after reaching a certain age.

The solution is to grieve for what has been lost. Older queer people need to arrive at a new relationship with their bodies. Their attractiveness can no longer be based on youth. It must be based on something else. And the loss of youth must be grieved. To grieve means not just to talk about this change in a bitter or longing manner but also to actively recognize the pain that loss creates. In time, an aging queer person can learn to accept the changes brought about by getting older.

Psychotherapists who have actively worked with the queer community for a number of years are often very experienced at dealing with loss. Because of the AIDS epidemic, many psychotherapists have been helping queer people deal with the loss of health and lives—their own, their friends', and their partners'. The same skill psychotherapists gained while helping queer people deal with AIDS-related losses can be used to help queer people deal with losses related to aging.

Older queer people also grew up in an era when being queer was considered sick, sinful, shameful, and criminal. This frequently had a profound impact on their self-identity. On top of that, many were expected to marry and have children. Thus, issues of childlessness can be particularly poignant for this group, even more so because older people with children usually expect those children to care for them when they can no longer care for themselves. Most older queer people, however, must make other arrangements. Older childless lesbians find it even more difficult because the economic discrimination women routinely experience leaves them with few resources upon which to rely. Loneliness also becomes a factor. The older one gets, the fewer of one's friends have survived.

There are, however, advantages to being an older queer person, particularly for lesbians. Older lesbians are affectionately referred to as *crones* and are valued by younger lesbians for their knowledge and wisdom. The same is true, if to a lesser extent, in the gay male community.

Irene

Irene was 72-year-old retired woman on a fixed income who was experiencing intense fear and loneliness. She had been an activist all her life but began to isolate herself before she started therapy. Irene needed more than just to have conversations with her psychotherapist. She needed a psychotherapist who could act as a resource person, helping her connect with available community services.

Irene's therapist helped her find a job at a queer nonprofit agency. There, she was viewed as an elder with wisdom to pass along. She worked only 10 hours a week, but that was enough to widen her social circle. Eventually, she became involved with an outreach program for elderly queer people. Despite her years as an activist, Irene had been unaware of this program. She needed the help of her psychotherapist to find out the program existed and also to convince her to take part in it. Through the help of her therapist, Irene was able to share her wisdom and activist background with those much younger than her and also to make new friends her own age.

BODY IMAGE

Our society does a great job of telling us that we are physically inadequate, regardless of how we look. It does not matter if we are large, medium, small, handsome, beautiful, or ugly. We all get the message that we are not OK. This makes it hard for us to feel connected to the physical part of who we are. In addition to the body image issues nearly everyone in our society has, queer people have a few others.

Transgender

For a transgendered individual, body image is an enormous issue, because his or her physical body is not consistent with his or her mental and emotional self-image. The oft-stated phrase, "I am a man trapped in a woman's body," and its converse, "I am a woman trapped in a man's body," say it all. There is no body image issue more basic than being transgendered.

Most people in our society are uncomfortable talking about transgender issues. They know little about being transgendered. But the one thing they do know is that some men have their penises surgically removed in order to look like a woman. Most men (and many women) become squeamish at the mere thought.

If for no other reason than that, transgendered people need a safe nonjudgmental place where they can discuss their true life experiences. Psychotherapy can provide that setting. But psychotherapists are often asked to become more involved in the lives of their transgendered clients.

It is a huge step to surgically alter the human body. Surgeons are cautious about performing the sex reassignment surgery needed for a biological woman or man to look like the other gender. The procedure involves removing parts of the body and using some of that removed tissue to construct organs resembling those of the other gender. These operations are radical and permanent. Most are irreversible. (Most body changes brought on by taking hormones are reversed when the individual stops taking the hormones.)

Thus, medical ethics and federal regulations mandate surgeons to make sure that the person requesting sex reassignment surgery gives informed consent to perform the operation. Informed consent for most medical procedures requires the surgeon to explain the risks involved with the given procedure and then ask the patient to sign a consent form. But because sex reassignment surgery is voluntary and so radically changes the body, medical ethics panels require that anyone requesting sex reassignment surgery first spend time discussing it in psychotherapy. Furthermore, the individual's psychotherapist must write a letter of support indicating that issues surrounding the desire undergo the surgery have been thoroughly explored in therapy. A good example of such a letter is included in the appendix.

Not all therapists are willing to write such a letter. Even those who are knowledgeable about transgender issues and willing to work with transgendered people sometimes refuse to write such a letter, no matter the circumstances. Consequently, if you are a transgendered individual considering sex reassignment surgery, it is best to ask your therapist in advance if he or she would be willing to write such a letter on your behalf.

Queer Women

The basic body image issue for lesbians and bisexual women is the same as for all women in our society. Simply put, a woman cannot be too thin. Women are taught from the time they are young to feel they could and should lose weight, regardless of their size or build.

Large women have it especially difficult. They are discriminated against in most sectors of society. But this insidiousness is not restricted to large women. Medium-size and small women are also affected. Anorexia, where a person starves him or herself to lose weight, and bulimia, where a person eats and then purges (vomits), are not uncommon. Both result from attempts to become thinner.

Karen Carpenter is one of the more well-known people to have died as a result of anorexia, but she is not alone. Thousands of others—nearly all women—have serious medical problems as a result of these conditions, including dental and gum problems caused by stomach acid being in the mouth of those who purge. Eating disorders can be attributed to how our society teaches women to relate to their bodies. Psychotherapy can help.

Mary

Mary weighed over 300 pounds when she first entered therapy at age 32. She came to therapy for two reasons. First, she had never had a relationship or even a sexual experience. Second, she wanted to deal with career issues, since she felt she was not as successful as she believed she could and should have been. Shortly after beginning therapy, she joined both Overeaters Anonymous and Fat Liberation. By joining the two groups at the same time she received an onslaught of cross-messages. In OA, she received a lot of support for watching her food intake, and in Fat Liberation she was told that it's all right to be a large woman. Mary liked both groups, though, and felt she got something from each. As a result, her attempts to control her body size were ineffective.

While Mary was concerned about self-image and body image, her therapist did not at first approach these issues frontally, but maneuvered around the side and in the back door. What the therapist focused on were Mary's genuine strengths: creativity, intelligence, and a sense of humor.

This helped Mary in her career. She got a much better job as the head of a thriving nonprofit, where her organizational and people skills were vital. She also got involved in a relationship with another woman. After they had been living together happily for two years, Mary decided to concentrate on her weight. The reasons for this, however, had changed. Whereas for Mary it had once been all about body image and how others viewed her, now it was about being healthy.

At first Mary had a hard time "coming out" about her weight program to her Fat Liberation friends. But more and more, she flexed the muscles she had built on the job and in her relationship. She found she was able to stay in the Fat Liberation movement while doing with her body what she wanted, which was to lose weight for health reasons.

Debbie

Debbie, 35, came into therapy just after being successfully inseminated. She was quite thin and suffered from bulimia. She wanted to deal with this problem because she did not want to harm the child she was carrying. She also did not want to pass her disease along to her child.

Debbie's therapy concentrated on attitudes about food and eating that she had internalized while growing up. Her childhood was filled with messages from her mother about how she should look, dress, and act. Debbie remembered that her parents used to go out on Saturday night, leaving her brother and her behind. Before leaving, her mother would dole out three potato chips apiece to each child and then staple the bag shut to make sure neither of them ate more than the allotted three chips. Once, while Debbie was a teenager, she put on bobby socks and loafers when her family went to visit an elderly uncle. Debbie's mother became incensed, holding a butcher knife to her chest and threatening to kill herself if Debbie did not wear nylon hose and dress shoes.

Obviously, Debbie had acquired a large load of parenting and body image issues. Her therapy centered on replacing images of appearance with notions of essence—who she actually was. During therapy, Debbie also looked at the kind of parent she wanted to be.

Debbie arrested her bulimia during the pregnancy and while nursing. In the year after her son's birth, she noted that she had not even thought about vomiting in a while. The therapy work then focused on allowing Debbie to have occasional thoughts about vomiting, should they occur. The emphasis was for Debbie to not have to try to keep a perfect record and thus set herself up for a letdown. Part of the treatment for any eating disorder or body issue is to let the person enjoy his or her success without trying to be perfect, recognizing that the underlying issues run so deep that relapse is inevitable. Therapy helped Debbie recognize that the issue was not whether thoughts of purging were going to occur but how she would manage them when they did occur.

Queer Men

Only the smallest percentage of men fit the image of what is generally considered handsome or beautiful, and even those who fit that image often feel inadequate. Queer men, unfortunately, have body image issues that are not shared by nonqueer men. Queer men are sexual objects in ways that nonqueer men are not. Women, in general, do not place the same value on physical attractiveness that men do. Consequently, nonqueer men are less concerned about how they look than are queer men. Queer men are both sexual hunters and sexually hunted. Thus, how other men look is important, and how *they* look is important.

While queer men have many body issues, several stand out. Those issues primarily relate to muscles, penis size, and the stereotypical image of a sexy man. While these are also issues for nonqueer men, they are generally more troublesome for queer men.

Starting after World War II, an artist using the pseudonym Tom of Finland drew images of men that soon became and are still extremely popular in the gay community. (A museum is dedicated to his work, and even now, years after his death, his drawings are hot sellers.) His images, both pornographic and nonpornographic, pictured queer men with exaggerated muscles and huge penises. He did much to change the image of queer men from frail sissy boy to macho male. This helped many queer men feel better about themselves. Tom of Finland single-handedly defined an exceedingly masculine look for queer men that many have tried to emulate.

"Tom's men," of course, are gross exaggerations. Yet many queer men go to gyms, lift weights, and take anabolic steroids to enhance their physiques. Anabolic steroids have several side effects. When used regularly, they push the user toward anger. The expression "roid rage" is well-known in the muscle-building community and used to describe an individual whose anger is out of control as a result of using anabolic steroids. Another side effect of taking steroids is testicle shrinkage. Steroids are similar to testosterone. When the body absorbs steroids from an external source, it stops producing testosterone, causing the testicles shrink. Many queer men feel that they can live with this since the benefits outweigh the costs. Two more side effects of anabolic steroids are unintended

erections and increased sexual desire. As with enhanced muscula-
ture, this combination proves hard to resist for many queer men
with low self-esteem.

While going to a gym and lifting weights is actually good for
most men and women, the reasons many queer men go to gyms can
cause emotional problems. No matter how often they go or how
often they take anabolic steroids, they will never look like "Tom's
men." Even competition bodybuilders fall short of this image. And
since most men do not have the genetic potential to be a competition bodybuilder, it is possible for them to feel bad about their bodies even when they have developed them to their fullest potential.

Frank

Frank was an effeminate boy who developed a masculine body
after puberty. But the inner image of being a sissy remained. As an
adult, he went to the gym daily, and although he worked out relent-
lessly, he never could achieve the body he wanted—a body, he said,
that would make him resemble one of "Tom's men." He was aware
those men were idealized images, but he still worked toward the
standard they represented. He took anabolic steroids, and they
worked. He became a 5-foot-10 225-pound man with more muscles
than he ever dreamed he could have.

One day when he was in a particularly bad mood, Frank found
himself stuck in traffic. The traffic got slower and slower, and he
felt his rage rising. He stayed under control until the driver behind
him honked, apparently feeling that Frank should have entered an
intersection instead of waiting until the other cars had cleared.
Frank lost it. He got out of his car, yelled at the driver who had
honked, and kicked the guy's car door. When the man reached for
his cell phone and dialed the police, Frank lost it completely. He
smashed his hand against driver's window, shattering it. He grabbed
the man by the collar and screamed obscenities. Finally, Frank realized what he was doing and stopped. He was arrested and charged
with assault.

As part of Frank's plea bargain, he agreed to seek counseling.
Frank was one of the few people who, when ordered by the court to
seek counseling, actually benefited from it. He had never done any-

thing like that before and knew that taking anabolic steroids had enhanced his rage. Until he was told to take part in counseling, he never realized how angry he was and how much he had disliked his body before he began working out and using steroids. After his court-ordered time in counseling was up, Frank continued on a voluntary basis.

The size of a man's penis is something that also concerns most men, queer or not. Virtually all men compare themselves to other men in locker room situations. There is a king-of-the-hill mentality that goes along with having a large penis.

There are a few controversial medical procedures that can make a man's penis larger, but for the most part, penis size is something a man has little control over. Genetics controls penis size; a man has whatever he has. But because of the unwarranted association of a large penis with virility and masculinity, men with average and smaller-than-average penises are often emotionally tormented. Queer men are no exception. Most have had a number of sexual partners, and they are well-aware of how large their penis is when compared with other men.

Lee

Lee, for example, agonized over the size of his penis until he was so depressed he could not work. As a college-educated professional, he commanded a high salary. He owned his own home, drove a new car, and had stylish clothes that fit his 6-foot-3 frame well. While not classically good-looking, he possessed a winning smile, and men cruised him constantly. But he rarely accepted their invitations.

What Lee was concerned about was the size of his penis. He claimed it was the smallest penis of any man he had ever met. While Lee was prone to exaggeration and oversimplification, his penis was probably on the small side. And to Lee, that meant he was unattractive.

Lee considered himself sexually versatile; he liked both the active and passive roles in sex. But he had experienced so many jokes and even outright rejections because of the size of his penis that he was shy about being sexual with men, and frightened about how they would react when he wanted to be the active partner. One day he came to his therapy session with a personal ad he had found in a local gay newspaper: Someone had placed an ad saying he was turned on by and wanted to meet people with small penises. Rather than finding comfort in the ad and responding to it—and without knowing anything about the person placing the ad—all Lee could say was "See, the only men who will like me are freaks."

Acceptance for Lee was a difficult and slow process. He never did become comfortable with the size of his penis, but he was able to accept that he had no choice. Eventually, he did meet someone who accepted him as he was, and they became lovers. While they never agreed to have a monogamous relationship, Lee decided early on he would only have sex with his partner because he could not stand the process of exposing himself to possible ridicule. Counseling was helpful in getting Lee to a point where he could let one man into his life, and that was enough for Lee.

Obviously, massive muscles and penis size are not the only body image issues important to queer men. The standards for handsome men are defined by the same general forces that define what is considered beautiful for women. And few men meet that standard. Queer men who vary considerably from that standard often feel rejected by the queer community at large.

Ian

Ian told me he was fat from the time he was born, weighing over 10 pounds at birth. He had heard stories again and again as a child about how much his large size had hurt his mother during delivery. How much he weighed was always the main topic at dinner while he was growing up. Furthermore, Ian was not only large but uncoordinated. He was taunted by other kids and had always chosen last in gym class.

At age 13, Ian began to buy *Playgirl* in order to look at pictures of naked men. They were all thin, muscular, and hairless. He had begun to shave when he was 11, and by 13 hair had begun to grow over much of his body. As he looked at the magazines and admired the men, he began to hate himself for being fat and hairy. Attempts at dieting failed, and Ian settled into a long-term depression that lasted through high school and college.

During college, Ian began going to male sex clubs with "glory holes"—places where men put their penises through an opening in a partition and another man on the other side of the partition performed oral sex. This seemed ideal for Ian: Regardless of which side of the wall he was on, the other man could not see him. This took care of his sexual needs, and in his early 20s that was enough.

As Ian grew older, though, he wanted to date. But he was so scared that no one would date him because of his size that he never tried. Though he managed to work and be successful in his occupation, his depression continued. He felt worthless. He continued to buy magazines with pictures of naked men, but they all showed photos of thin or muscular hairless men. He continued to hate the body he had.

The first time it was suggested to him in therapy that he try to love the body he had, Ian was repulsed by the idea and rejected it immediately. He cited many reasons for rejecting his body, from valid health concerns to invalid beliefs, such as that no one except a freak could love anyone so big.

Ian was aware of gay men who self-identify as "bears"—men who are big and/or hairy and who accept and love themselves as they are. Initially, he spoke of bears in condescending terms, calling them losers. It was only after reading stories that bears had posted on the Internet that he began to think that perhaps he was being too harsh on the bears and himself. Many hours were spent in therapy discussing this, and Ian slowly shifted from self-loathing to self-loving.

Ian continues to want to lose weight, primarily for health reasons. He also recognizes that the old messages go deep and that he may not ever love his size completely. As he became more involved with bear events, though, he was pleasantly surprised to discover that some of the men attracted to bears were not freaks but normal men who were sexually aroused by the sight of a large man. And, even better, some of those men were attracted to him.

RELATIONSHIP FORMATION AND DEVELOPMENT

The version of relationship development and formation that most of us grew up with was shaped by literature and Hollywood. Two people have a difficult time getting together. There are obstacles along the way—family, religion, class—that make it difficult for the partners to consummate their love. Finally, at the end of the book or movie, the pair is united, and we are left to assume they live happily ever after.

While such stories make for good entertainment, they are poor representations of life. For most people, the big problem is not overcoming the obstacles that prevent partnering; the big problem is staying partnered after getting together. Romantic relationships involve two separate personalities, each with unique ideas as to what a relationship should be.

Complicating matters is the fact that queer people form relationships that are significantly different from those of nonqueer people. Furthermore, most queer people have few or no role models for learning how to make a queer relationship work or even what a healthy queer relationship looks like.

Queer couples differ from nonqueer couples in numerous ways. For instance, queer couples tend to be egalitarian, meaning there is no designated leader. While nonqueer couples are becoming more egalitarian every day, studies show that generally the man is still more powerful than the woman in decision-making. In egalitarian relationships, decision-making is shared. And because of that, such relationships take more work than nonegalitarian relationships.

With the exception of transgender couples, for whom there often are designated male and female roles, queer couples cannot divide tasks and chores according to gender roles. That means queer couples, for the most part, must decide by mutual agreement who is to do what. Some of these decisions come naturally: One partner has an interest in a particular task and the other does not. But in general, when it comes to task allocation, there needs to be more negotiation between queer partners than between nonqueer partners. As a result, queer couples tend to be much more flexible than nonqueer couples. Roles change more frequently, and queer couples need to be prepared to deal with those changes.

Perhaps the most important way that queer couples differ from nonqueer couples is in the closeness they create. Most people would be intuitively correct if they assumed two women would form a closer romantic relationship than would a man and a woman. Where most would go astray, however, is if they assumed two men would form a *less* close relationship than would a man and woman. In fact, the closest couples are lesbian couples; the next closest are gay male couples; and the least close are heterosexual couples.

Queer partners try to be all things to each other. They try to be not only lovers and life-mates but also best friends. They do things together much of the time, have friends in common, share interests, and support each other to a great degree—much more so than heterosexual couples. The reasons for this are not clear. Speculation suggests that queer people do not get the family and societal support that heterosexuals normally receive, and therefore need to rely on and support each other to a greater extent.

This might seem quite loving, but it puts pressures on queer couples that nonqueer couples do not experience. Every couple, queer or nonqueer, has to deal with many issues, especially when the relationship is in its early stages. Any new couple might benefit from the services of a couples counselor who can help the partners understand their differences and build a common bond. Queer couples, because of their lack of role models as w`ell as societal and family support, are especially likely to benefit from couples counseling at an early stage in their relationship.

Richard and Robert

Richard and Robert, a queer couple, came to couples therapy to deal with constant fighting. They had been together 18 months and wanted their relationship to continue. They arrived dressed alike in jeans, polo shirts, and matching shoes. Even without considering their clothes, they looked quite similar. At first, it was difficult to remember who was Richard and who was Robert.

Although they looked alike, they were quite different in personality. Richard was passive and tended to defer to Robert, at least as far as Richard was concerned. Robert had a different story. Richard would always say yes to Robert but then would raise the subject again and again until Robert eventually gave in. Robert would then start to scream, and Richard would start to cry. This only added to Robert's resentment, since he felt he could never win. Richard also felt he could never win.

In the 18 months they had been together, Richard and Robert had done virtually everything together, other than going to work. After they got home at night—and all weekend too—they spent time together. They acknowledged that they intentionally dressed alike to make a statement to both the queer and nonqueer world that they were a couple. But Robert complained that he did not have a life or a personality anymore; it was all about Richard.

The first work of therapy was to get Richard and Robert to understand that they had created their enmeshed relationship and no one had forced them to be that way. They liked the closeness, but Robert found it overwhelming. This caused Richard to fear that Robert wanted to end the relationship.

Step 2 of therapy was getting Richard and Robert to recommit to their love for each other and their desire to be partners. In a quiet ceremony with only the two of them present, they went to a mutually very special place, exchanged rings, and promised to love each other as unique individuals. They wanted to do this with God as their only witness, feeling that would make it more special. This was to be their pact with each other and God.

Robert then became involved in queer politics while Richard stayed at home. Each did what he wanted during his free time. Robert agitated for the civil rights of queer people, and Richard tended the house. This worked for them until Richard developed full-blown AIDS. Several opportunistic infections left him weak and unable to work. He went on disability from his job and was not even strong enough to do much around the house.

Robert, at that point, gave up his political activities to take care of Richard and the house. He felt OK about doing this because he believed he was not being forced into it. Fortunately, this story has a happy ending. Protease inhibitor anti-HIV cocktails became available in early 1996, shortly after Richard developed full-blown AIDS. Richard's health improved enough that he was able to go back to maintaining the house, allowing Robert to return to his political work.

DOMESTIC VIOLENCE

Domestic violence is a physical assault on a family member. In essence it is no different than a physical assault on a stranger. It is, however, treated differently because after many domestic assaults the perpetrator and the victim continue their relationship, often in the same household. For that reason, treatment of domestic violence on a psychological level differs from the treatment for trauma resulting from an assault by a stranger.

Domestic violence happens in the queer community—in relationships between women, in relationships between men, in relationships in which one or both partners are transgendered. The existence of domestic violence between women was denied for a long time for political and social reasons, but it is now recognized and discussed. Domestic violence can and does occur in every kind of family relationship.

Depending on the particular situation, the usual treatment for someone assaulted by a stranger could be either individual, couples, family, or group counseling. For instances of domestic violence, though, a different set of rules applies.

If the incident of domestic violence was a single isolated event in a long-term relationship, it should still be treated as a serious matter. It should not be excused because it was a one-time event. It is indicative of something wrong with both the individual perpetrating the violence and the relationship of the couple. In cases of domestic violence, the perpetrator should at the very least immediately involve him or herself in individual psychotherapy and perhaps couples psychotherapy.

If this is not the first incident of domestic violence, an entirely different approach should be taken. The perpetrator should immediately enroll in a program to treat those who have committed domestic violence. Most of these programs focus on helping men, so it may be difficult to find a program that also treats women.

Programs for those who commit domestic violence involve a combination of individual and group psychotherapy, with an emphasis on group psychotherapy. There is power in groups, and someone who is prone to committing domestic violence needs both the pressure and support of the entire group to refrain from acting violently again.

Victims of domestic violence are also encouraged to seek individual or group psychotherapy. The purpose of such psychotherapy is twofold: to support the individual and help heal the wounds; and to help the victim understand how he or she might have contributed to the situation that caused the violence.

The second is a tricky area. There is no excusing the person who committed to violence. The common excuse that "he (or she) drove me to it" has no validity. Regardless of verbal or emotional provocation, the perpetrator bears full responsibility for his or her actions. However, there are patterns to the psychology of the victims. They tend to have low self-esteem. They tend to be angry inside with few ways of expressing that anger in a healthy manner. They tend to say and do things that are provocative. And perhaps most importantly, they seem to find one perpetrator of domestic violence after another. It is not unusual for someone to say that domestic violence was present in several of his or her relationships. That indicates the individual has at least some part in the violence.

The kind of treatment that should not occur in cases of ongoing domestic violence is couples counseling, because couples counseling can bring the couple back together before the perpetrator has taken full responsibility for his or her actions, thus making repeats of the violence more likely. After the perpetrator spends a significant period of time in both individual and group counseling, couples counseling may be appropriate. But this not recommended until at least a year after the perpetrator began his or her program of counseling.

FAMILY ISSUES

Family issues for queer people come in two varieties. The first variety relates to the family of origin, the second to the family the queer person creates. Often the intersection of the two families, particularly around holidays and family gatherings, is the cause of the stress.

Whether or not an individual is queer, the family in which he or she grew up often gives rise to considerable stress. All families are dysfunctional to some extent. If a family is only mildly dysfunctional, then the stress should be manageable. But most families are more than mildly dysfunctional, whether or not they admit it.

Families are generally headed by one or two people who were themselves brought up in dysfunctional families. There is much they do not know, but they rarely realize how unaware they are. Most heads of families believe they are doing a good or excellent job and know what is right. So they make authoritarian pronouncements and cause stress for other family members.

When one or more family members happens to be queer (and it could just as easily be one of the parents as one of the children), this causes problems for the family in all but a few cases. One third of all queer people report significant rejection from a member or members of their family of origin after coming out. This initial rejection often subsides, but most families still find it difficult to integrate a queer person into their ranks.

Queer people are acutely aware of this. Family-of-origin issues may involve the partner of the queer person. Should the partner be invited to family gatherings? Should the queer couple be permitted to share a bedroom when visiting? How should the aunts, uncles, cousins, and grandparents be involved? How should one partner address the other partner's parents? All these and a multitude of other questions are issues a queer person may want to sort through in psychotherapy, with the possibility of family psychotherapy as part of the mix.

In addition to their family of origin, queer people also create families. These families are of two varieties. First are multigenerational families created by birth, adoption, surrogacy, foster care, domestic partnership with someone who already has children, or some other means. The other—and more common—variety is an extended family of choice that often includes partners, ex-partners, close friends (queer and nonqueer), and blood relatives. Queer families, whether multigenerational or extended families of choice, are generally unsanctioned by society and often subject to discrimination and ridicule.

Psychotherapy with a queer-affirmative psychotherapist can help a queer person sort through his or her unique family issues.

Sandra

Sandra, now in her early 60s, is a good example of a queer person with family issues. In the late 1960s, Sandra and her lesbian lover were not out. They called themselves roommates. Because people might think she was a lesbian, Sandra's partner was told to not bring her "roommate" to her sister's wedding. Her lover chose to skip the wedding rather than go without Sandra. Several years later in the mid 1970s, Sandra's lover died. Sandra sought therapy then to deal with the grief over her lover's death. Because no one officially knew of their relationship, there were no offers of support or condolence commensurate with her loss.

Prior to her lover's death, Sandra had experienced a lot of trouble dealing with her lover's fundamentalist Christian family. But a strange thing happened after Sandra's lover died. The lover's family changed from being cold and hostile toward Sandra to being warm and accepting . Though it may seem strange, Sandra maintained a relationship with the family of her deceased lover. Ever since, when with the family, Sandra has maintained the fiction that she and her lover were roommates.

Sandra knows the lover's family *knows*. But there is an unstated agreement to not use the *L* word. Sandra believes the family knows the truth because the family honors Sandra in ways they would not if she had merely been a roommate. They invited Sandra to the weddings of younger members of the family, and in one case, when Sandra told them she would be traveling in Europe at the time of a wedding, they changed the date so she could attend. The family transferred the affection they had for Sandra's lover to Sandra, and they came to treat her as a widow of their daughter.

Though Sandra originally went into short-term therapy to deal with the grief she experienced when her lover died, she has continued to see a psychotherapist off and on over the years. One particular reason for her continuing therapy has been dealing with the feelings her lover's family brings up every time they invite her to another family gathering.

CHILDHOOD ABUSE

One of the major reasons people seek psychotherapy is to deal with the devastating impact of childhood emotional, physical, and sexual abuse. Interestingly, many people do not realize—until they have spent time talking about their childhood in therapy—that their childhood was in fact abusive. I am not discussing here the controversial subject of "recovered memory syndrome," in which people do not remember childhood abuse until they have spent time in therapy or hypnosis. I am referring to people who remember quite well what happened during childhood but have not been able to connect the dots and see that some of those memories have had a negative impact on them as adults. In fact, many people have had horrendous childhoods involving verbal, emotional, physical, and sexual abuse; they remember those events but do not recognize their childhoods as abusive. This was their only childhood—a normal childhood as far as they know as adults—and they view it that way until they begin talking to others who recognize the signs of an abusive childhood.

Childhood abuse is not restricted to queer kids. The percentage of women who have been sexually abused by family members is similar for queer and nonqueer women: about 38%. (From *Lesbian Passion: Loving Ourselves and Each Other* by JoAnn Loulan.) That is a strikingly high number, and it means that more likely than not a lesbian couple will have at least one person who was sexually abused as a child. Similarly, gay men, especially those who were effeminate as children, were often prey to verbal, emotional, physical, and sexual abuse from family members, peers, and strangers while growing up.

Otto

Otto is a 38-year-old gay man who has been in therapy intermittently for 15 years. His first therapy experience at 23 was couples counseling with his partner. During that session, he told the therapist and his partner that he was the second youngest in a large family, and had shared a room with a brother who was 10 years older. Every night Otto was terrorized by the older brother, who sexually molested him and threatened to kill him if he told.

Otto believed the threats and kept quiet. His mother, who was depressed and unable to cope with her large family, never noticed any of the signs that Otto was having difficulty. His father worked extremely long hours and was almost never home, so he too was unaware of the abuse.

During his 15 years of intermittent therapy, Otto would often refer back to the first session, saying that was the day that changed his life. It was the first time anyone had ever suggested to him that his childhood was anything other than normal. It helped him to understand why he felt unloved and would do almost anything to feel loved, including staying in abusive situations in his personal life and on the job.

SPIRITUAL ISSUES

Spiritual issues can be difficult for queer people, primarily because many of the world's religions have traditionally been queer-negative and instigated widespread discrimination and persecution of queer people. Recently, though, progressive factions in several major religions have attempted to change rigid doctrines and judgmental antiqueer attitudes among the faithful.

In the past, queer people had no supportive institutions to meet their spiritual and existential needs. In the past 30 years, however, queer-affirmative churches have emerged. The Metropolitan Community Church, a queer-Protestant-based nondenominational group, has formed congregations in many communities. There are queer-affirmative synagogues in major cities as well. And many mainstream churches and synagogues in queer neighborhoods have become welcoming of queer people. Still, the general attitude of the major world religions remains queer-negative.

Consequently, many queer people, especially those not residing in major metropolitan areas, do not have a place where they can openly discuss their spiritual and existential questions. Some view psychotherapy as a place to sort through these issues and find a way to integrate spirituality into their lives. Many queer-affirmative psychotherapists who recognize a spiritual element in their own lives have become adept at helping clients separate spirituality from religion.

Roberta

Roberta is a good example. She grew up in a Roman Catholic family, attended mass and Catholic schools, went to confession, received the sacraments, and even considered becoming a nun when she was young. She married a Catholic man soon after college, and they had two children. It was not a happy marriage, but it was not unhappy either. Several years after the birth of their second child, her husband announced that he was gay and wanted a divorce.

Roberta was emotionally paralyzed. She was more upset that her husband wanted a divorce than about his being gay. Divorce was unheard-of in her family. No one had ever, to her knowledge, been divorced. She was well-aware of how the Catholic Church treats the issue of divorce and remarriage, and felt her life was over. She spoke to her priest and was comforted but not helped. She decided to try psychotherapy.

She found a female psychotherapist who was also Catholic. She did not know when she began therapy that her psychotherapist also was a lesbian. She later learned that the person who referred her to the psychotherapist knew about her husband being gay and thought sending her to lesbian would mean she had a psychotherapist who was knowledgeable about these issues. For the first six months, the primary issue for Roberta was her grief over the breakup of her marriage and how she believed she could never remarry, lest she be excommunicated.

After dealing for months with spiritual issues, Roberta began to look more at her own existential issues: who she was and what her life was about. And then something surprising happened. Roberta realized she was a lesbian but had repressed her true feelings for many reasons. She realized she had been initially attracted to her husband because he had not put much sexual pressure on her. And she now understood that was because he, like she, had little interest in the opposite sex. Suddenly, the fact that she could not remarry without being excommunicated was no longer an issue. She looked forward to someday having a female partner, secure in the knowledge that she would not be excommunicated even if she had a commitment ceremony.

CHRONIC ILLNESS

One of the most stressful events that can occur in someone's life is to be told that he or she has a chronic or life-threatening illness. Such an illness affects not only the person diagnosed but also his or her family, friends, and caregivers. The AIDS epidemic has brought tremendous stress to the queer community, but even before AIDS, caring for someone with a chronic or life-threatening illness—or worse, being seriously ill oneself—took a heavy emotional toll.

Because of the prevalence of AIDS in the queer community, an entire spectrum of mental health services has been set up to help those living with or giving care to someone with AIDS. Many of these services have been duplicated to serve those affected by other chronic or life-threatening illnesses.

The need for mental health services is high for both the ailing individual and his or her loved ones and caregivers. The person who is ill has been told that his or her entire life is now different than expected, that he or she will probably experience debilitating symptoms as a result of the illness and/or its treatment, and that he or she may need to contemplate dying at a relatively young age. As the illness progresses, the person often becomes less functional and suffers from a changing appearance. For family and caregivers, there is a feeling of helplessness. For all involved, there is much anticipatory grieving over the losses, often including death, that are likely to occur.

Elisabeth Kubler-Ross in her groundbreaking book, *On Death and Dying*, wrote about the five emotional stages experienced by someone who has been told they have a life-threatening illness. The first stage is denial, in which the person believes an error has occurred. Initially, denial helps the person to cope. The initial stage is followed by stages of anger, bargaining, depression, and finally acceptance.

These are not discrete stages that someone goes through in a specific order until acceptance is reached, completing the process. Rather, these are general categories that describe the emotional states experienced by those either living with chronic or terminal illness or giving care to someone with a chronic or terminal illness.

People can be experience the different stages in any order and any number of times. An individual can go from a state of denial, to anger, back to denial, then to bargaining, depression, more bargaining, more anger, and eventually acceptance. The range of available psychotherapy services designed to help people through these stages is now impressive.

First, crisis counseling is often available. Some psychotherapists specialize in helping those who have recently learned of their diagnosis with AIDS and other debilitating illnesses. Once the initial crisis is past, there are both drop-in support groups and ongoing closed support and therapy groups for both patients and their families and caregivers. And should the person die, there are similar groups to help survivors through the grieving process.

Because of the AIDS epidemic, psychotherapists who primarily serve the queer community are generally more familiar with issues of death and dying than are any other group of psychotherapists. They can provide invaluable support and knowledge.

Harriet and Abbey

Harriet and Abbey had been together 23 years when Abbey first developed multiple chronic illnesses: hypertension, diabetes, and obesity. Out of love for Abbey, Harriet took responsibility for Abbey's medical treatment and well-being. Abbey came to expect Harriet to do things for her that she could have done herself.

Little by little, after working through issues in couples therapy, Abbey took responsibility for areas of her life she really could manage. She began to use Harriet more thoughtfully and effectively, such as accompanying her on visits to the doctor and acting as her advocate and to help her remember what questions to ask as well as the answers to them. (Abbey would get so upset when she went to the doctor, especially if she heard damaging news, that she could never remember what she was supposed to do.)

The other larger issue Harriet and Abbey addressed in therapy was individuation. Harriet had started to limit her activities based on Abbey's limitations and began to resent Abbey because of this. Through therapy the pair worked out ways that Harriet could do things with her friends away from Abbey. This had the added benefit of mobilizing Abbey to be more proactive. Abbey felt shut out and at the same time challenged to push her limits in order to take part in some of these activities. For instance, they used to go backpacking in their younger days, staying in the wilderness for days at a time. Now Harriet had begun to go camping with her friends, driving to a campsite and going on day hikes from the base camp. Abbey began to go along, staying at the campsite during the day, sitting and reading—essentially the same activity she would have been doing at home, only now she was out with her partner in the wilderness again. The women would hang out near the campfire in the evening, and when the other women went into their tents to sleep, Harriet and Abbey would drive a small distance to a nearby motel, where they could deal with Abbey's medical needs in a way they could not at the campsite.

Edward

Edward started psychotherapy to deal with the emotional fallout from his lover's AIDS illness. Edward was HIV-negative and felt sure he would outlive his partner. He wanted to be able to go on with his life afterward and knew from experience that doing so might be difficult. As a Vietnam veteran, he understood the psychological impact of having been in that war and felt many of the same emotional issues recurring. He was also a private person and did not want to tell his story to many other people. He felt one person, a psychotherapist, was enough for him.

Throughout the final six months of his lover's life, Edward came to psychotherapy each week. As he watched his lover's body deteriorate, he alternated between rage and helplessness—and did not deal well with either. He was not only a quiet and restrained man by nature but also a man of action who was used to being in charge and having his directions followed. His lover's illness proved to be a serious emotional challenge for him.

Edward and his partner had always had a sexually open relationship, and in the final months before his lover died he and one of the men with whom he regularly met for sex became close. While this was comforting for Edward in some ways, it also proved difficult because the agreement with his partner was that they could see others for sex but not more.

As Edward's lover slipped into the awful final stages of AIDS, he found himself feeling guilty over the comfort and pleasure he received when spending time with this other man. Psychotherapy was his place to sort through these issues.

Several months after his lover died, Edward decided to stop therapy. The relationship with the man who was once "the other man" was now in the open, and they told others they were lovers. Edward felt that he had received from psychotherapy what he needed to get and that it was time to move on.

Life sometimes takes tragic twists. Two years after the death of his lover, Edward died of a heart attack. His new partner, who was HIV-positive though otherwise healthy, suddenly found himself in a position he never though he would be in, having to grieve the death of an HIV-negative partner. Individual psychotherapy and a grief group helped him through the emotional impact of Edward's sudden death.

Death and Grieving

Nothing is as certain as death. All living creatures die eventually. And with death comes the need for those who survive to grieve for who or what has been lost.

Psychotherapists who serve the queer community, because of AIDS, are generally more familiar with death and grieving than other psychotherapists, with the possible exception of those who specialize in geriatric psychotherapy or working with the terminally ill. Many queer psychotherapists are now experts on the grieving process and regularly talk to nonqueer audiences about the subject.

Grieving is the process of changing your relationship with the person who died. The relationship changes from a present relationship that is ever-changing to a past relationship fixed in time. While you know intellectually that a person has died, you might still think and feel as if the deceased were still alive. You might walk down the aisle of the supermarket and find yourself reaching for the box of cereal your lover ate, though your lover has been dead for six months, or you might burst into tears each time a certain song comes on the radio.

Grieving can be smooth or difficult, depending on a multitude of factors. Each person mourns in his or her unique way. Psychotherapy is an excellent place to discuss feelings of grief. Talking about these feelings helps you to make the internal change from relating to someone in the present to in the past. I strongly recommend having someone with whom to discuss your ongoing and changing feelings about the loss of someone close to you, should that situation arise. It will make an extremely difficult process that much easier.

Barbara

Barbara, for instance, lost her lover to suicide. Neither she nor her lover were out as lesbians. Both held high-profile jobs in the straight world; it would have been difficult for either of them as professionals to have been open about their sexuality.

Consequently, when her lover committed suicide, Barbara could not find support for dealing with her grief. Everyone wondered why Barbara was so upset that her "roommate" had died. They could not understand why her grief lasted so long, why she was unable to function for a while, or why she needed to take a sabbatical from work.

Little by little, Barbara worked through her grief. She talked about her deceased lover's depression—what she felt were missed calls for help. She talked about her feelings of helplessness, of all the things she had tried that did not work. Barbara talked about her anger at her lover for killing herself. And most importantly, she talked about her guilt that she could have—and perhaps should have—done more.

Therapy helped Barbara sort through her feelings, which enabled her to accept what had happened and move on with her life. In her next relationship, both she and her partner were able to be out as lesbians and a couple.

WANTING TO TALK

To a significant extent, especially among individuals with only a few problems in their lives, the services of psychotherapists are utilized primarily to have someone with whom to talk. The client has no serious symptoms, no particularly stressful or difficult life cycle issues. But the client feels he or she could be happier and therefore visits a psychotherapist.

Some psychotherapists will not work with this type of client. For psychotherapists who adhere strictly to the medical model, treating this type of patient cannot be justified. There is no diagnosis, so no treatment is warranted. Publicly funded clinics generally subscribe to the medical model, as do health maintenance organizations. If you are honest with the representatives of either organization about merely wanting to talk, you will probably be rejected as a client.

Some psychotherapists are action- and goal-oriented and want to work on problems. Those psychotherapists are also not comfortable with clients who merely want to check in and discuss what is going on in their life.

To a great number of psychotherapists, though, these individuals are the most rewarding type of client. Often they are committed to long-term therapy, meaning the psychotherapist has an opportunity to help the client grow over a period of years.

Sometimes people begin therapy with "just talking" as their goal; other times it happens without being planned. A client sometimes begins therapy to deal with a particular problem, which may or may not become resolved, and then discovers that he or she *likes* talking to the psychotherapist on a regular basis. So the appointments continue.

The point is that there does not have to be a particular agenda for someone to be in psychotherapy. To those who are suspicious of psychotherapists, this probably sounds self-serving. However, having a "friend" with whom to discuss your life on a regular basis is important, and some people can only arrange that with a paid professional.

Dolores

A good example is Dolores. Dolores looked female when she walked into the therapist's office. She had long ago begun taking female hormones, and they had significantly changed her appearance. Though she had chosen to not have sex reassignment surgery, her masculine features were gone and she easily passed for female. She had been dating a man who really liked her. She had told him the truth about herself, and they continued to date.

Dolores wanted to start a family through adoption and relocated to an area where politics and local values would permit that. When she moved, though, her male friend broke up with her, threatening her dream. Dolores needed a place to talk about this, and came to therapy for that purpose. After she had dealt with her relationship issues and her desire for a family, she decided to continue therapy, feeling she could benefit from it even without having to deal with specific issues.

Part Two
Mental Health

Chapter 5
Models of Mental Health

What is Mental Health?

Mental health and mental illness are difficult and touchy subjects. They are not well-understood. Even among mental health professionals, there is no clearly accepted definition of what constitutes mental health or mental illness. And there is no generally accepted understanding of why a person becomes mentally ill.

Part of the problem stems from the history of our attempts to understand mental illness. For the past several hundred years, this task has been relegated to physicians, who use a *medical model* for understanding the problems people face. While the medical model may be appropriate for physical problems, such as the common cold, heart disease, broken bones, or AIDS, it is not appropriate for most mental and emotional problems. Yet even today many mental health professionals adhere to this approach.

However, many other mental health professionals use a different approach, the *growth model*. The definition of mental health and mental illness depends on which model of mental health is used.

Models of Mental Health

People want to understand things, especially themselves. This is one of the main reasons people involve themselves in psychotherapy. People also want to understand the world around them. They want to understand all that they see, hear, touch, feel, smell, sense, and experience. This is done by "connecting the dots." People connect miscellaneous facts in such a way that the facts are no longer disconnected but part of a larger picture. Someone looking at it can see both the dots and the picture formed by connecting them. When a new fact or experience happens, the person calls on his or her understanding of the larger picture to see where the new dot factors in.

To visualize the larger picture, some assumptions must be made about the connections between the dots. These assumptions have underlying principles and are called *models*. The models of understanding human behavior and mental health have changed considerably over the centuries and will probably continue to change. Depending on which model is used, people understand human behavior, mental health, and emotional problems quite differently. This is particularly important when seeking mental health services, especially if the client happens to be a queer person.

THE SUPERNATURAL MODEL

The *supernatural model* of mental health is very old. From the oral traditions of cultures that existed thousands of years ago, before there were written records of what people believed, and continuing through the present day, it is clear that some people have understood human behavior, mental illness, and emotional problems in terms of supernatural forces. God, Satan, ghosts, angels, spirits, elves, demons, or other supernatural forces were all believed to affect how people felt and behaved. If someone demonstrated a mental or emotional problem, it was believed that the causes and the cures were in the realm of the spiritual. A spiritual healer might be the only person who could help the afflicted person. Exorcism, for example, was one form of treatment. By driving out the demons, the person would be cured of the emotional problems or troubling behavior.

This conception of mental illness continues to have many adherents in both Western and non-Western countries. People pray to God asking for help with behavioral or emotional problems. In many non-Western societies, shamans are responsible for helping the emotionally and mentally afflicted. Going to see a priest or minister for counseling also stems from this tradition.

THE MORAL MODEL

Beginning with the period in Western civilization known as the Enlightenment, (roughly the latter part of the 18th century), people began to question the supernatural model of mental and emotional problems. Many people no longer believed that mental and emotional problems were caused by supernatural forces. Instead, they substituted the *moral model*. The basis of the moral model is that people make a personal choice to act in a particular way. Supernatural forces are not involved. This places the responsibility for change on the individual. In the moral model, homosexual behavior is seen as a choice.

Because people have a choice, they can choose to do the right thing or the wrong thing. If they choose to do the right thing, they are good. If they choose otherwise, they are bad and will be treated as such. Homosexual behavior and stealing are roughly equivalent in this model. Trent Lott, the Senate majority leader, recently equated homosexuals with kleptomaniacs and alcoholics. Around the same time, Reggie White, a minister and professional football player, made similar remarks. The views of both men are widely shared.

In the moral model, a person can and should refrain from stealing, just as a person can and should refrain from homosexual behavior. According to the moral model, the proper way of handling inappropriate behavior, including homosexual behavior, is through the legal system. Consequently, with the rise of the moral model, the euphemism "crime against nature" began to appear in our legal codes. (Since homosexual behavior was considered morally repugnant, any more specific description of the crime was also considered repugnant). People demonstrating homosexual behavior have at times been imprisoned, tortured, and even executed. Such punishments still occur in certain cultures.

THE MEDICAL MODEL

The *medical model* originated at the start of the 20th century. For queer people, the medical model was a great advance over the supernatural and moral models in understanding human sexual behavior. People were no longer thought to be acting as they did because they were possessed by demons or criminal in nature, but because they were sick. Sick people were to be treated with compassion, rather than scorned as sinners or criminals.

While the medical model was an advance over the supernatural and moral models, it still negatively impacted the way society looked upon and treated queer people. That impact is still felt. Many people believe the medical model urgently needs to be replaced as the dominant model of understanding mental and emotional problems, queer issues aside, because it is the wrong way of understanding the human personality and because, by itself, the medical model causes numerous problems.

The medical model approaches humans much in the same way people approach buying and owning an automobile. There is an ideal state in which a car should be. If the car was manufactured correctly and arrived at the dealer without any defects, it is a perfect example of that particular model of automobile. From there it is all downhill. Parts wear out or rust. Accidents occur. Age causes a natural deterioration. Regular maintenance will help, but things will go wrong and need to be fixed. At a certain point, things will go so wrong that it will not be worthwhile to fix the car. It goes off to the junkyard, and a new car is purchased.

For physical health, the analogy is valid. Most babies are born in perfect health or with a few defects that can be fixed. As a person grows, body parts begin to show wear and tear, accidents happen, and diseases cause the child, adolescent, or adult's body to no longer function properly. Humans begin at an ideal state and over the course of a lifetime develop problems, some of which can be fixed, many of which cannot. A physician, like an auto mechanic, is responsible for determining what is wrong and fixing whatever can be fixed. The end comes when the problems are so overwhelming that the person's body can no longer cope. The scrap heap of death is the result.

When applied to mental and emotional functioning, however, the medical model is less functional. With this model, there is an ideal state of mental health, just as there is an ideal state of physical health. A child is born as a blank slate and then has certain experiences. If the individual has good experiences, he or she will function as a mentally healthy person. If the person shows evidence of emotional problems, the medical model believes that something went wrong. The job of the mental health professional is to gather information, make a diagnosis, and prescribe a course of treatment, which might include psychotherapy, behavioral modification, and/or medication.

Mental health, from the perspective of the medical model, is defined as the absence of any diagnosable mental disorders. If a person's behaviors, feelings, ideas, and perceptions fall within what is considered the normal range, then the person is deemed mentally healthy. If a person meets the criteria for a diagnosis, they are deemed to have a mental illness. This is basically an all-or-nothing system. You either have a mental illness or you do not. There are some judgment calls, but mostly it is a fill-in-the-blanks approach. When a person meets certain criteria, they are given a diagnosis. When they no longer meet the criteria, they are cured.

For the first half of the 20th century, virtually all mental health professionals subscribed to the medical model. In this period, the mental health profession was dominated by psychiatrists, who were initially trained to use the medical model to treat physical illnesses, and then to use the medical model to understand and treat mental and emotional problems, unaware there might be a better way.

Using the medical model to understand mental health and emotional problems has many shortcomings, the worst of which being the subjective standards used in deciding what is normal (healthy) and what is a problem. Homosexuality, for instance, was originally deemed a problem that needed fixing.

From the very beginning, not all mental health professionals agreed with this. A letter from Freud to the American mother of a homosexual man indicated that Freud believed homosexuality was not a mental illness and should not be treated as such. He did, however believe that homosexuality indicated the person's personality had stopped developing at a very young age, when homosexual feelings were normal. But Freud did not speak for the entire professional mental health establishment.

The classification of homosexuality as a mental illness remained in force until 1973, when the American Psychiatric Association, by a majority vote of its members, finally declared that homosexuality was not a mental illness but instead a variation of normal sexual behavior. (Unfortunately, several still-existing diagnoses classify being transgendered or being a cross-dresser as a mental disorder.)

Despite its many problems, the medical model is widely used in the field of mental health. In fact, it is nearly always used when someone wishes to use medical insurance to pay their psychotherapist's fee. It is commonly used at community-based mental health clinics, as well. It is also the basis of how many mental health professionals view their relationship with you. You have something wrong and are coming to them to get it fixed. You will be cured when you no longer have the problem.

THE GROWTH MODEL

In the second half of the 20th century, another way of conceptualizing mental and emotional health appeared: the *growth model*. The growth model differs considerably from the medical model. Its basic assumption is that people have a desire and a need to grow over the course of their lives. To be emotionally healthy, a person must believe he or she is growing in ways that fit him or her.

The growth model recognizes that all people are unique, as are the ways they grow. Symptoms of emotional distress appear when growth is inhibited. Obstacles to growth are present in distorted ideas learned earlier in life or in a person's interactions with others. The removal of the obstacles will allow an individual to continue to grow.

An underlying assumption of the growth model is the theory of *positive intent*. Positive intent means that people *want* to grow. Unfortunately, notions of what will help them grow may have become distorted. The job of the psychotherapist is to help the client understand his or her innermost motives, grow in healthy ways, and see how he or she and others in his or her life are making that growth difficult.

Mental health professionals using the growth model help clients unlearn or change old ways of thinking, feeling, acting, and reacting. Rather than being experts on what is right and wrong with a client, growth model clinicians are experts on human functioning. They use their knowledge in conjunction with clients to help their clients grow and have more satisfying lives. Unlike a medical-model physician who does something *to* you, growth-model clinicians do something *with* you—mostly holding conversations until you have learned whatever it is you needed to learn in order to grow and get what you want from life.

How the Model of Mental Health Will Affect You

The model of mental health to which your psychotherapist subscribes, sometimes called his or her "orientation," will have a great impact on the form of treatment you receive. The questions asked, the statements made, and everything else that happens in psychotherapy depend to a large extent on this one factor. A therapist adopts a model for many reasons, but most basically there is something attractive to the therapist about a particular approach to understanding mental health.

Today there are few licensed psychotherapists who say they believe in a supernatural or a moral model of mental health. Almost all psychotherapists will tell you that they use either a medical model or a growth model. Certain supernatural elements are contained in what psychotherapists call a "transpersonal" approach (see chapter 6), but this approach is substantially different from the supernatural model as previously described. And elements of both the supernatural and moral models are used by therapists who work from a Christian perspective.

In comparing the medical model and the growth model, certain differences stand out. The growth model is based on and emphasizes the strengths of the client. It uses the client's own internal resources to ferret out obstacles to growth and to address issues, difficulties, conundrums, and concerns. The medical model approaches mental health quite differently. In fact, it might more appropriately be called the *disease model*. Having something mentally or emotionally wrong is considered a disease requiring treatment. The medical model is based in negativity.

The growth model is what many clinicians have come to use. However, the dominant powers in the mental health profession—psychiatrists, drug companies, and insurance companies—subscribe to the medical model. As such, even if you see a clinician who does subscribe to the growth model, he or she will probably use the medical model to describe you on insurance documents or in reports, if that is necessary.

Client Versus Patient

Earlier in this book I said that I would call consumers of mental health services *clients* rather than *patients*. This is because I use a growth model instead of a medical model.

Because the medical model was dominant for many years, consumers of mental health services were called patients. During this period, mental health professionals were almost all physicians who became psychiatrists, and these practitioners generally worked in clinics or hospitals. Consequently, nearly all mental health services took place within a medical model. Characterizing users of these services as patients—the same as users of other health services—seemed appropriate.

During the 1960s, however, the terminology began to change from *patient* to *client*. There has never been complete agreement about this change. Psychiatrists, who begin their careers as medical doctors and then receive further training in mental health issues, almost always refer to the people who come to them for services as patients. So do a significant number of older psychologists. But many, if not most younger and nonmedically trained mental health professionals now call consumers of mental health services clients.

The terminology change from *patient* to *client* is important for queer people. Patients go to a doctor to be treated and hopefully cured. The doctor is supposed to make them well. The term *patient* reinforces the societal notion that queer people are less than or not as good as nonqueer people. Referring to a queer person as a patient implies that the individual is sick. Needless to say, such notions are emotionally unhealthy.

Clients, however, are people in need of services and/or professional expertise. Most professionals see clients. Lawyers, accountants, and even housecleaners have clients for whom they provide expertise or perform services.

The sector of the mental health profession that still regards all consumers of mental health services as patients misses the point. Many and perhaps most of the people who will read this book will seek the services of a mental health professional not because they have a mental illness but because they want to lead happier and more productive lives.

One major roadblock to the change in terminology is the *Diagnostic and Statistical Manual of Mental Disorders*, which lists and describes all the "mental illnesses." It is published by the medical wing of the mental health profession, the American Psychiatric Association. It was in this book that homosexuality was once listed as a mental illness. Almost all mental health professionals are forced to use this book because insurance companies require a medical diagnosis before paying for mental health services. Technically, every individual who seeks mental health services and relies insurance to pay is a patient. But *client* is the term I have chosen to use in both my practice and this book.

QUEER-AFFIRMATIVE PSYCHOTHERAPY

The mental health profession has a long history of neither understanding nor accepting people who have romantic and sexual attractions to members of their own gender. And while the official policy of every American mental health organization is now positive and supportive of gays and lesbians (see Appendix A), we still live in a culture that continues to be homophobic and transgender-phobic. It is therefore wise for any queer person choosing a psychotherapist to make sure that psychotherapist is *queer-affirmative*.

A queer-affirmative psychotherapist is not necessarily queer. He or she is simply a person who has an orientation to life that says queer is great. A queer-affirmative psychotherapist is a positive, affirmative person who looks upon the ability to love another person as something wonderful, regardless of gender.

A queer-affirmative psychotherapist understands that there are more than two usually accepted romantic/sexual orientations: homosexuality and heterosexuality. A queer-affirmative psychotherapist understands that there is a romantic/sexual orientation in which people are to varying degrees attracted in love and sexuality to members of both genders. A queer-affirmative psychotherapist understands that people do not always emotionally identify with their physical gender or the roles usually associated with that gender, and that this phenomena can be independent of the gender(s) of the people to which that person is romantically or sexually attracted. A queer-affirmative psychotherapist understands that a person's romantic and sexual orientation is always changing and evolving. A queer-affirmative psychotherapist knows that what is most important is not where a person's romantic and sexual nature has been or where it is going. What matters is where it is now. A queer-affirmative psychotherapist understands that queer people have been taught to see themselves as sinful, criminal, or sick, and that helping queer people to not see themselves in those ways is part of the work to be done in therapy. A queer-affirmative psychotherapist is knowledgeable about the culture of being queer and understands that queer people form families different from the norm. A queer-affirmative psychotherapist understands that it's not easy being queer in a nonqueer world.

A queer-affirmative psychotherapist is also someone who has done introspective work to understand his or her own inevitable prejudices about being queer. He or she understands that everyone internalizes at least some of society's negative messages regarding queer people, and actively works toward minimizing how those prejudices interfere with the psychotherapeutic process.

CONVERSION THERAPY, A.K.A REPARATIVE THERAPY

To fully appreciate queer-affirmative psychotherapy, it helps to understand those mental health professionals who are not queer-affirmative. The following section describes the group of psychotherapists who are the most extreme in being nonqueer-affirmative. To a lesser extent, these beliefs and feelings exist among other mental health professionals. This information should help you when you try to assess if a psychotherapist is queer affirmative, regardless of how they label themselves.

The American Psychiatric Association officially declassified homosexuality as a mental illness in 1973, but a small group of highly vocal and media-savvy mental health professionals still insist that homosexuality *is* a mental illness. These practitioners claim to offer a treatment that will enable a homosexual to become heterosexual. This approach was known for many years as conversion therapy, but the popular term now is reparative therapy. Proponents claim that through the process of psychotherapy they can repair an individual who became homosexual as a result of the damage wrought by a faulty upbringing.

Reparative therapy has its theoretical basis in both psychoanalytic and behavior therapy. (See chapter 6 for a fuller explanation of these treatment approaches.) Using psychoanalytic theory, reparative therapy claims that homosexual orientation results from arrested development during the first few years of the child's life. Reparative therapists claim that if a relationship similar to the parent/child relationship can be established between the psychotherapist and the client, then the client can move forward from the point where his or her development was arrested and through the developmental process that they claim leads to heterosexuality.

As an adjunct to the psychoanalytic approach, many reparative therapy clinicians use a behavioral therapy technique known as aversion therapy. For example: A queer man is placed in a chair in a darkened room. A device known as a plethysmograph is attached to his penis. The plethysmograph registers any growth in the size of the penis (indicating that the man is becoming sexually aroused). Another device is attached to the man that can administer an electric shock. Images of both men and women in various situations, some highly sexual, are projected on a screen. If the plethysmograph indicates sexual excitement is occurring when viewing images of other men, an electric shock is administered. A variation of this approach involves administering nausea inducing drugs while homosexual images are shown. The claim is that individuals can be conditioned to not respond to homosexual stimuli, and will then, through the rest of the psychotherapy process, become attracted to the opposite sex.

Practitioners of reparative therapy have formed an organization known as the National Association for Research and Therapy of Homosexuality (NARTH) to give themselves the legitimacy they otherwise lack. NARTH releases to the media stories that portray all queer people as unhappy, and reparative therapy as the solution.

There are two major problems with reparative therapy. One is that it does not work. The other is that it harms people. Even reparative therapists acknowledge that sexual orientation is difficult to change, claiming that only a small percentage of their clients actually change sexual orientation. And their studies that claim to show this minimal success are fraught with problems. It is very likely that most of those people they claim to have changed from homosexual to heterosexual were in fact bisexual before the therapy began, and they are now simply not having homosexual relationships. Furthermore, the reparative therapists acknowledge that virtually all the successful clients continue to have erotic homosexual fantasies.

What is rarely discussed is what happens to those who "fail" at reparative therapy. The shame at failing has a negative impact on the self-image and self-esteem of these individuals. Even worse, some people subjected to aversion therapy find that half of the treatment works. Consequently, they no longer enjoy homosexual thoughts and fantasies, and have nothing in its place. They become asexual.

While the practitioners of reparative therapy are becoming more organized, so is the mainstream opposition. All of the major mental health organization in the United States have repudiated reparative therapy. The American Psychiatric Association, the American Psychological Association, the National Association of Social Workers, and the American Counseling Association, among other mental health groups have all issued strong statements condemning reparative therapy, stating that a homosexual orientation is not a mental illness. Members of these organizations are universally enjoined from treating queer people as mentally ill and in need of conversion to heterosexuality. So while practitioners of reparative therapy are good at getting media attention, they have been completely unsuccessful in gaining support within the mainstream mental health community. They are now on the radical fringe.

Chapter 6
Treatment Approaches

If you decide you want to see a psychotherapist, one of the most important facts to know is that there are at least 450 different types of psychotherapy, each with its own approach to mental health. A clinician who favors one approach will treat you differently than a clinician favoring a different approach. Plus, the individual personality of a psychotherapist will impact how his or her chosen approach is applied. What that means is no two psychotherapists are exactly the same. In chapter 9, I discuss individual therapists' styles. But this chapter is devoted to understanding the major approaches to psychotherapy. It will not, of course, cover all 450 forms, since many are small variations on the others and can be grouped under general headings.

Psychodynamic Psychotherapy

Psychodynamic psychotherapy is one of oldest and most popular forms of psychotherapy. It began around 1900 with the pioneers of psychotherapy, Sigmund Freud, Carl Jung, and Alfred Adler.

The key to understanding psychodynamic psychotherapy is in the word dynamic. Dynamic means "related to energy." Psychodynamic psychotherapy views the individual as a mass of conflicting forms of psychological energy that are kept in balance inside the person. When these forces meet the outside world, there exists the possibility that they will conflict with societal expectations. When that happens, the potential for problems arises.

The largest and most important school of psychodynamic psychotherapy began with Sigmund Freud and has been further developed by his followers. According to this school, the most important psychological forces in the individual are the life forces (Eros) and the death forces (Thanatos). The life forces are those related to love and sexuality; the death forces are those related to aggression. These forces conflict with each other and with the demands of the world at large. Social considerations override much of what we instinctually want to do, and we pay a price for our frustrations.

All psychodynamic approaches to psychotherapy believe that emotional and personal problems reside in and stem from the unconscious. The source of these problems is childhood. Psychodynamic clinicians believe that adults are likely to recreate childhood problems unless they are able to bring what is going on unconsciously into their consciousness and deal with it.

This "bringing to light" process occurs through psychoanalysis, or psychoanalytic psychotherapy. Psychoanalysis is considered by psychodynamic clinicians to be the Rolls Royce of psychotherapies. It is expensive, time consuming, and intense. A person involved in psychoanalysis might see his analyst (which is what these particular psychotherapists call themselves) as often as four times a week.

The initial goal of psychodynamic psychotherapy, from the point of view of the psychotherapist, is to develop a working relationship with the client (most psychodynamic psychotherapists still use the term patient). The client learns to trust the psychotherapist's understanding of what is happening in the client's life. To accomplish this, a psychodynamic psychotherapist will take a neutral stance on most issues. Psychodynamic psychotherapists tend to not share details of their personal life, thoughts, or feelings with the client. The psychodynamic psychotherapist attempts to create a space for the client to have his or her own thoughts and feelings without being bombarded by those of the therapist or anyone else.

Psychodynamic psychotherapists concentrate on what they call *transference*. Since they do not share their own thoughts and feelings, they assume that a client's beliefs about a psychotherapist are really just the client's own ideas about him or herself transferred to the psychotherapist. They further believe that the client does this with everyone in his or her life. They hope to make the client aware of this and help the client stop doing it, instead perceiving people as they actually are and not as the client believes them to be. Psychodynamic psychotherapists see this as the key to leading a happier life.

The first session with a client is likely to be when a psychodynamic psychotherapist will seem the most active. He or she will probably ask more specific questions in this session than in any other. After the initial session, the client will be instructed to *free-associate*—to say whatever comes to mind and follow where it goes. The psychodynamic psychotherapist listens for patterns and understandings on the part of the client.

What makes a conversation with a psychodynamic psychotherapist different from conversations with other psychotherapists is that the psychodynamic psychotherapist listens for certain themes in what the client says and responds only to those particular themes. One of the major themes that psychodynamic psychotherapists listen for is that of sexuality, especially as it relates to the client and his or her mother and father—what the psychodynamic psychotherapist calls the *Oedipus complex*.

After listening carefully while the client free-associates for an extended period of time, and sometimes after consulting with colleagues, the psychodynamic psychotherapist gives the client an *interpretation* often involving themes related to the Oedipus complex. This interpretation can be based on the content of what the client has said and on the observations of the therapist about how the client acts and reacts in the world. It might also be an interpretation of any dreams the client shared with the psychotherapist.

Psychodynamic psychotherapy is *insight-oriented*. Psychodynamic psychotherapists believe that understanding oneself—making conscious what is unconscious—is extremely important in dealing with emotional problems. They believe this process takes at least several years, and they often see their clients for a long time. This is not brief therapy; it is not a quick fix. While a crisis in your life might initially cause you to see a psychotherapist, the psychodynamic psychotherapist believes that crisis happened because of forces that had been building up over the years. And they believe that the solution will also take years.

Queer people should be cautious about choosing a psychotherapist from a psychodynamic background, especially if the psychotherapist subscribes to the *psychoanalytic theory* developed by followers of Sigmund Freud. Freud's record on homosexuality is at best neutral, and many of his followers are extremely negative in this regard. Psychodynamic psychotherapy, more than any other school, is based in the medical model, and more than a small number of subscribers to this theory still view queer people as sick.

When the American Psychiatric Association changed its official position in 1973, declaring that queer people are not sick simply because they are queer, the main opposition to this change came from psychiatrists who were trained in and subscribed to the psychodynamic and psychoanalytic theories developed by the followers of Freud. (Psychoanalytic psychotherapists are trained at special psychoanalytic institutes. Until very recently, some of the more conservative institutes would not admit an openly queer person.) Most of the psychotherapists who practice *reparative therapy* base their ideas on faulty psychoanalytic theories.

Much of the antiqueer sentiment in the psychoanalytic community is disappearing. Indeed, there have been sane and rational voices in the psychoanalytic community from the time of Freud onward. Several early psychoanalytic theorists were probably queer, including Anna Freud, the daughter of Sigmund. In addition, some forms of psychoanalytic psychotherapy not based on Freudian theories, such as the analytic theories descending from Carl Jung, have never subscribed to the idea that queer people are by their very nature sick (though Jung's attitude toward homosexuality is, like Freud's, mixed).

It is therefore especially important to find out if a practitioner who identifies as a psychodynamic or psychoanalytic psychotherapist is also *queer-affirmative*. If you do not unequivocally believe, after asking, that a psychotherapist is queer-affirmative, then look for another psychotherapist.

Humanistic Psychotherapy

Humanistic psychotherapy has its roots in existentialism, a movement that began in Europe during the 1930s. Humanistic psychotherapy resembles psychodynamic psychotherapy in so far it believes there are forces and counterforces in each of us that need to be kept in balance with each other and the outside world in order for us to grow and be happy. These forces are not the same, however, as those in the psychodynamic schools.

While psychodynamic psychotherapists believe that the forces competing within us represent life, love, and sexuality (and alternately aggression and death), the humanistic/existential model characterizes the basic conflicts within us as involving the deep "ultimate concerns" of human existence—death, freedom, isolation, meaninglessness.

Humanistic psychotherapists have a more open view of the human condition than do psychodynamic psychotherapists. This difference is evident in the themes a psychotherapist listens for. The psychodynamic psychotherapist listens for oedipal content. The humanistic psychotherapist listens for death anxiety and questions of meaning, will, and isolation. Conversations might focus on the meaning of life or who the client really is.

Humanistic psychotherapy is firmly based in the *growth model*, believing that within each individual is the desire and ability for growth and healing. The role of the psychotherapist is to work with the client to help him or her grow into the best person he or she can be. The therapist does this by helping the client understand and eventually remove the barriers to growth that exist in his or her life. Some of the better-known names associated with the humanistic approach to psychotherapy are Carl Rogers, Abraham Maslow, Rollo May, Viktor Frankl, and Fritz Perls.

Different approaches to humanistic psychotherapy have resulted in dissimilar techniques. Some are nondirective, such as *client-centered therapy*, the form proposed by Carl Rogers. In this form, the psychotherapist is nonconfrontational. The therapist takes a neutral stance on what the client should or should not do in both the therapy hour and life. The role of the psychotherapist is to reflect back to the client what the client is saying. The therapist believes that healing takes place because of what happens during the therapy hour. The Rogerian therapist aims for *empathy* with the client. He or she attempts to understand and feel what the client feels, and then to reflect this back to the client. Additionally, the psychotherapist strives to have *unconditional positive regard* for the client. This is expressed through the therapist's warmth and by respecting and affirming the client's humanness. An important task for the therapist is *congruence*, or genuineness, where the therapist remains authentic to who they are as a person. Unconditional positive regard can be especially healing for a queer person who feels rejected by his or her family and society.

A different approach within the humanistic model is Gestalt psychology, based on the work of Fritz Perls. Here the psychotherapist is directive and confrontational, telling the client what to do during the therapy hour, in much the same way as a movie director controls the action on a movie set. (Other Gestalt psychotherapists are not as confrontational as Perls.) The Gestalt psychotherapist does not interpret what the client says. The focus is on the present. Gestalt psychotherapists believe that the problems people have are based on a lack of acceptance or awareness of who they are, and the therapist works to correct this. This is accomplished through such means as role-playing and challenging the client to take greater responsibility for his or her life. Gestalt psychology believes in helping an individual to work through the impasses in his or her life, so the person can become self-actualized and happier. Gestalt also pays homage to the forces within an individual, often at war with each other, and helps the client to recognize these parts and to work toward having them operate as one.

The humanistic approach can be helpful to a queer person for a number of reasons. The most important, perhaps, is that it stresses that we need to be who we actually are. Since queer people have often been highly encouraged to *not* be who they are, a humanistic approach can help a queer person work through some of the mental and emotional impasses that prevent him or her from fully accepting him or herself as a queer person. Humanistic psychotherapy is an optimistic, positive approach.

Behavioral Psychotherapy

Behavioral psychotherapy, begun as a discipline around 1900, is an amalgam of various approaches to mental health and psychotherapy. Two significant names in this branch of psychotherapy are Ivan Pavlov and B.F. Skinner

Behavioral psychotherapists believe the problems people experience are based on faulty or inadequate learning. We develop habits as children because there were rewards to developing these habits. As adults, we need to unlearn our bad habits and learn new, healthier habits. Just as Pavlov's dogs learned to associate the ringing of a bell with food, and Skinner's rats were conditioned to expect food every time they pressed a bar, humans sometimes expect certain things to happen when they act in certain ways.

Behavioral psychotherapists are not particularly interested in the client's past, nor do they believe that insight into the client's problems helps to solve those problems. Behavioral psychotherapists are interested in the things that trigger the client to behave in certain dysfunctional ways. The goal is to help the client learn to not respond to the old triggers, and instead to respond to new, healthier triggers, thereby changing the client's old, bad habits into new, healthier habits. As a result, behavioral psychotherapy is particularly well-suited to people who are pragmatic by nature, who have specific behaviors or feelings they want to change, and who are not interested in searching for their inner person.

Behavioral psychotherapists use a variety of techniques. If a client is particularly anxious, the behavioral psychotherapist might use *systematic desensitization.* For instance, if a client is afraid of flying in an airplane, the psychotherapist takes the client through a series of progressively more difficult (anxiety-provoking) fantasies. The client imagines him or herself going to an airport, then walking toward the plane, then boarding, then taking off, etc. After the fantasies have been successfully managed, the therapist might accompany the client to an airport and later to the gate of an airplane until the time comes when the client can get on the airplane and fly without overwhelming fear. Psychoactive medication such as tranquilizers might also be used.

Biofeedback is another technique used by behavioral therapists. In this technique, the client is attached to a machine that alerts the client when he or she becomes anxious. The client learns to control his or her response through relaxation techniques. Other behavioral therapy techniques include *aversion therapy* and *flooding*.

Cognitive Psychotherapy

Cognitive psychotherapy is one of the newer forms of psychotherapy, and has been gaining in respect and popularity. It has been particularly beneficial in helping people deal with depression. Its main proponent is Aaron T. Beck.

Cognitive psychotherapists believe the problems people experience are based on faulty thoughts and beliefs. One belief that may lead to depression is "I am not a good person." A cognitive psychotherapist helps clients identify faulty, harmful beliefs and substitute healthier, more functional beliefs. Cognitive psychotherapists are not interested in the past. They are primarily interested in what the client is thinking in the present, and in helping the client identify his or her dysfunctional thought patterns so they can be replaced with new, more functional thought patterns.

Many health maintenance organizations favor cognitive therapy coupled with antidepressant medication for treating depression. If someone calls an HMO and says he or she wants to see a psychotherapist for depression, the HMO may intentionally refer him or her to a cognitive psychotherapist.

Transpersonal Psychotherapy

Transpersonal psychotherapy is based on the belief that, while we are all unique, there is a transpersonal dimension to human identity—a dimension that goes beyond individuality. Transpersonal psychology believes that everything that exists somehow shares in this dimension of our identity. This understanding of identity grew out of looking at cultures from all over the world and finding that in most of these cultures there is a connection between the psychology of the individual and spiritual practices and traditions.

Two of the foremost names in transpersonal psychology are Carl Jung, who coined the term *transpersonal*, and Abraham Maslow, mentioned earlier in the section on humanistic psychotherapy. Jung proposed that in addition to our individual unconscious, there is a collective unconscious containing thoughts, ideas, and feelings that are shared by all people.

On a practical level, psychotherapists who subscribe to a transpersonal approach are the ones most willing to integrate notions of spirituality. Transpersonal psychotherapists are also the most open to integrating both Western and non-Western concepts into their practice.

Family Systems Psychotherapy

Family systems psychotherapy, also called systems psychotherapy, grew out of post–World War II research with mothers and their children. The primary belief is that human behavior, for better or worse, is the result of our interactions with the environment and the important people in our lives, particularly our family. The significant pioneers in this field are Virginia Satir, Salvador Minuchin, Jay Haley, and Cloe Madanes.

Systems psychotherapists work on changing the interactional patterns between people in a system. The system can be a family, a workplace, or any other environment where a group of people interacts. A family does not necessarily mean mom, dad, and the kids; any group of individuals who define themselves as family and who interact in the ways families do would be considered a family by systems psychotherapists. As such, many family systems therapists are queer-affirmative.

Family systems psychotherapists are the modern marriage counselors. They are the ones trained to help couples work out their difficulties. If you and your partner want to see a psychotherapist together, it is likely that the counselor will, at least in part, identify as a family systems psychotherapist.

Family systems psychotherapy is a valuable tool for queer people. It can help a queer person resolve issues he or she has with his or her family of origin or with the family he or she created. The family a queer person creates may not fit the definition of family that some homophobic people use, but it is a true family and one in which a family systems therapist may be able to help that person better function.

Because there are many emotional issues concerning *family* in America, queer people are strongly advised to make sure any family systems psychotherapist they are thinking of seeing is queer-affirmative.

ECLECTICISM

Perhaps one of the most important but underrated approaches to psychotherapy is eclecticism. An eclectic psychotherapist is one who has studied various schools of psychotherapy, along with other sources of knowledge, and uses what he or she considers to be the best ideas, theories, and practical methods. The eclectic psychotherapist makes personal choices as to which ideas he or she considers the best and most useful and which should be discarded.

Most psychotherapists are eclectic, although few will acknowledge that when asked to state their orientation. In the pecking order of orientations, eclectic psychotherapists are seen by many as being at the bottom of the pack. There is constant pressure within the field of psychotherapy for a therapist to subscribe to a particular orientation. Those who say they are eclectic are often pictured as either not bright enough to understand the complexities of a particular orientation or not committed to a consistent approach.

Most psychotherapists who say they are eclectic are in fact heavily based in one of the theoretical orientations but want to leave the door open to integrating theories and methods from other schools. Eclectic therapists customize their work to each client, drawing from relevant approaches as needed but relying on some approaches more than others. If you ask a therapist for his or her theoretical orientation and are told he or she is eclectic, it is entirely appropriate to ask which school(s) of psychotherapy are most appealing to that therapist. By doing that, you will get a better understanding of how the therapist works.

If a therapist says he or she is eclectic, you know the therapist is bucking pressure to declare him or herself with a particular school. This is a free-thinking psychotherapist who follows his or her own inner voice. If that idea appeals to you, you might want to look for an eclectic psychotherapist.

Bodywork

Bodywork combines mental health theory and physical manipulation of the body. To some it may seem as if a psychotherapist who calls him or herself a bodyworker is merely a glorified masseur or masseuse, but in fact bodywork is a highly developed form of psychotherapy with a long history. Bodyworkers believe that our bodies have blocked energy that corresponds to emotional blockages. By directly manipulating the client's body, the psychotherapist believes that the emotional blockages can be lessened.

Bodywork is somewhat controversial because of the possibility for sexual abuse of the client. Many people become sexually aroused when touched by another person, and this sometimes happens during bodywork sessions. Furthermore, many professional sex workers advertise as masseurs, masseuses, and bodyworkers, thus confusing the issue. Professional bodyworkers walk a thin line between legitimate professional services and actions the client might interpret as sexual. At times, a bodyworker may believe his or her actions do not have a sexual overtone, but a client may feel otherwise. It is also not uncommon for clients to become sexually attracted to their mental health workers. A prospective client and body worker should discuss these issues before entering into a therapeutic relationship to avoid misinterpretation.

Expressive Therapies

Some forms of psychotherapy utilize expressive forms of the arts to produce a therapeutic change. Expressive therapies often combine the use of the art form with talk therapy. Psychotherapists using such techniques are *usually* trained and licensed as psychotherapists. Caution, however, is urged, as some are not trained or licensed as psychotherapists. Make sure to check an expressive therapist's qualifications before committing to working with him or her. Qualified expressive therapists, in addition to their training as psychotherapists, should have received additional training in a particular art form and how it can be used to enable a client to grow.

ART THERAPY

Art therapy involves the client using the visual arts—drawing, painting, sculpting, collage, photography, etc—to express him or herself. Sometimes the work is created based on directions from the art therapist. The therapist might ask the client to draw a picture of his or her family. Other times the process is nondirective, with the therapist asking the client to use the medium of his or her choice to express whatever he or she wants to express. Sometimes the client is asked to talk about the artwork; other times the creation of the art may be enough. The therapist, depending on how he or she works, might interpret the artwork or focus on how the client felt while creating it.

The essence of art therapy is that the creative process of the client is combined with the therapeutic process of emotional growth. Art therapy attracts some people because they have an extensive background in the visual arts. Others want to use art therapy for exactly the opposite reason: They have no experience with the visual arts. Many of us as children heard that we did not draw or paint well, and such messages in some way traumatized us, if only mildly. Art therapy enables a person who might otherwise be afraid to use the arts expressively to work in a medium that interests him or her.

DRAMA THERAPY

Jacob Moreno pioneered drama therapy in the 1960s, using what he called "psychodramas," during which a paid audience would come to an evening of "theater" and one or more audience members would volunteer to be the protagonist in a scene.

As currently practiced, drama therapy enables the client, usually in a group with several other clients, to use acting to achieve growth. With the therapist taking the role of director, clients act out scenes that are meaningful to one or more of the participants. Usually, by the end of a drama workshop, every client usually has had an opportunity to be the protagonist.

The miniplay might be an emotionally charged scene out of a client's deep past, or it may represent current issues in his or her life. Another possibility is for clients to work on an emotion or concept rather than a specific scene. When scenes are used, they are sometimes allowed to unravel of their own accord, while at other times the psychotherapist/director may pause a scene so that he or she can ask the actors to say or do something specific. Usually, each cast member and all those watching give feedback regarding the scene that was created.

DANCE THERAPY

Dance therapy involves the client, either alone or with others, using movement to express him or herself. The therapist may choreograph movements in ways that should enable the client to grow, or the dance may be less structured, enabling the client to experience spontaneity. In most situations, clients talk afterwards about what they thought and felt as they either moved or watched others move. Dance therapy tries to help clients gain greater insight through movement and to make the movements themselves a therapeutic experience.

MUSIC THERAPY

Music therapy is similar to other expressive therapies, except it uses the medium of music. The client may or may not have a background in playing a particular instrument. If the client is untrained in music, the therapist works to ensure that the client has a positive musical as well as psychotherapeutic experience. Music, like the other expressive arts, is used to help clients understand what the sounds might represent and grow through the experience of creating.

SANDPLAY THERAPY

If you walk into the offices of a psychotherapist and see shelves full of small objects: people, houses, animals, cars, boats, trees, and just about anything else you can imagine, plus one or two trays filled with sand, you have entered the office of a psychotherapist who uses sandplay therapy. Unlike art, drama, dance, or music therapists, sandplay therapists rarely identify themselves as such as a primary way of saying who they are. Most consider sandplay an approach to be used in addition to other forms of therapy.

Sandplay therapy involves a client taking some of the objects off the shelves and putting them into the tray of sand until a picture is created. When the client says the tray is done, it is done. Sometimes the client may talk about what she or he has created; other times the tray will speak for itself.

Sandplay therapy is closely related to art therapy in that a visual image is created. It is often easier for people to work in sandplay therapy than art therapy, though. Many of us were traumatized by elementary school teachers who claimed that the people or cars or houses in our drawings did not look as they should, and as a result we have become timid about drawing or showing our drawings to others. With sandplay, these fears are eliminated. Most people have no history with sandplay, so there are no bad experiences to overcome.

The underlying assumption of sandplay work is that the image created comes directly from both the client's conscious and unconscious, with an emphasis on the unconscious. Some think of sandplay as the equivalent of a dream, something that comes from deep in the client's brain. Sandplay is viewed as a way to access what is going on inside the client on a deep level. The trick, of course, is in understanding what something that is.

For others, sandplay therapy is less about understanding what is created than about simply doing it. It is thought that inner conflicts will emerge, and over a period of time the trays will help the client work through his or her conflicts. Therapists usually take photographs of the trays created and look for particular meanings or trends. Sometimes they share these photos with the clients, but many therapists believe it is best for the client to retain the image only in his or her brain.

Sandplay was invented by Carl Jung, one of the pioneers of modern psychotherapy. While relaxing at the beach, he had noticed how therapeutic it felt to create a picture in the sand and how the sand picture itself seemed to stem from the unconscious. The process was refined by Margaret Lowenfeld of the London Institute of Child Psychology in the 1920's, and further popularized by Dora Kalff.

Chapter 7
The How and Where of Psychotherapy Conversations

Like virtually everything else, there is a way that psychotherapy operates. The more you understand about this, the more likely it is that you will get what you need from psychotherapy.

Rules have been set up to meet the needs of both the providers and consumers of psychotherapy services. Compromises abound, but this set of basic guidelines enables the psychotherapy profession to function efficiently. It allows psychotherapists to provide a high level of service to a significant number of people in an orderly manner. But more important to you as the consumer are the guidelines defining the ethics of the mental health profession. These guidelines are designed to protect clients, and they impact how clients meet with psychotherapists.

During most psychotherapy sessions, only the client and psychotherapist are present in the office, and they engage in some sort of conversation. That is what clients seem to need and want most. At other times, though, more than two people are present. The form of treatment depends not only on the nature of your problem but also on the psychotherapist you happen to choose. Different psychotherapists work in different ways.

Psychotherapy may occur either inside or outside a mental health hospital. Most psychotherapy occurs outside such hospitals. Because people in hospitals are called patients, services provided inside mental health hospitals are referred to as *inpatient* services. Services provided outside mental health hospitals are called *outpatient* services, even though individual practitioners may prefer the term *client*. Many services are offered on both an outpatient and an inpatient basis, the difference being where the service is provided and how insurance companies reimburse clients for psychotherapy expenses.

INPATIENT TREATMENT PROGRAMS

Some psychotherapy takes place in a mental health hospital or the psychiatric department of a larger hospital. When a client stays overnight in such a setting, he or she is receiving inpatient psychotherapy.

CRISIS

The most likely reason to become an inpatient consumer of mental health services is a crisis so overwhelming that it is difficult or impossible to function in a normal manner. Time spent in a mental hospital is designed to provide relief from the stress, to protect the client from hurting him or herself or others, and to enable the client to work on issues without the distraction of other life tasks.

A client may be admitted to a mental health hospital either voluntarily or involuntarily. Voluntary admission means that the client agrees to hospitalization. Involuntary admission means that either the police or a physician believes the client is a danger to him or herself or others. Involuntary confinement can last up to 72 hours without a court order. Often, someone admitted involuntarily may be released in less than 72 hours if the hospital believes that person is no longer a danger to him or herself or others.

Sometimes, an involuntarily admitted person may wish to leave after the initial 72 hours have passed, but the hospital staff believes that person is still a danger to him or herself or others. In such cases a legal proceeding is convened, often at the hospital, during which a judge hears arguments on behalf of both the hospital and the client. If the judge agrees with the hospital, the individual may be confined for an additional period, usually two weeks. For longer involuntary stays, more legal proceedings are necessary. The individual in treatment does not ever lose his or her rights and may legally challenge an extended confinement.

What happens in the hospital crisis centers varies. In many hospitals, clients are confined to a locked ward, where they have access to various rooms on the ward but not the outside world. In many hospitals, little or no psychotherapy is provided. People are merely warehoused until they are no longer a danger to themselves or others. Television, telephone, reading, and conversation are the only activities. Other facilities try to provide individual or group therapy. In nearly all cases, the individual is evaluated by a psychiatrist. A social worker might also interview the person to help plan his or her discharge from the inpatient facility. Calls, with the client's permission, may be made to the friends, family, and psychotherapist to coordinate treatment after leaving the hospital.

SHORT-TERM

Sometimes it makes sense for people to be admitted to a mental health facility for a slightly longer period of time, usually anywhere from a week to a month. These stays are almost always voluntary. Some individuals come after a stay in a crisis center; others go directly to a mental health facility designed for extended stays.

There are two primary reasons why someone is admitted to such a facility, and often the two are related. One is that the individual has a substance abuse problem and needs a facility where he or she can work full-time on his or her initial recovery from substance abuse. The second is that the individual is suffering from depression or other serious symptoms that make it difficult to function in the world. In these situations, the individual or friends and family of the individual recognize that he or she is a danger to him or herself or others and therefore needs a rest and a break.

Extended-stay facilities provide both individual and group psychotherapy. Family therapy is also available, if the client's family is willing to take part. A portion of family therapy is usually spent working on the family dynamics of whatever brought the client to the hospital. Planning for the client's discharge may also be incorporated into family therapy.

Confinement in an inpatient mental health facility is very expensive, as much as $1,000 a day or more. Most people can afford this level of care only if they have medical insurance that covers inpatient mental health care. Many managed care health insurance plans need to approve inpatient mental health services in advance of admission.

Inpatient mental health facilities usually have locked wards to prevent disoriented or impulsive people from wandering off. However, most people are confined there voluntarily and may sign themselves out of the facility if they wish to leave, even against the medical advice of the hospital.

LONG-TERM

Long-term confinement in a mental health facility is relatively rare because of the expense. Few can afford it, and most medical insurance policies only cover a limited number of days. Managed care companies look closely at extended stays because of the great expense involved.

In today's world, the most common long-term mental health facilities are halfway houses. Halfway houses are group living facilities offering on-site mental health care, while allowing residents to take part in some normal life activities. Often, residents work or participate in community activities during the day and return at night. Staff and residents alike usually share in preparing meals, housekeeping, and other activities of daily living. People often go to halfway houses after short-term inpatient treatment.

Admission to a halfway house is usually voluntary, and residents normally may sign themselves out at their own discretion.

OUTPATIENT TREATMENT

Most mental health services are provided on an outpatient basis, meaning the person receiving the services is not in a mental health hospital when the service is provided. The trend in mental health is similar to the broader health care trend to provide as much service as possible outside expensive inpatient settings.

INDIVIDUAL PSYCHOTHERAPY

When most people think of the psychotherapy setting, they picture individual outpatient psychotherapy—one psychotherapist meeting with one client. Many people grew up with the idea that the client lies on a couch, while the psychotherapist sits unseen in a chair off to the side. The psychotherapist quietly takes notes and says little. Innumerable novels and Hollywood films have popularized this image of psychotherapy. And there is some truth to it. Some psychotherapists still use couches. Much more often, however, the psychotherapist and client sit in chairs facing each other and converse.

Individual psychotherapy is usually the appropriate form of psychotherapy when you want to take greater responsibility for your life and happiness. Through individual psychotherapy you come to understand what you need to do, and you work at whatever that is. Individual psychotherapy is sometimes used in conjunction with another modality.

COUPLES COUNSELING

What began years ago as marriage counseling is now generally referred to as couples counseling, and quite often the therapist is called a couples counselor. Almost no one in the field refers to it as couples psychotherapy, though it is a form of psychotherapy designed to help two people relate to one another. Couples counseling is actually a subset of family therapy but particular enough to be considered a specialty.

People come to couples counseling to deal with issues that affect them as a couple. Most who seek couples counseling are in the process of breaking up. Their thinking often runs thus: *We've tried to resolve this by ourselves, and it hasn't worked. Let's try couples counseling, and if that doesn't work, we'll split up.* Generally, the relationship has been bad for a while, and one or both individuals have one foot out the door already; they are simply seeking permission to throw in the towel. In such situations, couples counseling may help couples admit that they want to split up. Because of this, many people have the misguided notion that what happens in the couples counseling causes couples to separate. That is rarely the case.

Couples counseling can be a valuable tool, especially for queer couples. Queer relationships are not sanctioned by society. There are few role models and little legal, spiritual, or family support. Support for queer couples comes primarily from the queer community, and queer-affirmative couples counselors can be an integral part of that support network.

In my opinion, it is never too soon to begin couples counseling. I am in a long-term relationship that has now reached the 15-year mark. My partner and I began couples counseling early on because we felt it would be helpful to have an outsider comment on how we were setting up our relationship. We sought and found a queer-affirmative couples counselor. Over the first few years of our relationship, we went to the couples counselor periodically to discuss the ways we related to each other.

Then, for several years we did not see a couples counselor. At the 10-year mark of our relationship, however, we realized we had both changed, but our relationship had not. We had become locked into patterns of behavior that we had established years earlier. Again, we sought a queer-affirmative couples counselor. The goal of this round of couples counseling was to break certain patterns that were clearly not working for us but difficult to change. Over the course of the next few years, we met with the couples counselor on a weekly basis.

At no point did it ever seem that our relationship was in danger, but we realized that not making changes would cause each of us to be unhappy and possibly lead to problems down the road. Couples counseling used in this manner is good preventative medicine.

Reasons a Queer Couple Might Seek Couples Counseling

There are many reasons why queer couples seek couples counseling, but several stand out as particularly important. One is to start a relationship right. Relationships involve two people who have led separate lives before deciding to become a couple. Each learned ways to do things from the family in which he or she grew up. An aspect of family loyalty is the belief that the way things were done in your family is the right way to do things. Thus, whenever two people from different families try to form a new family, there are the inevitable conflicts. Couples counseling can relieve some of this friction.

Another reason is that queer couples have different dynamics than nonqueer couples. Queer couples form emotionally close and enmeshed relationships. This has long been recognized in lesbian couples, but it is also true for gay male couples and probably for couples in which one or both persons are transgender. Queer couples try to be best friends as well as sexual partners and partners in life. This means that each member of the couple has to put aside at least some of his or her desires to do things alone or differently. Over time this produces stress. The desires each partner initially put aside will reemerge at different points. One person either wants to do some things alone or do things that do not interest his or her mate. This can seem like a threat to the relationship. Seeking the help of a couples counselor at this point is often helpful.

The subject of children can put stress on queer couples. Virtually all young lesbian couples face questions about whether they plan to have children and, if so, by what means. Gay male couples are beginning to experience similar pressure. Parents of queer people once despaired over not having grandchildren. Because of recent advances in reproductive technologies, though, some parents are now asking their queer children about having children. In today's world, nearly all queer couples must decide whether they want children, and partners may disagree about that choice. Couples counseling can help when disagreements over having children arise.

Children of a different sort also cause stress for queer couples. Many queer people, at some point in their life, were in a heterosexual relationship that resulted in children. Thus, many queer couples find themselves dealing with young or adult children from previous relationships. If the children are young, then the queer couple deals with all the issues of a blended family, particularly the role of the nonbiological parent. If the children are adults, different sets of issues arise, such as how to deal with homophobic feelings the child might have. Couples (and/or family) counseling can help here as well.

In addition to the plethora of queer-related issues, queer couples need to deal with the issues facing all couples: money, sex, work, religion, families of origin, with whom to spend the holidays—let alone lying, cheating, and betrayals of trust. Couples counseling can provide a helpful and safe place to discuss these issues.

FAMILY THERAPY

In family therapy, several members of the same family see a psychotherapist at the same time. Family therapists are specially trained to work with families as opposed to individuals.

Family therapy is a product of post–World War II developments in mental health. Beginning in the late 1940s, psychotherapy clinics began to schedule meetings with troubled children and their mothers. Prior to then, the clinician usually saw the mother and child separately. It soon became apparent that at least one important person was missing from these sessions: the father. So fathers were invited, and family therapy developed. Over the next 30 years, family therapy expanded to include all family members, as it was recognized that one member's problem affected everyone in the family.

In the mid 1970s, family therapists began working with the families of queer people. In practice this usually means one of two configurations, either meeting with a queer person and members of the family into which he or she was born, or meeting with a queer person and the family he or she has created. This latter configuration is often a varied group. Some queer people have children by heterosexual partners; others have children by adoption or alternative forms of fertilization. Still others have created unique multi-generational families that do not fit most traditional conceptions but are families nonetheless. A queer-affirmative family therapist will be willing to meet with all individuals who consider themselves part of a family, regardless of whether the family is legally sanctioned.

A particularly good time to see a queer-affirmative family therapist is when someone is coming out and a family member or members are having difficulty with that. Family therapy can help family members communicate their concerns in a clear manner and resolve the differences of opinion that exist.

INTERVENTIONS

Interventions occur when a large group of people, usually the family members and friends of a particular person, gather with a family therapist for the specific purpose of trying to persuade that person that he or she has a problem with alcohol or drugs that needs to be addressed. Most frequently, this happens when a chemically addicted person needs to enter an alcohol or drug treatment program. Occasionally, interventions occur for other reasons: Perhaps the person has joined a cult or is a sex addict. The family therapist's role is to control the flow of the communication in order to maximize its effect.

The form of each intervention differs, but the general pattern is for each person to reaffirm his or her love for the person who is the subject of the intervention. The speaker then describes a specific incident where the subject of the intervention was out of control, for example, because of his or her use of alcohol or drugs.

Interventions are a powerful method for breaking through the denial of someone who is abusing alcohol or drugs and is unable to admit it. Intervention sessions usually last several hours. Friends and family members often come from other cities to attend.

GROUP PSYCHOTHERAPY

Group psychotherapy is based on the idea that psychotherapists can use the dynamics of group interaction to help clients. To those unfamiliar with group psychotherapy, this probably sounds strange and counterintuitive. And yet it is sometimes the best way to deal with problems. A powerful and efficient form of psychotherapy, group psychotherapy has helped a large number of people.

Group psychotherapy has the same purpose as any other form of psychotherapy: to help the members of the group function better in the world. Certain problems and issues are well-suited to group psychotherapy, such as coming out, shyness, self-loathing, grief, recovery from addiction, and support to live a healthy life.

There are many different forms of outpatient group psychotherapy (see Appendix B). The only common factor is that more than one client is present. The total number of clients involved can vary. Even the presence of a psychotherapist is optional, and sometimes more than one psychotherapist is in attendance.

The most commonly understood form of group psychotherapy is the general psychotherapy group. Usually, a single psychotherapist meets with between three to 12 clients on a regular ongoing basis. General psychotherapy groups usually meet on a weekly basis and last for 1½ to 2½ hours. The same people come to the group each week for an extended period of time. Occasionally, someone drops out or someone new is added. Each person has their own reason for coming. In any particular session, one or more of the group members may be the focus of the group's attention.

A generation ago, group psychotherapy was a bad place for a queer person to be. Groups almost always pressured the queer person to become heterosexual, often with the encouragement of the group leader. Regardless of the issues that brought a queer person to the group, his or her queerness quickly became the issue, making it difficult to work on the problems that brought them to the group in the first place.

Fortunately, this behavior has become a thing of the past. Group psychotherapy rarely focuses on changing sexual or romantic orientation—unless the group is run by those attempting reparative conversion therapy. In fact, group psychotherapy now offers a number of advantages to queer people.

Variations in Groups

General Psychotherapy Groups Versus Issue-Focused Psychotherapy Groups

General psychotherapy groups consist of individuals dealing with a variety of issues. If the group shares some commonality, it is that each member has *a* reason for being there. For one member, that reason might be depression; for another, it might be difficulty starting a relationship; and for a third, it might be fear of leaving his or her home. But the group has no overall theme or purpose than to help individuals with their problems.

Issue-focused groups differ in that all the members share something in common. It might be that they are all over 50, or they are single parents, or they are single and interested in forming relationships. Or it might be that all of the group members are queer. There is always at least one commonality between each group member. At times that may seem to be the only thing they have in common.

Open-Ended Groups Versus Time-Limited Groups

Some psychotherapy groups go on for years, while others begin and end on specific dates. Those that continue indefinitely are known as open-ended groups. Individuals may stay in the group for a few months or many years. One psychotherapist in San Francisco has been facilitating the same Tuesday evening psychotherapy group for 22 years.

Open Groups Versus Closed Groups

Usually, almost anyone may attend open groups, so it is likely that different people will participate in each meeting. Sometimes called drop-in groups, open groups are often sponsored by a mental health agency or a nonprofit organization that advertises the existence and purpose of the group. Open groups almost always have a specific focus, such as to help caregivers to persons with AIDS. Open groups usually meet at a regularly scheduled time and do not require the participants to contact anyone in advance or commit to a certain number of visits.

Most psychotherapy groups, though, are closed. Only individuals who are group members may attend, and the same people attend each meeting.

Groups With Leaders Versus Leaderless Groups

Most groups have one designated leader. Sometimes there are two leaders, although only very rarely are there more. The leaders are the same every week and are almost always either psychotherapists, interns, or peer counselors.

Leaderless groups are much less common but do exist. Mental health agencies or nonprofit organizations usually sponsor such groups. Occasionally, a group that has previously met with a leader will decide to continue as a leaderless group. In leaderless groups, it is common for one or more of the group members to take on the role of group facilitator.

Queer Groups Versus Mixed Groups

If you are considering joining a psychotherapy group, one of the first questions to consider is whether to join a group in which all the members and the leader(s) are queer or a mixed group in which some are queer and some are not. There are good reasons to join each kind of group.

If you are in the early stages of coming out, you should strongly consider an all-queer group, which can expose you to the tremendous diversity within the queer community. This can be very helpful to someone who has primarily been exposed to media stereotypes, often negative, of what a queer lifestyle is. You might also look for a group cofacilitated by two leaders. Group members tend to look to group leaders as examples and role models. Being able to observe how the two facilitators can live quite different lives should help you find your own path as a queer person.

You might also want to choose an all-queer group if you are dealing with a significant amount of self-loathing or self-hatred related to being queer. It is impossible for anyone to grow up queer in America without internalizing *some* self-loathing. And for some queer people, such feelings are a constant burden. These individuals find themselves wishing they were not queer and disliking queer people in general. An all-queer group can help heal these internal wounds, since there a poorly adjusted queer person will get to interact with group members who have a higher level of self-acceptance and are functioning better in the world.

A good reason for joining a mixed group is that it frequently reflects the makeup of society. A mixed group allows a queer person to learn to be comfortable with him or herself in the company of nonqueer people. A mixed group can also recreate the dynamics of the family of origin for a queer person, allowing him or her to learn how to deal with the reactions of his or her nonqueer relatives in a healthier manner.

Therapy Groups Versus Support Groups

When looking for a group, you might find that some groups call themselves therapy groups, while others call themselves support groups. The underlying idea behind this distinction is that therapy groups are for people who want to change, while support groups are for people who need support around a difficult issue in their lives. Thus, a shy person who wants to be more outgoing should join a therapy group, while a person living with AIDS should look for a support group.

In reality, though, there is little difference between therapy groups and support groups. Therapy groups are also support groups, and support groups help members change the way they cope with life issues and situations.

The Process of Group Therapy

Group psychotherapy can seem intimidating. You are asked to share your most private thoughts and feelings with strangers. This alone is enough to scare people off. Knowing a little in advance about what usually happens in group therapy can help you overcome such fears.

If the psychotherapy group is just beginning, and all the members are strangers to one another, the group usually begins with the members and leader(s) all getting acquainted. This is usually an easy stage, during which members say who they are and a little about why they are there. This usually takes one to two group sessions. Then the work begins.

The next task for the group is usually to build mutual trust. This happens through members telling more about what has brought them to the group and watching the reactions of others in the group. If each group member feels understood and accepted, trust begins to build.

As trust builds, the group begins working on the issues that have brought the group members together. This is the real work of the group. It is an opportunity for each member to report regularly on his or her progress or problems and get feedback.

Finally, if the group is time-limited, there is the stage of saying good-bye. The work is wrapped up, at least for the time being. The issues that brought the members together in the first place may still need work, but the group ends and the members move on, perhaps continuing the work on their own, in individual therapy, or in another group.

This explanation is, of course, oversimplified. Groups tend to be much more complicated, and problems do develop. Some members will not get along; others will not develop trust. In effect, the group becomes a microcosm of the world. The beauty of this microcosm is that it permits members to work on their issues with the world at large in the controlled setting of the group.

If you join a psychotherapy group already in progress, the process is slightly different. It is likely that the other group members have developed a degree of trust, since they already know each other and why everyone is in the group. As the new member, you have to get to know and trust the other members, just as they need to get to know and trust you. Since you may be the only new person in the group, this usually takes less time than when everyone in the group is new.

You will still find that everyone brings their own interpersonal issues into the group. However people are in the outside world is how they will behave in the group. While in the group, every member will have many opportunities to work at getting along better with others.

Most psychotherapy groups have a set of ground rules by which they operate. The most basic of these rules is that what is said in the room stays in the room. Another ground rule is that each person speaks only in the first person: They make "I" statements, as opposed to "you" statements, about how they think or feel and about what other members say. Couples counseling sometimes uses this same rule.

Workshops

Workshops are a specialized and time-limited form of group psychotherapy. They are generally an all-day or weekend affair with a particular focus, such as intimacy or midlife issues. Sometimes a psychotherapist will ask individual clients to take part in an all-day workshop with other clients. Other times, the workshops are advertised to attract those interested in a particular focus or leader. Weekend workshops are sometimes held at resorts so those attending the workshop can be away from their home and things that usually distract them.

The Focus of Groups

Both within and outside the queer community, innumerable psychotherapy groups either have a specific focus or limit attendance to those who share some common trait. Appendix B illustrates the breadth and variety of existing queer therapy groups.

Most queer psychotherapy groups are restricted by gender. If you want to be in a psychotherapy group that includes both men and women, you will probably have to look outside the queer community. Queer psychotherapy groups for both men and women generally exist only when there is a particular cogender focus, such as being a queer parent.

TELEPHONE AND CYBER-COUNSELING

Sometimes a client cannot make it to the office of a psychotherapist, perhaps because the client lives in a remote area, is constantly traveling, or has a physical condition that makes getting to the psychotherapist's office difficult. Or the client may be too fearful of leaving home to make it to the office. Any number of reasons could make getting to a psychotherapist's office either difficult or impossible. In such situations, there are alternatives to meeting face-to-face with a psychotherapist.

Counseling over the telephone is probably as old as psychotherapy, since modern psychotherapy and the telephone came into existence at approximately the same time. It is a natural fit; the telephone seems ideal for psychotherapy, which is often mostly about talk. Some psychotherapists even believe that the "distance" of talking on the telephone gives the client the safety he or she needs to reveal things that otherwise would remain unsaid.

There are, however, psychotherapists who believe that to be effective psychotherapy requires face-to-face contact. The only way to find out if a psychotherapist is open to telephone consultations is to ask, stating your reason for wanting this form of therapy. Do not be surprised if the psychotherapist says no and cannot tell you the reason why. Psychotherapists are intuitive by nature and may know something is not right for them without being able to say why.

Martha

Telephone counseling worked out well for Martha, who began therapy after breaking up with her lover and stayed in counseling after the crisis passed to deal with her alcoholism and feelings of low self-esteem. She met regularly with her therapist for several years, during which she became clean and sober as well as successful in her career. She started a new relationship with a woman who was also career-oriented, and they lived happily for a year—until Martha was offered a huge promotion. The promotion meant relocating to a city far away.

Martha was given one week to decide whether to accept the promotion, which caused tremendous stress for her and her partner. There were several emergency meetings between Martha and her therapist, one of which also included Martha's partner, who opposed the move because there was no way she could move to the other city without giving up her job and much that she had accomplished.

After considerable anguish, Martha accepted the position. Within two weeks, she found herself living in a corporate apartment in the new city without her partner, friends, or the support network she had built. She and her partner had decided to continue their relationship, but they both felt they needed help with adjusting to the sudden changes.

Martha soon felt overwhelmed by the mountain of tasks set before her: finding a permanent place to live, moving her possessions, attending AA meetings, and learning the new job. She had few remaining support systems on which to rely during the difficult transition. Martha's therapist, though, appreciated the impact of the rapid changes. To Martha's surprise, her therapist suggested they continue their weekly conversations on the telephone until Martha felt settled enough to find a new therapist.

Telephone therapy lasted longer than either Martha or her therapist had expected—almost a year. During that time, Martha repeatedly said that the phone contact, though not as personal as meeting face-to-face, was quite helpful. Several times Martha visited her former city of residence to be with her partner. On those occasions, Martha set up in-person appointments with her therapist, two of them including Martha's partner.

Martha did eventually establish a relationship with another psychotherapist—who was in no way threatened by Martha continuing her telephone conversations with her former therapist. Martha and her former therapist continued to meet via telephone, though the frequency of their conversations dropped over time. The telephone therapy had given Martha something stable at a time of great change in her life.

Alan

Telephone therapy also benefited Alan, an actor touring in a play. Insecure about his masculinity and what he had to offer a boyfriend, Alan began to date another member of the cast, whom he described as "dark, brooding, and masculine." Alan soon found himself in turmoil over the on-again, off-again attitude of the man he was dating. The play was in San Francisco for an extended run, so he began psychotherapy to deal with these issues.

A month later, the play's run in San Francisco came to an end. For the next year, the company was scheduled to play in a different city every week or two. Clearly, under those circumstances, it would have been impossible for Alan to have ongoing face-to-face meetings with any psychotherapist. He asked his therapist if they could "meet" on the telephone each week, and because of the circumstances the therapist agreed.

An appointment time was established based on the time in San Francisco. Each week, Alan checked to see what time zone he was in and called right on the hour for the telephone session. For Alan, telephone psychotherapy was the only way to have continued contact with his psychotherapist and the work he had begun in person. In his case the arrangement worked well.

Psychotherapy is adapting to other communications media as well, including the Internet. Narrative therapy seems well-suited to the Internet. Narrative therapy usually means that the psychotherapist and client(s) not only meet face-to-face but also correspond with letters that summarize or respond to their in-person sessions or previous written communications. When done on the Internet, narrative therapy may only involve writing, or it may supplement face-to-face meetings or telephone conversations.

Obviously, this form of psychotherapy works only for people who want to read and respond to correspondence—and can regularly allow time for that. Narrative therapy can also be done through the mail, although the Internet provides for a quicker response. As the Internet develops, other innovative methods of conducting psychotherapy will likely emerge.

BENEFITING FROM OUTPATIENT THERAPY: AARON

Aaron is a high-functioning professional in his 50s. Over the course of his life, he has used many forms of psychotherapy to help him to cope with personal, relationship, and family issues.

Aaron had been an unhappy teenager, unaware that much of the unhappiness he experienced was related to his dysfunctional family of origin and the repressed knowledge that he was gay. This was an era when the need for psychotherapy was considered shameful, so even though Aaron knew he was unhappy, he put off visiting a psychotherapist until his mid 20s.

By the time Aaron finally entered therapy, he had so deeply repressed his gay nature that he felt asexual. He did not have any interest in dating women, but he thought he was supposed to want to do so. The thought of dating men did not occur to him.

Aaron called a private psychotherapy clinic and began seeing a psychotherapist twice and sometimes three times a week. During this period, he started to date women, losing his virginity to one of them. With that, the floodgates of sexuality opened, and he began to intensely feel his gay side beckoning to come out. When he and his girlfriend broke up, he decided that he would not date women, at least for a while, and he gave himself permission to meet, date, and be sexual with men. This felt so freeing to Aaron that he decided to stop therapy. He had gotten all he needed out of therapy–or so he thought.

About a year later, Aaron decided to come out to his parents. He had come out to his siblings who were accepting of and comfortable with his homosexuality. He was not, however, prepared for his parents' shock and hysteria. They were determined to prevent him from making what they believed was the biggest mistake of his life. They insisted that the three of them—Aaron, his mother, and his father—see a family counselor, who they were sure would discourage Aaron from continuing to come out.

Because Aaron had had a positive experience in individual psychotherapy, he agreed to go with his parents to family counseling. At the first session, he asked the family counselor if she thought homosexuality was a mental illness, and the counselor told him she did not. This was before homosexuality was officially declassified as a mental illness, so Aaron was relieved and felt he could continue the family counseling.

Aaron and his parents met with the family counselor for a total of six meetings. While nobody changed their mind about what had brought them to the family counselor's office, they agreed to disagree. Aaron remembers this experience as one of the few times he was able to have a direct conversation with his father. Years later, after his father died, Aaron would come to cherish those conversations.

During this same period, the early 1970s, workshops called encounter groups became popular. Encounter groups were often large, sometimes with 100 or more attending. Attendance was open to whoever could afford the nominal entrance fee. Usually led by a psychotherapist, encounter groups were designed to help attendees to get in touch with their feelings. Aaron went to a number of these workshops and felt they helped him to be more in charge of his life.

At one of these workshops, the leader announced that he was forming an ongoing psychotherapy group. He said the group would be similar to the large encounter group, except it would be restricted to eight people, who would be expected to attend each week. Because Aaron liked the leader, he applied for admission to the group and was accepted.

For the next two years, Aaron attended the group on a weekly basis. He got to know the other group members at an emotionally intimate level, something new to Aaron. And perhaps more important, Aaron let himself be known by the other group members. He was able to tell all of his secrets, especially his sexual secrets, and have other people hear and understand him and give him feedback. After two years, some members dropped out, and the group leader decided to dissolve the group.

Aaron did not see a psychotherapist for the next 13 years—happy ones for him. He moved to another city, become successful in his field, and had friends and an occasional boyfriend. Then came AIDS. Aaron had been sexually active and felt certain he had contracted the HIV virus. He took an HIV test to make sure. When the results came back positive, as he had expected, he was surprised to find himself shocked and stunned. For days Aaron could not say anything about his feelings. So he decided to once again see a psychotherapist. He wanted to talk about what he thought was a terminal illness that would probably kill him fairly soon.

Through a mutual friend, Aaron knew of a particular psychotherapist, so he called to make an appointment. Aaron met with that therapist for a total of seven sessions, during which he did virtually all the talking. The psychotherapist, probably trained by a psychoanalytic institute, said very little. A number of times, Aaron asked for feedback, but the psychotherapist claimed not to know Aaron well enough to have anything to say. This was not the feedback Aaron was looking for. Plus, this therapy was expensive. The lack of feedback and the cost caused Aaron to discontinue. But the talking he had done, even if it was only one-way, had been enough to get him over the shock he had been experiencing. Aaron was able to function once again, even with the knowledge that he was HIV-positive.

About a year later Aaron met Frank, and it was love at first sight. Both were HIV-positive and wanted to have a wonderful life together, however short that life might be. Soon after becoming lovers, they went to a couples counselor. They wanted their relationship to work and felt a couples counselor would help. Over the course of the next two years, they saw the couples counselor intermittently. Eventually they discontinued, having achieved what they wanted in therapy.

Then a funny thing happened to Aaron and Frank. Neither of them died. Their health was stable, and when protease inhibitors became available, their blood test results, which had already been steadily improving, came out even better. They both realized they were going to be around for a while.

Aaron and Frank had put off dealing with certain issues in the belief that one or both of them would die, thus ending their relationship. There were many things that each had felt he could put up with for a short while but not for an extended period. They had gotten into a rut and could not get out of it by themselves. So they began couples counseling once again.

For over two years now, Aaron and Frank have continued couples counseling. As a result, Aaron has realized that he needs to change how he responds to Frank and to life in general. To that end, Aaron has recently begun to see a counselor individually. Likewise, Frank has begun seeing the couples counselor alone sometimes in order to work on his own issues. Over the course of their changing relationship, both Aaron and Frank feel they have benefited from the different forms individual, family, couples, and group psychotherapy can take.

Part Three

Clinicians

Chapter 8
Who are Psychotherapists?

It becomes easier to decide whether you are going to put your faith, time, and money into seeing a psychotherapist, once you have a clearer understanding of who psychotherapists are. Almost any psychotherapist can truthfully make the following statement with small variations:

"I am a person who likes to help other people. In one way or another, I've done this since I was young. I have always been drawn to people, have always been interested in people, and have always enjoyed trying to help people feel better. In the family in which I grew up, I naturally gravitated toward the roles of the mediator, peacemaker, and comforter. I listen carefully to what people are saying.

"As I got older, I thought long and hard about how I wanted to earn my living. I decided I was interested in sitting and having conversations with people about what is going on in their lives, and trying to help them lead happier lives. I am not sure as to why this is right for me, but I know it is.

"I am now considered to be a specialist in how people live their lives. The subject fascinates me. I studied it in school. I read books and articles, I listen to lectures, and I talk to my colleagues about it. I am spending my life trying to understand how people and groups of people operate.

"Before I was allowed to do this on my own, I went to school to be trained. When I was in school, my professors listened to tapes of conversations I had with my clients. They pointed out to me where I was helpful and where I was not so helpful. I have learned from their teaching. Mostly, what I learned was to listen to what was being said, verbally and nonverbally. People did not always say what they wanted to say, so I had to learn to listen carefully to understand what they wanted me to understand. Now one of my greatest skills is my ability to listen and understand.

"After many years of school, I took an examination to be licensed as a psychotherapist. An agency of the state government has now verified that I have gone through these years of training and am competent to help some people—but not all of them. I am supposed to know whom I can help and whom I cannot help. Those who are beyond my ability to help I am supposed to refer to others who might be able to assist them.

"Most of my day is spent sitting and talking with people. I often see the same people at the same time each week, but that can vary. These conversations are ongoing. Like most ongoing conversations with friends or families, I hear some stories over and over. Other times, people tell stories I have never heard before.

"Like physicians, I have pledged to first do no harm. Therefore, I must be sure of what I do and do not know, and I must be aware that my actions (or inaction) can cause pain and damage. I am dedicated to promoting the health and well-being of my clients, and I understand that at times I will have to put their interest above my own. I am willing to accept this sacrifice."

Although most psychotherapists could make such a statement, how they became psychotherapists can be quite different. This chapter will enable you to understand the similarities and differences between various types of psychotherapists.

Not long ago, this chapter would have only had to explain the differences between psychiatrists and psychologists, because they were virtually the extent of the mental health profession. But times have changed. In addition to psychiatrists and psychologists, there now are marriage and family therapists, clinical social workers, pastoral counselors, peer counselors, counselors who specialize in treating alcohol and drug abuse, and a variety of other therapists. While many of these professionals provide similar services, the cost to the client can be quite different.

PSYCHIATRISTS

Psychiatrists occupy the top of the status hill among mental health professionals—and have been there for most of the 20th century. More than any other mental health professionals, psychiatrists are trained in the medical model of mental health. They see "patients" who have "illnesses" and prescribe medications and treatments that are to be strictly followed. The most powerful group in the field of mental health, psychiatrists are often deeply entrenched in the medical model.

Psychiatric training is extensive. Because of the time involved, it is rare to meet to psychiatrist younger than 30. After high school, a person planning on a career in psychiatry will go to college for four years, followed by four years of medical school. When he or she graduates from medical school, the Doctor of Medicine (MD) is awarded. Then the doctor goes through another three to four years of specialized training to become a psychiatrist. And the education never stops. All psychiatrists are required to attend a number of classes each year so that they may maintain their licenses.

To a greater extent than most mental health professionals, psychiatrists are educated in the sciences. As college undergraduates, they commonly major in either biology or chemistry. If they major in another subject, they still must pass an extensive number of classes in these two subjects in order to be admitted to medical school. Medical school is science-based; most classes examine different topics concerning how the human body functions.

Every medical student must take a small number of classes in subjects related to mental health, since all physicians regardless of their specialty are expected to know something about the topic. It is after medical school, however, that psychiatrists-to-be finally receive extensive training in mental health.

Until recently, psychiatrists were trained in a combination of psychobiology, which is the biology of mental health and how people react to various medications, and psychotherapy, which is the skill of working with patients in talk therapy. Today, however, the emphasis has shifted to psychobiology, as more nonphysicians become trained in psychotherapy Psychiatrists trained in recent years who wish to perform psychotherapy usually need additional post-residency training.

A psychiatrist must be licensed by the state in which he or she wishes to practice, first as a physician and then as a psychiatrist after completing a psychiatric residency. Licensing often involves taking a series of exams, both written and oral. Medical boards also certify psychiatrists.

Psychiatrists provide a number of services, the most frequent being medication evaluation and management. They are the only mental health professionals permitted to prescribe psychoactive medication. This includes medication for anxiety, depression, mood disorders, sleep disorders, and psychosis (such as schizophrenia).

Psychiatrists function as the gatekeepers for many programs and benefits for people who are emotionally disabled, whether offered by the government or a private insurance company. Most any client claiming an emotional disability will need a psychiatrist to validate that claim. Psychiatrists are also the gatekeepers for admission and discharge from mental health hospitals.

Perhaps the greatest advantage to seeing a psychiatrist is being able to receive all mental health services from the same provider. Psychiatrists can perform evaluations, prescribe medications, certify disability, arrange for admission and discharge from mental health facilities, and, if he or she is so trained, provide psychotherapy.

The greatest disadvantage to seeing a psychiatrist is the cost, since psychiatrists commonly charge the highest fees of any mental health professionals. And there is no guarantee that their services are superior to those provided by other psychotherapists.

PSYCHOLOGISTS

Professional training for psychologists, like that of psychiatrists, usually begins after the completion of undergraduate studies. While undergraduates contemplating careers as psychologists can major in almost any subject, many chose psychology or the social sciences. Some students especially interested in research major in a science such as biology.

Traditionally, psychologists-to-be have first completed a master's degree in psychology or a related field before applying to a doctoral program in one of the various branches of psychology. Today, however, many doctoral programs do not require a master's degree in psychology or any other subject prior to admission. Upon completion of their doctoral training, psychologists are awarded one of three degrees: Ph.D. (doctor of philosophy), Psy.D. (doctor of psychology), or Ed.D. (doctor of education).

Graduate-level training in psychology involves classes, internships, and research. Classes focus on a variety of subjects related to human development and psychology. Internships take place in a clinical setting supervised by faculty members or practicing psychologists. With a client's permission, an intern may tape-record a psychotherapy session in order to replay it later for a supervisor who then gives professional feedback. Supervisors also routinely review interns' notes about clients they are seeing.

All doctoral candidates must complete a research project and present the results in a dissertation submitted to the faculty. The psychologist-in-training gets to choose the area of psychology or mental health he or she wishes to research—and that choice often begins a course of professional specialization.

After receiving a doctorate, a psychologist must be licensed by the state in which he or she wishes to practice. Most states require further supervised clinical experience before granting a license. This often means that the psychologist-in-training must spend another year or two working under supervision in a clinic or from a licensed psychotherapist.

Upon successfully completing all the other requirements, the psychologist-in-training must pass one final hurdle: an examination usually given in two parts, written and oral. The written part often has multiple-choice questions, while the oral part contains "vignettes," short stories of imaginary cases, about which the testee must state how he or she would proceed. Only after passing this final exam will a psychologist become licensed to practice.

Psychologists provide many different types of services, only two of which are relevant to readers of this book: psychotherapy and psychological testing. Psychologists provide psychotherapy services in much the same fashion as other clinicians. However, some psychologists specialize in administering and interpreting psychological tests such as the Rorschach test, in which a client examines irregular inkblot patterns and tells the psychologist what they might represent. Others tests include intelligence and personality profiles, which can uncover information that helps the psychotherapist better understand the client. The results of these tests can sometimes tell a psychotherapist how much of a problem is related to physical problems in the client's brain and how much is related to the client's personality.

MASTER'S-LEVEL MENTAL HEALTH WORKERS

One of the major changes in psychotherapy in the past 30 years has been the emergence of the master's-level mental health professional. Today, the great majority of psychotherapists entering the field are neither psychiatrists nor psychologists, but people who have a master's degree in a mental health discipline and become licensed as psychotherapists. What this means for you as the consumer of mental health services is that you use "Mr." or "Ms." instead of "Dr." when addressing your therapist.

The training for a master's-level psychotherapist is remarkably similar to the training for a psychologist, only scaled down. Instead of three years of classes and clinical training, the master's-level psychotherapist normally completes course work and clinical training in two years. And instead of presenting original research in a dissertation, a master's-level psychotherapist is usually required to write a thesis. The requirements for a thesis are considerably less rigorous than those for a dissertation.

Master's-level programs cover the same subjects as doctoral programs. Both include the study of child, adolescent, and adult development as well as clinical skills, psychopathology, ethics, and psychological testing. Clinical training for both master's-level and doctoral students is supervised in similar ways.

There is, however, a difference of emphasis. Doctoral programs in psychology usually emphasize the individual clinical aspects of mental health, whereas master's-level programs tend to focus on the social work or marriage and family aspects of mental health.

Schools of social work were the first to establish master's-level programs in mental health. Students in these programs receive training in both psychotherapy and social work, and after completing all their professional requirements, they become clinical social workers. Because of their training, it is not unusual for clinical social workers to pay particular attention to their clients' living conditions. Clinical social workers may even attempt to arrange for services needed in addition to psychotherapy.

The newest training programs for psychotherapists are designed for master's-level trainees who will eventually be licensed as marriage and family therapists. (The exact title of the marriage and family therapy license differs slightly from state to state, but it is always similarly worded.) These programs contain the same basic courses as doctoral programs in psychology and other master's-level psychotherapy training but emphasize working from a family systems perspective. Many of the classes teach students to view the client as not just an individual, but as a member of several families—the family into which the client was born as well as the one or more families the client has created.

Because *marriage* and *family* are right-wing buzz words, a queer person might think twice before seeing someone trained as a marriage and family psychotherapist. However, virtually all marriage and family training programs teach students about the wide spectrum of both traditional and nontraditional families.

Master's-level psychotherapists hold a variety of degrees: master of social work (MSW), master of arts (MA), master of science (MS), or master of education (M.Ed.). The licensing process for master's-level psychotherapists is similar to the licensing process psychologists undergo. After graduation, the candidate must work in a supervised clinical setting for a year or two and then take the licensing exam, which usually contains both written and oral portions. Unlike the licensing exam for psychologists, the master's-level exam will contain questions directly related to the area of specialization (social work or marriage and family issues). In addition, the testers will be specialists in that particular field.

A host of initials often follows the name of a master's-level psychotherapist. In addition to the degree (MSW, MA, MS, M.Ed.), there will also be licensing initials: LCSW for licensed clinical social worker, LMFT for licensed marriage and family therapist, or LPC for licensed professional counselor. Many master's-level psychotherapists also hold a doctoral degree and will therefore display licensing initials such as Ph.D. for doctor of philosophy, Psy.D. for doctor of psychology, or Ed.D. for doctor of education.

Some clinical social workers receive further certification from their professional organization after additional training and experience. You may see the initials ACSW, which means Academy of Certified Social Workers, a two-year post graduate national credential; BCD, which means Board Certified Diplomate, a five-year post-graduate credential; or DCSW, which means Diplomate of Clinical Social Work, also a five-year post-graduate credential.

The myth surrounding master's-level clinicians is that they are third best after psychiatrists and psychologists. Supposedly, only clients who cannot afford a psychiatrist or psychologist would be willing to see a master's-level clinician. This reasoning partly may have to do with misogyny: most master's-level psychotherapists are female—but that hardly means they are not talented clinicians.

Perhaps the greatest advantage to seeing a master's-level clinician is the expense, or lack thereof. master's-level clinicians are usually less expensive than psychiatrists or psychologists. The greatest limitation is that a master's-level clinician cannot prescribe medication, as a psychiatrist can, or administer and interpret psychological tests, as a psychologist can. However, most master's-level clinicians can and will arrange for their clients to obtain specialized services elsewhere when such services are necessary.

PASTORAL COUNSELORS

The very first psychotherapists were probably pastoral counselors. Thousands of years ago, spiritual leaders were in all likelihood the ones with whom people talked when they had spiritual, emotional, or life problems.

Today, many people are more comfortable talking with their minister, priest, rabbi, or emir than with a psychotherapist. Often, they have a previous relationship with the religious leader and view that person as someone they can trust. Some religions have even institutionalized this relationship. Roman Catholics, for instance, there is the sacramental rite of confession in which parishioners talk to a priest about matters they might never discuss with anyone else. Military units, hospitals, legislative bodies, prisons, and other organizations often have a chaplain assigned to handle people's spiritual issues and emotional problems. In the military, there is no stigma associated with talking to the chaplain, whereas talking to a psychiatrist is looked upon negatively.

Whether religious leaders desire the role or not, people see them as someone to whom they can tell their secrets and from whom they can receive advice. (This is, of course, identical to how many people view psychotherapists.) Religious leaders who set aside time for this purpose are known as pastoral counselors.

The training for pastoral counselors ranges from none at all to years of study. Because of our constitutional separation of church and state, the government cannot require religious leaders to be trained or licensed before declaring themselves pastoral counselors. As long as they do not present themselves as a psychotherapist, psychiatrist, psychologist, or as any other of a number of regulated titles (unless, of course, they are trained and licensed), pastoral counselors are free to offer therapy. After the name of a pastoral counselor, you may see the initials M.Div. (master of divinity), Ph.D. (doctor of philosophy), or Th.D. (doctor of theology).

This does not necessarily mean that pastoral counselors are not trained in the art of counseling people. Most religious leaders spend years in religious training, and that training almost always includes the study of philosophy and morality. And in the past generation, many religious leaders have recognized that a significant number of people come to them for counseling similar in nature to psychotherapy. Therefore, many religious training programs now place greater emphasis on pastoral counseling.

In addition, a significant number of people are fully trained as both religious leaders and psychotherapists. When working as psychotherapists, they may or may not choose to make their religious training obvious. Similarly, they may or may not emphasize their psychotherapy training when functioning as religious leaders.

The bottom line when it comes to seeing a pastoral counselor is that you should check his or her credentials and decide if he or she deserves your trust. Remember, because of the separation of church and state, almost anyone can claim to be both a religious leader and a pastoral counselor.

A queer person should be very cautious about seeing a pastoral counselor. The major religions of the Western world—Christianity, Islam, and Judaism—have historically been misinformed as to the nature of homosexuality. In fact, some people have interpreted the Bible as mandating a penalty of death for male homosexual behavior. Today, few religious leaders call for such extreme punishment, but there remains a heavy antiqueer bias in most organized religions.

Many such religions have established counseling organizations to serve the spiritual and emotional needs of their members. The practitioners at these centers often identify themselves as pastoral counselors. Some of these organizations are specifically designed to counsel queer people not to have relationships with other queer people. Though packaged with words of love, acceptance, and understanding, these ministries have an agenda: to change homosexuals into heterosexuals. A queer person unhappy with his or her life is only likely to be even more unhappy after involvement with one of these ministries.

Queer people should at all times avoid organizations that identify themselves as Christian counseling centers. Christian counseling centers and their counterparts in other religions are designed to provide psychotherapy services to members of that particular Christian (or other religious) community. These organizations are almost always firmly antiqueer and can do more harm than good.

This is not to imply that all religious leaders and pastoral counselors are to be avoided. Exactly the opposite is true. Just as the mental health profession has reversed its views on homosexuality in the past 30 years, significant segments of the world's religions have followed suit. Even in the most homophobic religious organizations, there are growing numbers of leaders and pastoral counselors who are queer-affirmative. It is up to you to find out if the pastoral counselor you might wish to see is queer-affirmative.

As mentioned earlier, pastoral counselors have no licensing requirements. And anyone can declare him or herself a religious leader. It is easy to get an official document to hang on one's wall. Indeed, in the back of various magazines are advertisements for entities that will ordain anyone as a minister for a small fee. So in addition to finding out if a pastoral counselor is queer-affirmative and has training in counseling or psychotherapy, you should also check his or her religious credentials.

Pastoral counselors provide the same range of services as other psychotherapists. Primarily, they counsel individuals, but some also see couples, families, or other groups. Some religious leaders require engaged couples to undergo premarital counseling with a pastoral counselor before they will agree to perform the ceremony.

Many pastoral counselors specialize in short-term counseling of clients in crisis over issues related to spirituality or life-cycle events. Death, marriage, and divorce are subjects that often bring people to see pastoral counselors. It is not completely unheard-of for a pastoral counselors to do long-term psychotherapy. If the pastoral counselor is also the head of a congregation, though, his or her time is likely to be limited. Pastoral counselors who work as therapists full-time usually have greater flexibility.

ADDICTION COUNSELORS

Addiction counselors are a new and distinct sub-specialty in the field of psychotherapy. They specialize in helping people addicted to alcohol or drugs (and sometimes other things such as sex, food, or gambling). Since substance abuse is widespread, there is a great need for people with this particular expertise. Many, though not all, addiction counselors are recovering alcoholics or addicts who, at some point in their recovery, decided to change careers and attempt to help others with similar problems.

Training for addiction counselors ranges from very little to years of study and experience. There are now formal training programs specializing in addiction counseling. After finishing an addiction counseling program, usually one or two years in length, the graduate receives a certificate of completion. Accredited universities sponsor many of these programs.

Addiction counselors are not licensed by the government. There are, however, professional organizations that certify individuals formally trained in addiction counseling as certified addiction counselors. Depending on their level of training and experience, certified addiction counselors may display the initials CAC together with the Roman numerals I, II, or III after their names.

Most addiction counselors work for private or nonprofit agencies that serve clients attempting to become clean and sober. A few addiction counselors are in private practice. Some medical insurance plans, such as health maintenance organizations, include certified addiction counselors in their lists of service providers and will refer clients to such professionals for evaluation and/or treatment when appropriate.

The advantage to working with an addiction counselor is that he or she has probably been recovering from an addiction too and therefore is intimately familiar with the scams an addict can and does perpetrate on him or herself and others. Addiction counselors have "been there, done that." Such knowledge is invaluable. An addiction counselor who is also a recovering addict is usually more sensitive to signs indicating a client may be headed toward a relapse than a therapist who has not personally gone through the process.

The disadvantage to seeing an addiction counselor is the flip side of the same coin. Addiction counselors get their credibility more from personal experience than professional training. As such, they are likely to be less learned in other areas of mental health than most clinicians.

INTERNS

Interns are psychotherapists in training. They see clients just as other psychotherapists do but are supervised by licensed psychotherapists. Some interns are still in graduate school and seeing clients to fulfill the requirements for graduation. Other interns have completed graduate school but are not yet licensed and can legally see clients only under the supervision of a licensed psychotherapist. Interns are generally required to tell you what level of training they have received.

An advantage to seeing an intern is the cost, which is generally less than what licensed psychotherapists charge. Another advantage is that at least two people, the intern and the intern's supervisor, are working to help the client. Nevertheless, some people refuse to see an intern, believing they will be better served by talking with a fully licensed psychotherapist. While this seems intuitively correct, it may not actually be so.

Research into the effectiveness of psychotherapy is a tricky subject. Most of this research has used a medical model to measure efficacy and is somewhat questionable. Yet even those who adhere to a medical model admit this research makes an interesting point: there is no hard evidence showing that psychotherapists become more effective with more training. If true, these findings should comfort anyone who chooses to see an intern.

Interns are not licensed, but many states require those who have completed their training and are working in private practice under the supervision of a licensed psychotherapist to register as interns. An intern still in school or a training program might not have to register but will still be required to tell clients about his or her intern status, usually before or during the first session.

Interns provide most of the same services as other psychotherapists. They are, however, ethically bound not to see any clients or provide any services that are beyond their training and competency. This rule, by the way, applies to all psychotherapists.

Peer Counselors

Peer counselors are not psychotherapists, although they provide essentially the same services. Peer counselors are usually volunteers at counseling agencies who wish to help others by sitting and talking with them. Peer counselors have often gone through experiences similar to those of the people they are counseling:

being queer, coming out, HIV or AIDS, cancer, loss of a child, etc. Peer counselors often staff mental health and suicide prevention hotlines.

The training a peer counselor receives depends to a large extent on the agency at which he or she has volunteered. All mental health agencies utilizing peer counselors are ethically obligated to provide at least a minimal amount of training. Some agencies provide extensive ongoing training. The only way to know how much training a peer counselor has had is to ask either the peer counselor or the agency.

At most agencies, peer counselors are taught basic listening skills and how to not cause additional problems for clients or other service providers. Peer counselors' training is as much about what *not* to do as about what *to* do. Most agencies that provide peer counseling try to limit the scope of the responses of their peer counselors. For instance, most peer counselors are not allowed to give their opinions or tell their clients what to do. They are taught to listen and reflect back to the client what the client is saying, both verbally and nonverbally.

Generally, peer counselors, like interns, are supervised by more experienced clinicians, who sometimes work at the agency. But it is just as likely that the supervisor is a working professional in private practice who, like the peer counselor, is volunteering at the agency.

SPECIALIZATIONS IN PSYCHOTHERAPY

As psychotherapy has evolved and become more complex, psychotherapists have come to specialize in helping only certain people. Psychotherapists limit themselves to working with those whom they are competent to help. In fact, they are ethically bound to refer to other clinicians any client with whom they are not competent to work. A therapist who specializes in individual psychoanalysis, for instance, may not be competent to facilitate family therapy.

Queer-affirmative psychotherapy can be looked upon as a specialty. But even within the world of queer-affirmative psychotherapy, most psychotherapists have particular specialties. When an insurance company, for instance, asks about my specialties (and they usually ask for no more than four), I list marriage and family counseling, queer issues, AIDS-related concerns, and grief work. Those are the areas with which I am most familiar. Those are the areas in which I am most experienced. Those are the areas I know the most about. And people dealing with those issues are the people I feel most able to help.

Chapter 9
Locating and Choosing the Right Clinician for You

If you decide psychotherapy might be of help to you, the next step is to find the right therapist. For a number of reasons, that may not be as easy as it seems. First, because most of us have been taught to be ashamed of having "emotional problems," it is difficult to ask others for help in this search. Beginning psychotherapy may seem like another coming-out process—having to acknowledge to yourself and others that you need help. This can be difficult. Furthermore, when most people finally decide to see a therapist, they are in the middle of an emotional crisis—not a good time to search for the *right* psychotherapist. It is not unusual for someone to get the name of one therapist and then decide they cannot search any further. But if you have the energy to search, there are ways to find an appropriate therapist

Referrals

Satisfied clients can be the best source of referrals to a psycho-therapist whom you may be interested in seeing. They know that psychotherapist best; they know how he or she works. Most impor-tant, they know if that psychotherapist has helped them. Perhaps someone you know—a friend, neighbor, acquaintance, or coworker—is seeing a particular psychotherapist. If you feel comfortable doing so, ask that person whether he or she would be willing to refer you to that psychotherapist.

Other health professionals—physicians, dentists, chiropractors—can also provide reliable referrals. Health professionals often know one another and have interacted professionally. They may even have clients in common.

A recent phenomenon has involved providers who have banded together and formed referral services accessed at toll-free phone numbers. After an electronic query or a brief conversation with a referral service operator, the caller is usually given one or more names of clinicians providing the requested services.

There are three different types of referral services for psychotherapists. The first is run by professional organizations to which the psychotherapists belong. These professional organizations can be organized along a number of lines, ranging from areas of specialization to treatment modalities. Many cities have queer-affirmative referral services, likely to be the best source of referrals for queer people.

The second type of referral service may be reliable as well, but the potential client should proceed a little more carefully. These are referral services set up by an independent group of psychotherapists, sometimes because they share a common interest in some area of psychotherapy. Or the psychotherapists may have banded together simply for economic reasons. It is difficult for individual psychotherapists to afford the advertising rates charged by newspapers, radio, and television, but by pooling their money, they are sometimes able to utilize these forms of advertising. Queer-affirmative therapists sometimes join together to form such referral services.

The third and relatively new type of referral service is actually an independent business, often started by professionals in the field in conjunction with business people. The purpose of this type of referral service is to make money for its owners. Professionals pay a set fee to join these services. Potential clients, though, are not charged by the service. Also, these services may not charge professionals for individual referrals, a practice known as fee splitting, which is considered unethical and is illegal in many states.

The potential client should be aware of what kind of referral service he or she is calling. It is perfectly acceptable to ask the referral service if it is associated with a professional organization that assures a certain level of quality.

ADVERTISEMENTS

Until relatively recently, it was considered unethical and in some states illegal for health care professionals (as well as other professionals such as lawyers) to advertise. The only acceptable form of advertising was a business card, which the professional could distribute. The information on that card was often limited to the professional's name, address, phone number, college degrees, and the type of service provided. But times have changed. It is now both legal and ethical for professionals to advertise. What a psychotherapist is permitted to say in an advertisement is still regulated by both law and professional ethics. (See Appendix E for sample advertisements.)

For practical reasons, advertising by psychotherapists is usually restricted to a few media. Because of the great expense, few individual psychotherapists use radio, television, or major daily newspapers. Psychotherapists tend to advertise in small-circulation newspapers focusing on particular audiences. Queer-affirmative psychotherapists, for instance, often advertise in newspapers aimed specifically at the queer community or in neighborhood newspapers serving communities where large concentrations of queer people live.

If you are looking in these newspapers to find a psychotherapist, read the ads carefully. They contain a lot of information about the professional placing the ad. In addition to the name, license, and phone number of the psychotherapist, the ads usually contain specific information about the services the psychotherapist offers. Some ads will state that the psychotherapist uses a sliding scale; others will mention that the psychotherapist accepts insurance coverage. Psychotherapists who are fluent in two or more languages or who are willing to see clients at unusual hours will generally include that information as well.

While queer and neighborhood newspapers are the greatest source of advertising for psychotherapists serving the queer community, they are not the only way psychotherapists advertise. The yellow pages contain not only the names and phone numbers of psychotherapists but also advertisements. Some editions of the yellow pages are not published by the phone companies but by other businesses that make money from their advertisers. These directories often target specific markets, such as speakers of a foreign language or the queer community, and can be another good way to find a queer-affirmative psychotherapist.

Psychotherapists also advertise their services in informational brochures or flyers often left in places where queer people congregate: community centers, bars, churches, bookstores. Brochures and flyers usually contain much more information about the psychotherapist than can be included in a newspaper advertisement.

SWITCHBOARDS

Another source of psychotherapy referrals are telephone switchboards, sometimes called hotlines or information lines. Most switchboards are either local or toll-free phone numbers that individuals can call to ask questions and get information. Switchboards serving the queer community will have information on a wide range of subjects, from where the bars are located to the names of psychotherapists serving the queer community.

INTERNET

The Internet has made finding the right psychotherapist easier than ever. If a psychotherapist has a Web site, it is possible to learn a lot about him or her prior to personal contact. Flip through the reference section at the end of this book, which lists several Web sites containing lists of mental health professionals.

WRITERS AND SPEAKERS

Starting in the 1970s in many major cities, queer "rap groups"—places where queer people could come together and talk about any number of subjects—formed as social alternatives to bars and bathhouses. Once I was asked to help facilitate a queer rap group, and about 50 people showed up. Along with seven other discussion leaders, I introduced myself and announced the topic I would facilitate. As it turned out, all but one of the eight discussion leaders were psychotherapists.

That is not as surprising as it may seem. Psychotherapists are trained to facilitate discussions. In fact, doing so is the essence of group psychotherapy. Psychotherapists, especially those in private practice, enjoy opportunities to show their stuff away from the office: rap groups, talk shows, news programs, or any other public forum. Going to hear a psychotherapist speak or facilitate a discussion is an excellent way to become familiar with him or her. If you like what you hear and see, then that psychotherapist might be a good fit for you.

For many of the same reasons, psychotherapists write articles and books (such as this one). And many newspapers have "advice columns" written by psychotherapists. Reading what psychotherapists have written is another way to get a feel for their beliefs and values as well as how they work. If you like what a psychotherapist has written, he or she might be right for you.

FINDING A PSYCHIATRIST

As mentioned earlier, not all psychotherapists are psychiatrists. The psychotherapist with whom you eventually decide to work may or may not be a psychiatrist. If not, once you begin therapy, you might find that you need a psychiatrist in addition to your psychotherapist. For instance, you may wish to go on psychoactive medication.

The best of all situations is when you have the financial ability, through your own resources or a point-of-service (POS) medical insurance plan, to see whichever psychiatrist you choose. If you are already in psychotherapy, ask for a referral from your psychotherapist. He or she probably has a working relationship with and confidence in one or more psychiatrists to whom he or she can refer you.

If you have preferred provider organization (PPO) medical insurance, you should have a directory of all physicians and specialists who are approved providers. Many insurance companies post an updated list on the Internet. Share the approved provider list with your psychotherapist and ask for recommendations.

If your insurance is through a health maintenance organization (HMO), try to get a list of all the psychiatrists in your area who are approved by your HMO and share it with your therapist. Do not be surprised, however, if obtaining this list proves difficult. Not all managed care insurance companies are willing to release such lists to their subscribers.

Additionally, some managed care companies have trouble recruiting psychiatrists. They may have an adequate number of psychotherapists to fill the needs of their policyholders, but psychiatrists may be scarce. It is not unusual for someone with managed care insurance to be given the names of several psychiatrists, only to later discover that their caseloads are all full. If this should happen to you, it is advisable to put the responsibility back on your managed care company by telling them that they are not fulfilling their responsibility to provide you with a psychiatrist.

If you are not involved in psychotherapy but want to see a psychiatrist, try to get a referral from your primary care physician, if you have a good relationship with him or her. I have yet to meet a primary care physician who does not know of several psychiatrists to whom they can and do refer their patients. Be sure to remind your primary care physician that you want a psychiatrist who is queer-affirmative.

If you are not in psychotherapy and do not have a primary care provider, use the same techniques you would to find a psychotherapist. Check the queer newspapers, attend lectures. Eventually you will get some names. If you are not sure whether the psychiatrist is queer-affirmative, ask directly. Be aware that many nonqueer people do not yet understand the meaning of the word *queer* in queer-affirmative, so asking if the psychiatrist is gay affirmative may be easier.

Choosing the Right Clinician for You

The search process does not end when you have located a queer-affirmative therapist. Now you need to make sure that person is the right queer-affirmative therapist for you. There are three questions for you to consider: What kind of mental health services do you need? What practical considerations (time, place, money) will impact those services? With what kind of person will you likely work best?

WHAT KIND OF MENTAL HEALTH SERVICES DO YOU NEED?

You may have a clear reason for seeing a psychotherapist and, if so, that will help you find the right person. If your reasons are less than clear, you will need to take a slightly different approach.

If you have specific needs, you should only consider a therapist capable of meeting them. For example, if you are a single person living alone and want to talk with someone about your long-term feeling of sadness, you should seek a psychotherapist who provides either individual or group psychotherapy. If you and your partner are fighting constantly and feel your relationship is in jeopardy, you should only consider couples counselors. If you and your teenage child are locked in a seemingly endless argument about nearly everything, you ought to see a family counselor. If you need psychoactive medication, you need to see a psychiatrist. And so on.

If you are unsure of your needs, I recommend that you make an appointment with a psychotherapist who seems willing to listen to what is going on with your life and to give to you his or her assessment of your issues. Then you can discuss together the ways you might proceed, whether with that particular psychotherapist and/or other providers.

Be skeptical of any psychotherapist who claims that the only form of psychotherapy that is likely to help you is the one he or she practices. If that psychotherapist's vision is so narrow as to not see value in other forms of psychotherapy, then he or she will also probably not see the value in the diversity of approaches to life. He or she will probably feel his or her approach to life is the one all reasonable people should follow—not a prescription for good psychotherapy.

WHAT PRACTICAL CONSIDERATIONS WILL IMPACT THESE SERVICES?

Practical considerations such as when and where therapy can occur, or how much you can afford to pay, will limit your choice of psychotherapist. But they will also point you toward providers with whom you can possibly work. If you can only meet during the evening or on weekends, do not have a car, and have a limited income, you will need to find a provider in your immediate area or near public transportation who works either evenings or weekends and uses a sliding scale or will accept your insurance.

WITH WHAT KIND OF PERSON ARE YOU LIKELY TO WORK BEST?

The chemistry between you and your psychotherapist can make the difference between an experience you'll consider a success and one you'll feel was a waste of your time, money, and effort. The importance of the personal fit cannot be understated. Finding a clinician competent to meet your needs and working out the practical considerations of psychotherapy are important, but finding a good personal fit between you and the psychotherapist is paramount. Appendix D contains an exercise for determining the kind of person with whom you are likely to work best. And the following discussion should help you focus on some meaningful variables affecting the relationship between you and your psychotherapist.

THERAPIST CHARACTERISTICS

A question many people ask themselves before starting therapy is whether it is important to have a therapist who shares their gender, sexual orientation, ethnicity, or some other characteristic. It is not uncommon for me to pick up the phone and hear someone say near the beginning of the conversation, "I am looking for a gay male therapist." Occasionally, the question is about another personal characteristic: my religion, whether I have a partner, if I am in recovery from substance abuse.

Gender, sexual orientation, ethnicity, and sobriety only begin the list of characteristics you might want to take into consideration when choosing a therapist. A person who is transgender might want a therapist who has dealt with that issue. A person who is into kinky sex might want a therapist who personally understands that lifestyle, which has been mistakenly pathologized in much the same way as queer sex was in the past. A person whose primary language is other than English may want a therapist fluent in that language.

It all comes down to what is important to you. Regardless of whom you choose, you will need to educate your therapist about some aspects of your life and lifestyle. But if certain characteristics are important to you, use them as criteria to sort through the therapists in your area. If you find what you believe you need, so much the better. If, however, the search proves difficult, at some point you should consider broadening your requirements.

One of the most common limiting characteristics is gender. It is not hard for people to say with certainty that they would prefer either a male or a female therapist. Usually, the preference matches the gender of the person seeking psychotherapy, but occasionally it is different. The common basic belief is that a man will be more able to understand male clients, and a woman will be more able to understand female clients. This raises the larger question of whether only someone like you can understand you. If that were true, you would need to find a therapist who is your virtual twin, which of course is impossible. So the question then becomes how similar or different.

A Queer Therapist Versus a Nonqueer Therapist

If you are queer, you might want your psychotherapist's sexual and romantic orientation to be as similar to yours as possible. Some queer clients feel it is absolutely necessary for their therapist to be queer because they believe the experience of being queer is so unique.

Others disagree, feeling that many nonqueer but queer-affirmative therapists have enough understanding and empathy to successfully work with queer people. They believe a therapist's willingness and capacity to understand and empathize can overcome differences between the psychotherapist and the client.

Both positions have merit; it is up to you to decide what you need. However, there are at least two situations where a client should absolutely choose a therapist who is queer. The first is when the issue bringing the client to therapy is coming out. The second is when the issue bringing the client into therapy is discomfort with being queer.

When a person is coming out, the therapist can be a role model and an information resource. A queer therapist has personally experienced the same questions and issues as the client. The therapist, in all likelihood, also knows what community resources are available to someone who is coming out.

When a person is upset, sad, uncomfortable, and wishing they were not queer, a therapist who is also queer can help the client learn to accept and love his or her romantic and sexual nature. The therapist can act as a role model or mentor. Just knowing a well-adjusted queer person, which the therapist is likely to be, helps the client to be more accepting of him or herself.

For someone who has been out for a while and is comfortable with their romantic and sexual nature, choosing a therapist who self-identifies as queer is less important, though it is still essential that the therapist be queer-affirmative. If the issue that brings the client into therapy is depression, for instance, a queer-affirmative but not necessarily queer therapist who is knowledgeable about depression might be a very good choice.

If the issue bringing you into therapy is not coming out or discomfort over being queer, my advice is to find the best therapist you can, whether queer or queer-affirmative.

ETHNICITY

The reason a client would seek a therapist who shares the client's ethnic background is identical to the reason a client would choose a therapist who is queer or a particular gender: Only someone who has had the same life experience can truly understand the issues the client faces.

There is no denying that being a member of an easily identifiable ethnic minority is a dominating experience in a person's life. Lawrence, an African-American man, told me that when he walks down a street in a neighborhood that is not predominantly African-American, he and every black man he sees make eye contact, saying, in effect, "Hi, brother." He feels an overriding kinship for those of African-American descent—a recognition of the prejudice, discrimination, and rejection black people have felt from non-African-Americans, and an affirmation of that common bond.

When he began therapy, Lawrence had a difficult time finding an African-American psychotherapist who was queer. Even though Lawrence lived in the gay ghetto of a major American city and was knowledgeable about how to find a therapist, he came across only two mental health professionals who were queer, male, and African-American. One was a psychologist whose caseload was filled; the other was a psychiatrist who specialized in medication evaluation and monitoring. Lawrence eventually chose a Caucasian therapist from a socioeconomic background similar to his own.

If the issue bringing you to psychotherapy relates to some aspect of your ethnicity, finding a therapist who shares your ethnicity might be a good idea. If, like Lawrence, however, you are unable to locate such a therapist, keep in mind that it is almost always possible to educate a therapist about your issues. In fact, this actually happens in some way with everyone in therapy.

CLEAN AND SOBER

The queer community has a significant problem with substance abuse. Some estimates state that one quarter to one third of the queer community are substance abusers. This estimate includes both men and women.

Not surprisingly, many queer people are in recovery from substance abuse. Sometimes the largest contingent in pride parades is composed of queer people in recovery. Many of my clients identify themselves as "clean and sober," meaning they have had a problem with alcohol or drugs in the past but are no longer drinking or using drugs. Many of those who identify as clean and sober also identify as being "in recovery," particularly if they attend 12-step program meetings such as Alcoholics Anonymous, Narcotics Anonymous, Sex Addicts Anonymous, Overeaters Anonymous, Gamblers Anonymous, or any of the many other AA offshoots specializing in helping people to cope with addictions and compulsive behavior.

Part of the underlying philosophy of all 12-step programs is that no one can help the addict in the same manner as someone who is also a recovering addict. And there is validity to that argument. The question you need to ask yourself if you are in recovery and looking for a therapist is this: Is it important for you to have a psychotherapist who is also in recovery?

Many psychotherapists will not reveal whether they are in recovery. Though some psychotherapists are comfortable disclosing personal information, many—perhaps most—are not. Several schools of psychotherapy insist that the psychotherapist remain a "blank slate," revealing as little about him or herself as possible.

Whether it is better to have a psychotherapist who is in recovery is open to debate. There is no hard and fast rule, but I would suggest this. If you are still in your first year of sobriety, you should consider seeing a therapist who has experienced challenges similar to those you are facing. The first year in recovery is often the most difficult. It is a time when you will need as much support as you can get to make the radical changes needed in your life.

Finding a therapist who is in recovery can be a little tricky. Almost no therapist advertises that she or he is clean and sober. But some therapists advertise that they specialize in helping clients in recovery or that they facilitate groups restricted to people in recovery. Such a therapist would likely respond to a direct question about being in recovery. If you attend 12-step meetings, you might hear someone share that he or she is a psychotherapist. While anonymity is the hallmark of 12-step groups—and it is improper in the context of a 12-step meeting to break anyone's anonymity—it is permissible to ask the psychotherapist after the meeting if he or she is accepting new clients and, if so, would be willing to see you. Hearing the psychotherapist share at the meeting should give you some sense of whether you want to talk with him or her. The psychotherapist may also be aware of colleagues in recovery whom you could contact.

TRANSGENDER OR KINKY

If you identify as transgender or kinky and have considered psychotherapy, you probably have thought about how much easier it would be if your therapist were also transgender or kinky. You might even be aware that being either transgender or kinky can cause you to be diagnosed as having a clinical disorder, much as homosexuality was formerly diagnosed as a clinical disorder.

Perhaps more importantly, being transgender or kinky means that you engage in self-identifying behaviors that bring up feelings of discomfort in others—sometimes great discomfort. Society as a whole has in recent years become more educated about homosexuality and therefore more accepting of it. Unfortunately, the same cannot be said for gender dysphoria or kinkiness. These topics are foreign to most people, who therefore fear them.

Does this mean you have to find a therapist who is transgender or kinky? No. Would that help? Yes. These issues are emotionally loaded, too much so to leave your therapist's opinion to chance. It is absolutely necessary, if you are transgender or kinky, to find out in advance if a therapist is competent and willing to deal with you. If that therapist has not learned the facts, and unlearned bad reactions to your orientation, then he or she is not competent to help you. In all likelihood, if a therapist identifies as transgender or kinky, he or she can understand clients belonging to the group of which he or she is not a member. His or her questioning of cultural norms has probably resulted in greater sensitivity to issues affecting what some would call the sexual fringe.

THERAPISTS' STYLES

How comfortable you feel about working with a psychotherapist may be more influenced by his or her manner of talking with you than either professional orientation or personal characteristics. If the conversation feels comfortable, you are more likely to get whatever it is you are seeking from psychotherapy.

Therapists of the same professional orientation do not necessarily conduct psychotherapy conversations the same way. While most treatment approaches are restrictive in various ways, the personality of the psychotherapist inevitably comes through. There are many choices a psychotherapist must make about how they hold conversations with clients. Those choices are influenced as much by who they are as individuals as by psychological theories that underlie their orientation to psychotherapy. Regardless of that orientation, most psychotherapists can justify what they say and how they say it within the bounds of their psychological orientation. So it is up to you to determine with what you feel comfortable.

Blank Slate or Personal Disclosure

Whether a psychotherapist should disclose personal information to a client is a controversial subject within the mental health community. Followers of Sigmund Freud dominated the field for many years. They have believed that the psychotherapist should remain a blank slate, although that is but one small part of their approach. For many clients, though, it is the most obvious part of the psychoanalytic approach. When I question clients about their prior experiences with psychotherapists, they often complain, "He (or she) didn't do much more than say 'Uh-huh.'"

"Uh-huh" usually means the psychotherapist practices a form of psychoanalytic psychotherapy. Remaining a blank slate is quite important to these psychotherapists. Some of these practitioners will cross the street if they see you coming toward them rather than have you interact with them outside their therapy office. They are that serious about this approach.

On the other hand, there are many other forms of psychotherapy that do not require the therapist to be a blank slate. Some approaches even *require* the therapist occasionally to talk about his or her personal experience in order to help the client. In reality, there is a continuum of disclosure from very little to a moderate amount of information. Most psychotherapists, however, keep most personal information to themselves. Certain areas of disclosure are almost always off-limits, such as the intimate details of his or her sex life. Much other information lies in a gray area and is usually not disclosed. An example of that gray area would be how your therapist and his or her life partner are doing. If they are not doing well together, disclosing such information can be considered seductive toward clients and therefore inappropriate.

Very few psychotherapists are open books. The amount of disclosure is a factor to consider in choosing a psychotherapist, especially if you anticipate a long-term psychotherapy relationship. In that situation, you and your psychotherapist are likely to spend a lot of time together. It is natural for you to become curious about your psychotherapist. This curiosity may or may not be satisfied, depending on the style of psychotherapy practiced by your psychotherapist.

On the other hand, some clients do not want to be burdened by information about their psychotherapist. They are seeking someone who will focus on and talk about the client. In those cases, a psychotherapist who remains a blank slate is appropriate. Again, it all depends on the client's needs and desires.

Active or Passive

Another aspect of a therapist's style to consider is how active or passive he or she is while conducting a psychotherapy conversation. An active psychotherapist will steer the conversation toward certain issues, while a passive psychotherapist will allow, and even insist, on the client setting the agenda for each meeting.

The psychoanalytic school is filled with therapists who seem to take a passive approach. They ask the client to free-associate, to say whatever it is that comes into their head. This is the "Uh-huh" school of psychotherapy. In fact, though, this is not a passive approach. It only appears that way from the perspective of the client. It is part of the psychotherapist's plan to have the client come up with material by letting his or her mind wander. The therapist takes careful notes about what the client says, and then eventually uses that information to help the client better understand him or herself.

Other psychotherapists truly are passive in their approach. They want the client to decide what he or she wants to discuss and then go with that. If a client asks what he or she should talk about, he or she will likely be told "Whatever you want." This is not a request to free-associate. It is a request for the client to think about his or her needs and to talk about what he or she considers important. Passive therapists often believe they cannot know what the client's needs are, and that if they actively direct the conversation, it is likely the conversation will be about what the psychotherapist, rather than the client, feels is important.

On the opposite end of the spectrum are therapists who are active in their approach. They believe that clients come to them for their professional expertise and are stuck in some way, unable to see either the forest or the trees. A therapist, they believe, might offer a broader perspective on the client's life by virtue of being not as close to the situation or as emotionally involved. That enables the therapist to see where work is needed and to take an active part in directing the client toward working on those areas. This kind of therapist will come from a nonpsychoanalytic background.

Directive or Nondirective

The issue of directive or nondirective is quite different from the issue of active or passive. The terms *active* and *passive* refer to the agenda of the psychotherapy hour. The terms *directive* and *nondirective* refer to the agenda of the client's life.

Some therapists are born advice givers, meddlers, and controllers. They believe they know what their clients need. They happily give advice, and they expect their clients to follow that advice. These individuals are directive therapists.

If you go to a directive therapist and say you are lonely, depressed, and isolated, the therapist will, after learning of your interests, direct you to do something specific, such as joining a club or going to a social event you would not otherwise attend. Directive therapists often come out of a social work tradition, and they sometimes actively help clients find and connect with outside resources.

Directive therapists are relatively rare. Most psychotherapists are loathe to give specific instructions to their clients. Many believe the client needs to make the decisions, regardless of his or her track record. If the therapist makes decisions for the client, the client will never learn how to make decisions for him or herself. In fact, many psychotherapists feel people learn more from their failures than their successes.

Once again, the choice comes down to what you want and need. If you decide you want a therapist who is directive, though, I must give you the following advice: Be wary of anyone who thinks that he or she knows all the answers about what is best for you. No one can know you like you know you.

Talking About the Past Versus the Present

The great majority of psychotherapists believe it is important for clients to talk about their past. They believe the origin of most problems is in the past, and that by talking about the past a client can get a better understanding of what happened and what he or she needs to do. Many psychotherapists also believe that by talking about past events a client can bring issues into his or her conscious mind, which often helps to resolve problems. Virtually all psychodynamic psychotherapists, as well as many others, spend considerable time talking with clients about the past, especially childhood.

A minority of therapists have no interest in talking with clients about their past. They are interested in helping the client with his or her current problems and do not believe discussing the origin of the problems is particularly helpful. If you were to go to a behavioral psychotherapist for help with your fear of flying, for instance, that psychotherapist would likely show little interest in the fear's origin. He or she would focus on helping you overcome that fear, probably by using relaxation techniques.

Talking About Thoughts, Behaviors, or Feelings

Yet another crucial factor affects the tenor and tone of psychotherapy, whether active or passive, directive or nondirective, or focused on the past or present. That factor concerns what information the psychotherapist concentrates on. For instance, when discussing something that happened, a client may describe what he or she did, thought, and felt. There are many directions a psychotherapist can go with that information. Typically, a psychotherapist will consistently proceed in the same direction.

Some psychotherapists concentrate on behavior: what the client *does* in certain situations. They believe it is important for the client to be aware of his or her behaviors and their impact. Other therapists, particularly those of the cognitive school, concentrate on the client's thoughts. They want to know what the client told him or herself upon becoming unemployed or receiving a phone call from his or her mother. They believe that looking at destructive thought patterns is the most valuable way to spend time in therapy.

And then, there are many, many psychotherapists who concentrate on the client's feelings. They ask again and again, "How did that make you feel?" Underlying their repeated questions is the belief that individuals are often not consciously aware of their feelings, yet those feelings control actions, words, and thoughts.

So by continually asking the client to discuss how he or she feels, the psychotherapist is presumably getting to the source of the client's problem.

NEWLY TRAINED VERSUS EXPERIENCED

One final consideration is whether to choose someone who is relatively new to counseling or someone experienced. Good arguments can be made in support of either choice.

Experienced therapists tend to know their way around the field of psychotherapy. They have learned what does or does not work based on years of experience. Experienced therapists are, however, in greater demand than those who are newly trained and licensed. If you see an experienced therapist, you are likely to be one of many clients. Some psychotherapists see 20 or more clients each week. Experienced psychotherapists also tend to be more expensive.

Newly trained clinicians generally charge lower fees than more experienced clinicians. However, just because someone is less experienced as a clinician does not mean he or she is less experienced in life. More and more, people are becoming psychotherapists as a second career. They have had significant life experience and then gone back to school in their 30s, 40s, 50s, and even later in life. These individuals can use their life experience to help their clients. In addition, training programs and licensing requirements today are more stringent than ever. A newly trained clinician is likely to have better training than an older professional and also be more familiar with the latest theories and practices. Recently trained clinicians have also been through rigorous licensing processes. Often, more than half of the licensing candidates fail the oral part of a professional certification exam and have to take it more than once. Just to become fully licensed, a psychotherapist's skills need to be sharp.

Chapter 10
Settings Where Psychotherapists Work

Psychotherapists work in a variety of settings that can be grouped under two general headings: clinics and private practice.

Clinics

Clinics are settings where a number of psychotherapists practice under one umbrella. One of the advantages to seeing a psychotherapist at a clinic is that it is likely that someone, though not necessarily your psychotherapist, will be available to assist you if you have an emergency at unusual hours.

Public Mental Health Clinics

Usually organized under the auspices of public health departments, public clinics provide a wide range of health care, including mental health services. Sometimes the mental health services are connected with larger clinics providing physical and/or dental care; other times the mental health clinics are separate facilities.

Community-based mental health clinics are usually subsidized with public funds and therefore tend to offer services at a lower cost than mental health providers in private practice. Often, a sliding scale is used to determine fees.

There are some significant limitations to seeing a mental health provider in a public clinic. Because of the low cost, demand for services is high. It is not uncommon for there to be a waiting list for seeing a psychotherapist. Since clients are usually assigned to a particular provider, they cannot interview possible psychotherapists and choose the one best suited to their needs.

In addition, confidentiality can be compromised at public mental health clinics. While all clinics have strict guidelines regarding confidentiality, in reality a lot of people may have access to a client's records. This is partially because clinics are required to keep extensive records, not only to provide quality service but also to justify government funding. It is possible for a nosy clerk or psychotherapist who is not your provider to snoop through your records.

However, if you do connect with a good provider and are willing to take the risks concerning confidentiality, public mental health clinics can provide excellent care at reasonable rates. It is a good idea, though, to ask the psychotherapist to whom you are assigned whether he or she is queer-affirmative. If not, you should attempt to switch to another psychotherapist.

HOSPITAL-BASED CLINICS

Many hospitals have an outpatient mental health clinic connected to the department of psychiatry. A training hospital will have a clinic with psychotherapy residents working under the supervision of a staff of psychotherapists who are there on a long-term basis.

The pros and cons of hospital-based clinics are similar to those of public mental health clinics. Fees are often lower, but the choice of whom a client can see is limited, and loss of confidentiality can be a factor. But again, if you connect with a queer-affirmative therapist, the lower cost can outweigh the negatives.

NONPROFIT CLINICS

A wide variety of nonprofit mental health clinics are set up as free-standing clinics, though some are associated with hospitals or charities. Some of these clinics specifically serve the queer community. Others have been established because some psychotherapists prefer not to work for a large bureaucracy but still want to practice in an environment with other mental health professionals. Some nonprofit clinics offer a particular form of therapy, such as psychoanalysis or family therapy. If a clinic is located in or near a neighborhood where queer people live, clinicians there are probably used to serving queer people and may be queer-affirmative.

It is still important, however, to find out if the clinic is in fact queer-affirmative. It could be a Christian counseling center that located in a queer neighborhood as part of its mission trying to "convert" queer people to heterosexuality.

PRIVATE, FOR-PROFIT CLINICS

Private, for-profit clinics are relatively rare, compared to non-profit clinics. That a clinic is for-profit should not deter anyone from using its services. Nonprofit clinics might be receiving some governmental support, but in the end all clinics must pay their rent and salaries. If a clinic is designed to make a profit, it must offer a service for which people are willing to pay. Otherwise, the clinic will not stay in business. Once again, you need to find out if the clinic is queer-affirmative before going there for treatment.

SCHOOLS AND TRAINING INSTITUTES

Schools and training institutes are places where those learning to become psychotherapists receive training. Some are connected with major universities; others are free-standing institutions. They are occasionally difficult to locate, but the effort is often worth it. They can be a great source of high-quality, low-cost psychotherapy.

To be trained as a psychotherapist, someone can read books, listen to lectures, and engage in supervised practice sessions with fellow students in which one acts as client and the other acts as psychotherapist. But at some point psychotherapists in training must start seeing real clients. Schools and training institutes, therefore, have clinics where individuals studying to become psychotherapists can begin to see clients under the watchful eyes of their teachers.

There are two major disadvantages to seeing a psychotherapist in this setting. One is that the students will only be at the clinic while they are being trained. They will not be able to see a client for long-term psychotherapy in this setting. The second is that many (though not all) of these students are relatively inexperienced, especially if the school is training psychotherapists just beginning their careers. There are, however, advanced training institutes that only accept fully trained psychotherapists. These institutes often provide training in a particular approach to psychotherapy.

On the other hand, there are major advantages to seeing a student at a training institute. Students in these programs usually have a small caseload and are intensely supervised by experienced professionals. This means that instead of one psychotherapist thinking about your case, often two, three, or even more professionals will be consulted about the best course of treatment. A second advantage is that, because the client and psychotherapist-in-training need each other equally, schools and training institutes often use a generous sliding scale to determine fees. So if you have very little money and want to get high-quality treatment, a school or training institute might be the way to go.

PRIVATE PRACTICE

Private practice means the psychotherapist is in the business of psychotherapy. A psychotherapist in private practice is just as much an entrepreneur as the corner grocer, a private music teacher, or the plumber you call when the drain does not work.

Usually, a private practitioner will have an office, either in a professional building or in his or her home. They are sole practitioners, though clinicians in private practice will often rent an office in a suite where other health care professionals are located. They might share a waiting room, support staff, and other common facilities, but each practitioner is an independent business.

Private practice suits the personality of some psychotherapists. They do not have a supervisor, they make their own hours, and they can choose to not work with a particular client or group of clients (such as people with a history of violence).

The other side of this story is that the psychotherapist in private practice must also run a small business. Schools that train people to be psychotherapists do not also train them to run a small business, which can be tricky. Psychotherapists in private practice must arrange their own continuing education by attending workshops and conferences. Private practice can also be isolating.

Perhaps the greatest advantage to seeing a psychotherapist in private practice is privacy. There is the psychotherapist, no one else. Clients concerned about privacy—especially queer clients—can be reasonably assured that what is said in the office will stay in the office. Only that psychotherapist will have access to notes about what is said during the sessions.

The major disadvantage to seeing a psychotherapist in private practice is that it may be difficult to get in touch with him or her if a crisis happens at night or on a weekend. If you were being seen in a large clinic, an emergency psychotherapist should be on call. All psychotherapists are ethically bound to check their answering services regularly. However, with some private practice clinicians, there might be a seemingly long delay between when you first left your message and when your call is returned.

Chapter 11
Paying for Psychotherapy

Fees

Money is a touchy subject. It is not unusual for people to feel bad about having to pay for psychotherapy. Some say it feels weird to have to pay someone to listen to their problems. This is the kind of thing, they believe, that friends and family are supposed to do. But in reality this is often not possible, so a psychotherapist is needed. And therapists need to pay their bills. The way they do that is by charging fees for their services.

The amount that people pay for psychotherapy varies widely, from nothing to more than $200 per hour. The most important thing to remember is that fees for psychotherapy services are determined by the same factors that determine the price we pay for almost everything: supply and demand. Thus, the number of psychotherapists in an area and the demand for their services will affect the fees they charge.

You are likely to pay a lower fee in a clinic than in a private practice. The reason is simple. Psychotherapists in private practice usually make their living from the fees they charge. That is all the money they get. Clinics, however, are usually subsidized by governments, charities, foundations, schools, or other health care institutions. This gives clinics more flexibility when charging for services.

Another factor that has great bearing on the fee is the training and license of the psychotherapist. Psychiatrists, who have had a long and costly training, tend to charge the most. The next highest fees are usually charged by psychologists with doctoral degrees. master's-level psychotherapists generally charge less than psychologists, and pastoral counselors and peer counselors usually charge the least.

SLIDING SCALE FEES

If you are shopping for a psychotherapist and cost is an issue, it is important to know if the clinic or the private practitioner uses a sliding scale. A sliding scale means the fee for the service can slide up or down depending on the income and overall financial situation of the client.

Assertiveness on the part of the client is helpful when it comes to determining the fee. If a person calls a psychotherapist or clinic and simply asks the fee, they are usually quoted the standard rate, which is also often the highest rate. It is up to the client to ask if there is a sliding scale and how it works.

Many psychotherapists in private practice use a sliding scale. This is often determined by demand, or lack thereof. If a psychotherapist is relatively new to private practice, he or she may not have as many clients as he or she would like to have. Talking to clients for less than the full fee may therefore be appealing.

Some might wonder if they are getting second-class treatment from a psychotherapist who uses a sliding scale. Their reasoning is, "If my psychotherapist was good, he or she would not have to use a sliding scale." There is some truth to this. Psychotherapists who do good work often acquire a strong reputation, and demand for their services is high.

A sliding scale, however, does not always signify lower-quality service. There is both a clinical side and a business side to psychotherapy. Individual practitioners and clinics may be great at providing psychotherapy but clueless about business. They may not know how to get the word out that they have a service to offer. They may be sitting in their office waiting for the phone to ring, not understanding that it is up to them to make themselves known. A private practitioner may have done spectacular work for years at a clinic where the clients came through their door because the clinic was good at the business side of psychotherapy. Then, after deciding to go into private practice, he or she finds that clients do not just magically appear. That psychotherapist might be willing to use a sliding scale.

There is another factor that affects sliding scale fees. The code of ethics for most psychotherapist professions says that in some way psychotherapists are expected to serve those less able to pay for their services. Psychotherapists are rarely if ever held accountable for this, but it *is* in their code of ethics. A psychotherapist is expected to see some people at a reduced rate or even for free. This is called *pro bono*. It is almost impossible to find out if a psychotherapist is seeing anyone pro bono, but it is advantageous for you, the client, to know that clinics and private practitioners are expected to do so.

There are also clinicians in private practice specifically because it gives them the freedom to charge whatever they want to whomever they want. Some of these people are motivated by a desire to serve those less fortunate. They are, from their perspective, doing the work of social justice by serving a more diverse population.

BARTERING

In the not-too-distant past, before the invention of money, all transactions were done by barter. I would give you a dozen eggs and you would give me a piece of cloth. Even in the last century, in countries where for one reason or another the national currency had become worthless, people resorted to barter. Each individual determined what a good or service seemed to be worth and then negotiated its value with others. It's an old method, proven to work.

Many people cannot afford a private therapist but do have goods or services they may wish to trade for psychotherapy. For example, an unemployed carpenter wants to see a psychotherapist, and that psychotherapist needs to have bookshelves built. Why not trade the psychotherapist's services for the carpenter's services?

Such barter arrangements between psychotherapists and their clients, however, have fallen out of favor with the boards that set ethical standards for psychotherapists. Thus, you cannot barter for psychotherapy.

One problem with bartering is that it creates a dual relationship between the client and psychotherapist. Anything other than a clinician/client relationship compromises the relationship and potentially diminishes the effectiveness of therapy. In the bartering relationship mentioned above, the carpenter is the client of the psychotherapist, and the psychotherapist is also the client of the carpenter. If the psychotherapist is unsatisfied with the carpenter's work, there is no place for the psychotherapist to go. He or she cannot complain to the local contractors' board without possibly revealing confidential information about the carpenter as a client. And if the carpenter has already built the shelves but is dissatisfied with therapy, it is hard to quit seeing that psychotherapist before receiving services equivalent in value to the cost of the work done while building the shelves. It is easy to see how a seemingly simple situation can get messy.

If you trade a tangible object, the situation can get just as thorny. Let us say you are broke and want to see a therapist because of low self-esteem and depression over your shaky finances. You have no money to pay for therapy, but for years you have been amassing a large art collection. You meet a therapist who is also an art collector and happens to like the artists you have been collecting. Why not trade art for therapy?

There are good reasons to not do so. You and your therapist would need to negotiate a price for a piece of art. Because you are suffering from depression and low self-esteem, you might undervalue an artwork. What happens when this becomes apparent? You may feel the therapist took advantage of you in a time of personal crisis. The therapist may disagree with that allegation, but if you believe it, it could undermine the work done in therapy.

The answer is cash. Money has a widely accepted value. $100 is worth exactly $100—no more, no less. The potential for abuse, hurt feelings, or confusion is eliminated.

INSURANCE

Insurance companies are not your friends. They are businesses hoping to make a profit. (A few insurance companies are nonprofit, but many of those are considering becoming for-profit.) Insurance companies make money by collecting premiums, not by paying claims to policyholders. And therein lies the problem. The interests of the insurance company and the interests of the policyholder are diametrically opposed. It is important to understand that you have an essentially adversarial relationship with your insurance company.

INSURANCE COMPANIES AND THE MEDICAL MODEL

All insurance companies that pay part or all of the fees for psychotherapy use the medical model. They require providers to make diagnoses using the *Diagnostic and Statistical Manual of Mental Disorders*. Regardless of whether the service provider uses a growth model or a medical model in working with a client, the provider communicates with the insurance company using a medical model.

TYPES OF INSURANCE

If you work for a major employer, it is likely that your medical insurance will be provided through your job. In many cases, you will have a choice of medical plans. Some are more expensive than others, and employers often pass along a part of the cost to the employee. The benefits of the different plans vary considerably, and knowing about the types of plans makes it easier for you to choose the plan best suited to your needs. The various types of plans are discussed below.

Point-of-Service (POS) Insurance

Prior to the 1990s, point-of-service (POS) insurance was the kind of medical insurance most people had. POS insurance plans permit the person insured to seek services from almost any licensed heath care provider and to be reimbursed for part or all of the cost of those services. POS insurance plans allow insured persons great leeway in choosing their own health care provider(s). Usually, a deductible amount needs to be met before the insurance company begins to reimburse the insured. These deductibles range from as little as $50 per year to as much as $2,000 per year. The higher the deductible, the less expensive the policy.

Most POS insurance plans only reimburse a percentage of the actual charge, usually 80% of the fee for physicians, 50% of the fee for mental health services. Often, there is a limit to what the insurance company will pay. The insurance company determines a "usual and customary fee" for a particular service in a geographical area, and will reimburse up to 80% of that amount (50% for mental health services). If the insured goes to a provider who charges higher fees, the insurance company will only reimburse for the percentage of the usual and customary fee. Though inflation has increased the cost of virtually all goods and services in recent years, many insurance companies have *lowered* their "usual and customary fee." Thus, POS insurance allows flexibility to see the provider of your choice, but it is often the most expensive type of plan.

With POS insurance plans, the service provider has the option of asking the insured to pay the entire fee at the time of service and then get reimbursed by his or her insurance company, or to ask the insured to pay whatever portion of the fee is not likely to be covered by the insurance company and then to bill the insurance company directly for the remainder. This is called accepting assignment of benefits: The insured assigned his or her benefits (the reimbursement) to the service provider.

Mental health professionals are under no ethical obligation to accept assignment of benefits. It means more paperwork for them, and they are likely to get the money weeks or months later than they otherwise would. Often, they need to call to straighten out errors insurance companies make. On the other hand, some providers will want to help clients, especially clients who have a limited income, by accepting the assignment of benefits.

To be reimbursed under the terms of a POS contract, either the client or the psychotherapist must submit a claim form to the insurance company, signed by both the client and the psychotherapist. In small print on the claim form, just above where the client signs his or her name, are the following words: "I authorize the release of any medical or other information necessary to process this claim." By signing the form, you have given the insurance company permission to ask your psychotherapist most anything.

In practice, insurance companies under POS contracts rarely ask a psychotherapist for any information other than the diagnosis. However, if for any reason an insurance company wishes to know more about why you are seeing a psychotherapist, your signature on your claim form permits additional information about you to be released. Insurance companies are much less intrusive with POS contracts than with health maintenance organization contracts but retain the right to question claims in any manner.

POS insurance is expensive. As a result, the percentage of people with this type of insurance decreases each year. The shift is away from POS medical insurance plans and toward preferred provider organizations and health maintenance organizations. Most large employers are still required by law or union contracts to provide point-of-service insurance. But the employers are permitted to charge the employee additional money for these contracts, and the difference in out of pocket expenses to the employee is often hundreds of dollars each month. Thus, fewer and fewer workers are choosing point-of-service contracts.

Preferred Provider Organization (PPO) Insurance

Preferred provider organizations (PPOs) are a modified form of POS insurance. The primary difference is that with a PPO, you must choose your psychotherapist (or doctor) from a list provided by the insurance company. The list will contain only providers who agree to accept a certain rate of reimbursement, generally lower than the rates charged by providers under point-of-service plans. Psychotherapists and doctors agree to be a part of a PPO because it virtually assures a steady stream of clients.

When you select a PPO plan, you sign a contract agreeing to its terms of coverage. Within that contract are words to the effect that you will see providers on the insurance company's list, and in return, you will only pay a set amount for each visit. This fee is called a copayment and is also commonly charged under health maintenance organization plans. The provider agrees to bill the insurance company for the rest of the amount owed to the provider. Basically, this is an automatic assignment of benefits.

Similar to the point-of-service contracts, PPOs require that you release any information determined necessary to process your claim. In reality, as with POS contracts, insurance companies rarely ask for more information than a diagnosis.

Health Maintenance Organization (HMO) Insurance

Many feel the introduction of the health maintenance organization (HMO) was a successful attempt to ration health care.

HMOs, not surprisingly, prefer a different term: managed care.

Managed care is based on the assumption that a higher level of care can be provided at a lower cost if an outside organization oversees that care. The assumption is that the managed care company (the HMO) will stop doctors and psychotherapists from authorizing unnecessary services that cost the insurance company and, indirectly, the clients money. The client, theoretically, will receive a more appropriate level of care.

That said, many people believe that HMOs are more interested in managing costs than care. In fact, there is a joke that typifies the problem most clients and psychotherapists have in dealing with managed care companies:

Q: What is the difference between a managed care company and a terrorist?
A: You can negotiate with a terrorist.

In the 1980s, as new technologies made medical care more expensive, and as the stigma against mental health care began to dissipate, the cost of medical insurance policies to employers increased dramatically. Consequently, employers sought ways to control the cost of the insurance policies they bought for their employees, resulting in the movement toward managed care. Most employees were offered a choice between HMO policies and POS or PPO insurance. If the employee chose one of the latter two options, he or she usually had to pay the difference in cost, often as much as several hundred dollars per month. Needless to say, most employees opted for managed care, despite its many drawbacks.

Foremost among the drawbacks is that you and your physician or psychotherapist no longer have the final say on your treatment. Instead, your health care provider decides what is necessary, and then contacts the HMO to seek its approval for treatment. If the HMO approves, you get the service. If the HMO does not approve, you either do not get the service or you must appeal that decision.

A typical line in Human Resources Department booklets to explain a company's mental health benefits might read: "You are entitled to 25 (or some other number) visits with a psychotherapist each year, as long as those visits are medically necessary." Sounds fairly straightforward. If you have a problem, you know how many sessions you are entitled to receive, right?

Wrong!

The two words at the end of the sentence—*medically necessary*—might not mean the same thing to you as to your insurance company. This is the big loophole in managed care mental health benefits. While you and your therapist might feel treatment is medically necessary, the HMO might not. The HMO has its own guidelines for determining what is medically necessary and will rarely share this information with you or your therapist. The HMO almost always defines "medically necessary" as narrowly as possible while still fulfilling policy obligations.

In reality, it is difficult for any individual to get approval for the entire amount of available sessions without being in a deep and unrelenting crisis. Many HMOs feel treatment for long-standing problems such as a lifelong anxiety or mild depression is not medically necessary. An HMO may assert that the proper treatment is antianxiety or antidepressant medication. The client will be asked to see a psychiatrist for evaluation and prescription of medication. If the client refuses, the insurance company will claim the policyholder declined what was offered as medically necessary treatment.

In my own practice, at times I have tried to get the maximum number of sessions available to a client authorized in the first part of the year, only to learn that the HMO determined it medically necessary to hold a certain number of sessions in reserve, in case the client should go into crisis later in the year. So be advised that just because your human resources department may say a certain number of psychotherapy sessions are available does not mean the HMO will agree.

Another way HMOs try to control costs is through capitation. Capitation is when an HMO pays a clinic or provider a set amount each year in order to provide all the medical or psychotherapy care for a certain number of clients. Providers receive the same amount of money whether they see a client just one time or 100 times—or not at all. Thus, the HMO knows exactly how much your medical care and/or psychotherapy will cost.

This leaves the issue of how often clients will be seen in the hands of the provider instead of the HMO. This puts your psychotherapist (or physician) in an unusual position, because he or she receives the same amount of money regardless of how often you are seen. Under this system, it is in the psychotherapist's financial interest to see clients as little as possible. This is not a good foundation upon which to build a psychotherapeutic relationship.

Perhaps the most controversial aspect of psychotherapy covered by HMOs is confidentiality. In the world of managed care, confidentiality does not exist. The entire basis of managed care is that a third party, someone hired by the HMO, reviews the case and makes a determination as to how to proceed.

Different HMOs handle case management in different ways. Some attempt to micromanage the treatment process, requiring large amounts of information about the client before making a decision. Others require smaller amounts of information. A few require only a diagnosis. For instance, an HMO may have an established relationship with a psychotherapist and already know that psychotherapist will see referred clients for only a small number of visits. The HMO will then automatically refer clients to that psychotherapist, sometimes not even bothering to review individual client cases.

Many managed care companies require the psychotherapist to fill out a report after the first or second session. The report generally asks for a complete five-axis diagnosis (see chapter 14 for an explanation of the five-axis diagnosis). Most reports also ask for a psychiatric history of the client: how many times the client has seen a psychotherapist in the past, or if the client has ever been hospitalized for mental or emotional reasons. Most reports include a mental status exam, in which the psychotherapist evaluates the client's affect, mood, and possible hallucinations, delusions, etc. Any history of the use of prescription psychoactive drugs such as antidepressant or antianxiety medication is also generally required. Many reports include information about family history of mental illness or psychiatric hospitalization.

The heart of most reports is the description of the symptoms the client is experiencing. Of primary interest to HMOs are anxiety, depression, suicidal ideation, homicidal ideation, sleep disturbance, appetite disturbance, bingeing and purging of food, sexual dysfunction, anger, isolation, withdrawal, phobias, panic attacks, violent acts, destructive behavior, bizarre behavior, obsessions, compulsions, loss of impulse control, self-mutilation, and thought disorders. Reports also commonly ask for information on the client's support system: who is there for the client. The psychotherapist might have to evaluate how helpful that support system is likely to be.

Frequently, the psychotherapist is required to perform an alcohol and drug assessment. The provider asks the client if he or she has consumed alcohol and/or any other mind-altering drugs—legal or illegal—and if so, how often and in what quantity. The provider also asks if the client has a history of alcohol or drug abuse and has ever been in a 12-step program or other drug or alcohol treatment program. Some companies also want providers to inquire about any family history of alcohol or drug use.

Some HMOs, though fewer now than in the past, also require a narrative description of why the client is seeking psychotherapy at the present time. Insurers' interest in narrative descriptions is decreasing, primarily because most reports are designed so that a computer can scan the information. Narrative descriptions make scanning difficult.

Lastly, an HMO often asks the provider to estimate the number of sessions the client will require to complete the course of treatment. Since the managed care treatment model advocates short-term, problem-focused psychotherapy, HMOs as a rule contend that most therapy issues can be resolved in eight to 12 sessions. Requests for more sessions should be handled cautiously.

The big unanswerable question is what happens to the information in these reports. It is supposed to be confidential. The employer who has purchased the policy is not supposed to have access and, in practice, generally does not. What is less clear is who at the HMO can access the information. Can a secretary who is handling the paperwork access it? Is the information protected? There is no good answer to questions like these.

HMOs are reluctant to reveal, even to their providers, what happens to the submitted information. And even if a client can find out what the policies of an HMO are at the moment, there is no guarantee those policies will not change. HMOs do occasionally change their information storage policies, and mergers and acquisitions within the industry have also resulted in changing policies.

Once your therapist has filled out the initial report and sent it to the HMO, a specific number of sessions will usually be authorized. If it turns out that you and your therapist agree that more sessions are needed, either another report will have to be sent to the HMO, or the therapist will be asked to consult with a case manager. Case managers are usually, but not always, other mental health professionals. The case manager will ask your therapist to explain why additional sessions are needed and will then decide whether to grant them.

Any telephone conversations between your therapist and the HMO are recorded by the managed care company. There is no way to know what happens to these recordings—yet another confidentiality issue when dealing with an HMO.

Breaches of confidentiality occur in yet another way. HMOs are regulated by the states in which they operate and must meet minimum standards to remain in business. They are generally expected to be accredited by organizations such as the National Committee on Quality Assurance, which periodically reviews the practices of HMOs. To show accrediting organizations that they are meeting expected standards of care, HMOs periodically audit the records of their providers. Thus, your therapist might receive a letter from your HMO asking for photocopies of certain client records, possibly yours. Your therapist is then given feedback as to whether his or her record-keeping, general procedures, and treatment methods meet the standards set by the HMO. What happens to the photocopied records is, once again, not disclosed to the therapist or the client.

There already has been some backlash to HMO breaches of confidentiality. California, for instance, passed a law that took effect in January 2000, requiring the client to be informed about any information that has been released, why it has been released, and how long the information will be kept before it will be destroyed. This informs the client and the therapist of what is happening but does not stop the release of information. Most other states do not yet have this kind of law.

Denials of Care

Every managed care company has a process through which denials of care can be appealed. The process is different for each company but almost invariably is likely to be lengthy. While the denial is being appealed, you will be required by most clinicians to pay the fees for treatment from your own pocket. If you win the appeal, the services previously denied will be covered by your insurance, and you will be reimbursed for out-of-pocket payments. If you lose, though, and most appeals are lost, you will not be reimbursed, and you will receive no further care unless you continue to pay out of your own pocket. Under these circumstances, many people decide to stop seeing their psychotherapist.

If you feel you have suffered damages from the denial of care or mismanagement by a managed care company, you might attempt to sue the company. However, such lawsuits are rarely successful. In fact, under federal and state laws, HMOs are immune from most malpractice suits.

EMPLOYMENT ASSISTANCE PROGRAMS (EAPS)

In addition to insurance plans, psychotherapy services are sometimes available to through employee assistance programs (EAPs). These programs differ considerably from POS, PPO, and HMO insurance plans.

EAPs are short-term psychotherapy programs offered to employees. The cost of the programs is almost always paid by the employer. Large employers may even have psychotherapists on their payroll as part of the human resources department. Other EAPs contract with psychotherapists in clinics or private practice to provide psychological assessment and short-term psychotherapy services to employees.

EAPs are based on the theory that if an employee is distracted by issues in his or her personal life, he or she may not be able to perform at full capacity in the workplace. Thus, a wise employer will provide a quick and efficient method for employees to deal with those issues.

Employees wind up utilizing EAPs in one of two ways: self-referrals, and management referrals. An employee who believes he or she has a problem that can be addressed by short-term psychotherapy can self-refer by calling a designated person in the human resources department and asking to see a psychotherapist as part of the company's EAP. Management referrals occur when management believes an employee has a problem that is interfering with job performance. In these cases, management tells the employee that he or she is required to talk to a particular psychotherapist. Refusal on the part of the employee can lead to dismissal. Management referrals are most commonly made when a supervisor suspects that the employee has a problem with alcohol or drugs, or if an employee is having trouble dealing with coworkers or supervisors.

In almost all cases when an EAP is utilized, some form of report is made to the employer. If the employee is there on a self-referral, the report may be limited to a diagnosis or a general statement of the issue (marital problems, financial issues). In the case of a management referral, the report may be quite specific, such as the number of drinks an individual admits to consuming. Management can and often will use psychotherapist's report to decide how to proceed in dealing with the employee.

Part Four

The Nuts and Bolts of Psychotherapy

Chapter 12
Beginning Therapy

First Contact

For many people, the scariest and most difficult part of psychotherapy is the beginning. After you have gone through the process of finding the name of a psychotherapist or clinic, contact must be made. In most cases, the first contact will be via the telephone.

Making the first call sometimes proves difficult. "I was given your business card by a friend about six months ago," one person told me, "but I couldn't get myself to call. It stayed on my dresser, and I looked at it each morning and evening. I kept saying, 'I'll call today,' but six months passed before I actually made the call."

If you are calling a clinic, the odds are fairly good that a person will answer. If you are calling an individual psychotherapist, you will probably end up talking to an answering machine. It is very rare for a therapist to answer phone calls while in session. Be leery of any therapists who answer the phone and say they are in session but will call you back later. If a psychotherapist interrupts someone's session to answer your phone call, it is likely he or she will interrupt *your* sessions to take calls too.

If you get an answering machine, you only need to leave your name, information on when and how you can be reached, and the nature of the call. You could start by saying "I'm interested in talking with you about possibly starting therapy," or you could open with "Your name was given to me by a friend who suggested you may be able to help me."

If you want to talk with a therapist directly, try calling at five minutes before the hour. Most therapists begin their sessions on the hour, and sessions usually last 50 minutes. If there is a time when a therapist can answer the phone, it is during this 10-minute window between clients. Of course, this will not work if the therapist does not start sessions on the hour.

Another good way to make initial contact with a therapist is via the Internet. Many therapists are listed on Internet referral services, which usually provide E-mail addresses, making it easy to send inquiries. If a therapist is listed thus, it is just as proper to first contact him or her via E-mail as by telephone.

The first phone (or Internet) contact between a therapist and a client is actually something therapists discuss and practice as part of their training. Many training programs include role-plays of first contacts: One student acts as the potential client, while another acts as the therapist. Both the teacher and class critique these mock conversations to help the therapists in training sharpen their skills.

The time it takes for your initial call to be returned might be an indication of how quickly that therapist gets back to clients. If your call is not returned the same day or the next, ask if such a response time frame is usual for the therapist or an aberration.

Therapists' styles of response to initial inquiries vary widely. Some will simply give you an appointment time and then answer other questions during the first session. If you get that sort of response but want more information, it is up to you to ask.

Most therapists, however, will conduct a more extensive interview over the phone. They may want to make sure the issues with which you are dealing are within their areas of competence and interest. They may want to establish a rapport with you on the phone, to make you more comfortable, or to let you see a little of their style of working. Some will want to discuss their fee structure, since that is often an awkward subject. Many will also want to find out if you intend to use medical insurance to pay for the therapy. If you do, you should have your insurance information readily available. A therapist may also want to gather information about you to decide if he or she wants to work with you. One therapist once told me, "I can only have so many depressed clients on my caseload at one time. Depressed clients are a drain on me. So whenever I get a phone call from a prospective client, I not only want to know why he or she wants to see me, I also want to start getting to know that person. That information that will help me decide if I want to work with him or her."

A therapist's response to your initial inquiry tells you a great deal about his or her style. Listen to what is said and how it is said to determine if you want a first session with that therapist. If you have the names of several therapists, call several and then make your initial appointment with the one with whom you instinctively feel the most comfortable.

After all the anxiety you may have experienced over making the first contact with a therapist, it is disheartening to hear the therapist say his or her caseload is full and that he or she is not accepting new clients. One way to respond to this is to ask the therapist for the name and phone number of a colleague who might be able to see you. Because they are usually in contact with one another, therapists are perhaps the best source of knowing who might be available to help you with your particular issues.

Another approach is to ask the therapist if he or she has a waiting list. Some, though not all, do. If what brings you to therapy are long-term issues that do not require immediate attention, then waiting for the right therapist may make sense.

If the therapist's caseload is full and he or she agrees to put you on a waiting list, suggest to the therapist that you come in for an initial session as soon as possible to make sure there is actually a fit between the two of you. Most any therapist will have at least a few cancellations each week, and he or she may agree to call you when an hour opens up. This will enable both of you to decide if you want to wait to work with each other. If at that meeting the therapist feels your problems need immediate attention, he or she is ethically obligated to refer you to someone who can see you sooner.

The First Conversation

It is difficult to be relaxed before your first meeting with a therapist. You are about to share a lot of private information with a stranger. Anxiety is natural is such a situation. In fact, I have found that therapists, when seeking my services as clients themselves, are just as anxious as everyone else before they meet me. So, if you find yourself nervous before the first meeting with a psychotherapist, just tell yourself that what you are feeling is normal and proceed from there.

When you arrive at the first session, your therapist may give you a therapist/consumer disclosure statement. Doing so is encouraged by ethics and licensing boards, as well as therapists' professional organizations. The statement will contain information about education, licensing, and practices of the therapist, such as whether sessions are 50 minutes or 45 minutes, whether clients are financially responsible for missed appointments, whether clients are charged for phone calls between appointments, or what happens if a client's check bounces.

Some therapists will ask you to read the disclosure form and to sign a copy indicating you understand and accept the terms. Others will ask you to take the information home and read it there. Either way, it is in your interest to read disclosure statements carefully. Otherwise, you might be surprised when you are charged for a session you canceled.

In the first session the fee should be discussed, even if it was previously discussed in your initial phone conversation. It should be clear to you what the fee will be and when and how it is expected to be paid. This discussion will likely be initiated by the therapist, but it is up to you to ask questions about anything that is unclear or not covered by the therapist.

Some therapists want to be paid at each session. If this is the preference of your therapist, writing out your check before getting to the therapist's office will leave you with more time for non-business matters. Other therapists prefer to send a statement at the end of the month, expecting the client to pay the balance due by a certain date. A few will ask that you pay for the month's sessions in advance. You should make known whether you prefer to pay each time, at the end of the month, or in advance.

If you have point-of-service insurance, some therapists will accept partial payment of their fees from you and will bill your insurance company for the rest, while other therapists will ask that you pay the fee in full and then be reimbursed by your insurance provider. If you have point-of-service insurance, this is something you might want to ask about at the initial session.

Another good topic to discuss is the psychotherapist's policy for raising fees. We all expect to pay more over time for the goods and services we get, but when and how those rising costs occur can be a touchy subject. Most clients would be unhappy if the fee they agreed upon at their initial session would increase only two months later. Some therapists raise their fees every year on a particular day. Others raise their fee when they feel economic conditions warrant a raise. Be wary of a therapist who cannot guarantee that your initial fee will not change during the first year of therapy.

During your initial phone conversation, you may have already discussed that you can only see a therapist at certain hours or on certain days. If not, your first session is a good time to broach that subject. The hours when therapists are willing to see clients can vary considerably. Some therapists schedule early morning hours; others work evenings or weekends. One psychotherapist in New York City works from midnight to 8:00 A.M. and claims he has a full caseload.

In the past, therapists rarely if ever answered any questions of a personal nature or about the views they held. They would directly answer only those questions related to the business side of therapy. Even today, therapists remain reluctant to answer such questions, and when they do, it is often during the first session, before the real work of therapy begins.

This is especially true of psychoanalytically oriented therapists, who usually give limited personal information during only the first session. Thereafter they will probably not respond directly to any question that is not related to therapy. Even when a question is therapy related, the client may or may not get a direct answer. The same is true for therapists who are not psychoanalytically oriented, but to a lesser extent.

The flip side of this is that very few people actually do interview a therapist, even when the therapist is open to answering questions. It is rare that I get interviewed by a potential client. I usually ask somewhere during the first session if the client has any questions for me. Usually, he or she says no—or asks just a single question.

If you have questions, the first session is the time to ask them. In Appendix E are checklists you can use to help organize the information you would like to learn from the psychotherapist. Making a photocopy of those pages and take it with you to the first session. It should help you to remember the questions you would like to have answered.

AFTER THE FIRST CONVERSATION

The first question to ask yourself after your first session with a potential psychotherapist is this: "How well did the therapist understand my issues?" For instance, one woman came to me in tears. She said she'd had one session with another therapist, during which she had shared what she wanted to achieve in therapy as well as her problems with her lover's unfaithfulness. In response, the therapist kept going back to one small part of what she had said: that her mother had been depressed and committed suicide. The woman could not have been more disappointed. She knew her mother's depression and suicide had impacted her, but she wanted to talk about her more immediate feelings of being betrayed by her lover. Perhaps the previous therapist did not adequately explain to her why he wanted to concentrate on her mother or how that aspect of her life related to her current problem. Regardless, she felt she was not understood by that therapist and decided not to return.

The old saying, "First impressions are lasting," reflects the understanding that we get accurate impressions of people based on limited interactions with them. The late Virginia Satir, one of the pioneers of family therapy, used to tell her students, "Everything you need to know about how a family interacts you will see in the first five minutes that a family is with you in the therapy room. But don't worry if you miss anything. All the information will be there in every five minute period."

In a similar fashion, during the first hour with most any therapist, you will gather a tremendous amount of information. Some of it will be objective: the fee, scheduling considerations, etc. But much more of it will be subjective: how and to what this therapist responds. Those subjective considerations, more than anything else, should help you decide if you want to work with a particular therapist. The key is to understand and trust your feelings.

For many reasons, clients usually come into a therapy office for the first time with a desire to like the therapist. In a small number of situations, clients arrive with a predisposition to *not* like the therapist. Both situations make recognizing how you actually feel about a therapist difficult. If you arrive with a predisposition toward liking the therapist, you may deny feelings of discomfort. If your predisposition is to dislike or distrust a therapist, you will probably come away with a negative impression regardless of what went on during the session.

Thus, the question to ask is not whether you liked or disliked the therapist but how it would feel to work with that particular therapist. Try to imagine an ongoing series of conversations with the therapist. Try to imagine him or her responding to you over the course of those conversations. How would you feel about that interaction? Is it appealing? Was there anything that bothered you? Answering those questions should give you a good idea about whether you want to continue with that therapist.

The other thing you might want to consider at this point, if not before, are the therapist's credentials and competence. Credentials are the degrees, certificates, and licenses a therapist has earned. Competence refers to the knowledge and ability of a therapist to work with you on your issues or problems. It is usually easier to check out credentials than competence, but competence is ultimately more important.

While it is good to be aware of a therapist's credentials, only a very few people will go through the process of checking out whether they are legitimate. In fact, I am not aware of any client having ever verified my credentials.

The license of a psychotherapist is actually easier to verify than the degrees or certificates. And since therapists are required to have various degrees for certain licenses, you can be reasonably assured that if they are licensed, they do possess those degrees. Some states have established Web sites where you can check whether a clinician is licensed and if the license is still valid. This process is usually easier if you know the clinician's license number(s) in addition to his or her name. Some states require psychotherapists to list license numbers in advertising or on business cards. Sometimes psychotherapists list license numbers on professional stationery or receipts.

Competency is more difficult to determine. One way is to be direct: Ask the therapist why he or she is competent to deal with your particular issues and then listen carefully to the answer. Assuming he or she is being honest, you should hear something useful about his or her training or experience. Another way is to ask others who have seen that psychotherapist, if possible. A difficulty here is that psychotherapists, because of confidentiality, cannot give the names of other clients, as other professionals sometimes can. But the therapist may be able to give you the name of another professional who knows the therapist and can vouch for his or her competency.

Chapter 13
Aspects of Psychotherapy

There are many aspects of psychotherapy that do not fit elsewhere in this book. This chapter will address some of them.

Brief Therapy Versus Long-Term Therapy

There is a long-standing debate among psychotherapists about brief (short-term) versus long-term psychotherapy. Psychotherapists remains split on this issue, partly since no one has precisely defined what *brief* and *long-term* mean. Brief psychotherapy can last anywhere from one to perhaps 50 sessions. Usually, it is thought of as less than 20 sessions. Long-term psychotherapy is defined as lasting anywhere from a few months to many years. The debate about which approach is better has intensified in recent years, with insurance companies, not surprisingly, championing brief psychotherapy.

Each side hypes the merits of its approach and questions the motives of the other. Long-term psychotherapists are accused of financially exploiting their clients. Proponents of brief therapy are accused of either being shills for insurance companies or merely working on surface symptoms, while ignoring underlying problems and condemning the client to unhappiness as other symptoms inevitably arise.

There is no clear winner in this debate. It comes down to this: If there are particular symptoms you want eliminated, such as a fear of flying or a nervous tic, brief therapy with a behaviorally oriented clinician might be best. If, however, you need therapy for support during a difficult period in your life, or to work on identity issues, or to try to have a healthier approach to life, then you may want to consider working with a psychotherapist who does long-term work.

Patterns of Psychotherapy

Your involvement with psychotherapy can take many forms. Some of the more common forms are discussed below.

Versions of Long-Term Therapy

Every individual can come up with his or her own version of a long-term commitment to therapy. It is possible to see the same therapist for many years, sometimes starting and stopping at various points. It is also possible to integrate a variety of short-term therapies into a long-term commitment.

Emmanuel

Emmanuel, for instance, had been seeing the same therapist for eight years, for both individual and couples work. When his partner died, he saw therapy as a place of continuity and support, so he went on seeing the same therapist. But a year after his partner died, Emmanuel became curious about what was going on inside of him on a deeper level. His therapist did not do this kind of work. So with his therapist's blessing, Emmanuel began in-depth psychotherapy, meeting three times a week with a psychoanalytically oriented psychotherapist, who happened to be a trainee at a psychoanalytic training institute. By seeing someone in training, Emmanuel was able to afford an intensive therapy process. What enabled Emmanuel to make this choice was the knowledge that in the future he could return to his former therapist with the knowledge he had gained in psychoanalysis and then continue the work they had been doing.

Gloria

Gloria's story is somewhat different. She had been in psychotherapy with her female therapist for over 20 years, but it was never continuous. Gloria would start and stop therapy. Sometimes it would last a few months; sometimes it would go on for a year or two.

Gloria liked to participate in group encounter workshops. During the 1970s she stopped therapy for two years and became deeply involved in EST, which was then popular. Eventually, she became an EST trainer herself. Once several years had passed, though, Gloria felt she had gotten all she could from EST. She then began seeing her former therapist again and processed what she had learned from EST into her individual therapy.

Later, Gloria met her partner. They both wanted to do couples counseling. The partner, though, felt Gloria's therapist would tend to side too much with Gloria, so they began couples counseling with a therapist neither of them knew. As she had with EST, Gloria incorporated what she learned in couples counseling into her individual therapy. Her individual work, in turn, solidified the gains she made in couples counseling. Thereafter, Gloria would occasionally stop therapy for a year or so to "test her legs." Her goal in doing so was to see how much she had integrated into her life what she had discussed in therapy, as opposed to what issues she still needed to tackle.

"TWO-YEAR THERAPY"

Another pattern to therapy that has emerged over the years is what I call "two-year therapy," which falls somewhere between short-term and long-term therapy. In two-year therapy, a client comes to a psychotherapist for help with a specific problem. For a year and a half, the client talks about the problem and makes only small amounts of progress—two steps forward, one step back. Sometimes the person takes three steps back and feels no progress has been made. In fact, the individual feels worse. Then, after a year and a half, a different attitude emerges. There is a seriousness to the work that was not there earlier, an earnest willingness to change that differs from before. The major part of the work is then accomplished in the last six months, after which the client ends therapy.

Marcia

Marcia had worked for a nonprofit organization that had not handled its finances well. As a result, everyone was fired one day, and the agency closed. Marcia had put her life into her job; it had meant everything to her. She had never had a meaningful romantic relationship. When she was laid off, she did not know what to do with her time.

Marcia received unemployment payments, and she came from a middle-class family who was more than willing to help support her. After six months, though, her unemployment was running out, and she had not made any real efforts to seek a new job. She took a friend's advice and started counseling to find out why she was procrastinating.

For the next year and a half, Marcia continued to procrastinate. She felt victimized by the former head of the agency, who had mismanaged the agency's finances, causing it to close. She kept saying the only job she really wanted was the one that no longer existed. She was critical of herself and always found a reason to not apply for jobs that were available.

In therapy Marcia came to realize that she was the biggest cause of her not having a job, and she began to look at the ways she undermined herself. She had a habit of saying "Yes, but..." to all suggestions made by her therapist or anyone else. After a year and a half of therapy, though, Marcia started to listen to suggestions with new ears, instead of fighting them. Finally, she began an earnest job search. Her therapy ended at about the two-year point, when she took a job similar to her former position, except that it was in the city where she grew up, and that meant relocating.

Numerous possibilities were available to Marcia long before, but she could not look at them seriously for a year and a half. Once she convinced herself to move forward, though, she quickly completed the work she had needed to do.

Flights Into Health

The fear of psychotherapy that prevents some people from seeking help paradoxically enables some to become healthy. Some people see psychotherapy as the final resort and try almost everything else beforehand. After everything else fails and they find themselves in the office of a psychotherapist, it is a shock. In their first session they often hear the therapist say what they already know to be true. They then realize the path they have been resisting is the one they need to take. They call the psychotherapist after the first session to cancel the second appointment, choosing to make the necessary changes by themselves. While the psychotherapist might want to give him or herself a pat on the back for "curing" the client in one session, it is actually the client who does the work. For such individuals, the thought of seeing a psychotherapist on a regular basis is enough to cause a flight into health.

Miguel

Miguel, who sought therapy to deal with his feelings of depression, provides a good example of a flight into health. He thought he was in a monogamous relationship with his lover Louis. They had been involved for two years but did not live together. Miguel suspected Louis was sleeping with other men, but Louis always denied it and said he was faithful to Miguel. One day Miguel went to Louis's house unannounced and found Louis and another man getting dressed, presumably after having just had sex. Dejected, Miguel went home and began to sink into a deep depression. He felt betrayed but kept his emotions bottled up inside. Louis tried to apologize, but Miguel could not accept his apology. He could not bear the thought of no longer having Louis all to himself.

Over the next few months, Louis and Miguel saw each other as often as they had in the past, but Miguel's depression continued unabated. Louis no longer lied to Miguel about wanting to sleep with other men. He admitted he could give up neither other men nor Miguel. He wanted to continue as Miguel's lover, but he also wanted the freedom to have sex with other men.

Miguel was disgusted with himself. He was a proud, independent man who always had taken care of himself. Now, however, he could hardly function. His primary care physician noticed his depressed mood when they met for Miguel's regular HIV treatment follow-up appointment. When the physician heard Miguel's story, he suggested adding an antidepressant drug to Miguel's already considerable drug regimen. Miguel refused, saying he did not want to take any more pills, and he definitely did not want to take pills that would "mess with his head." His physician then referred him to me for psychotherapy.

Miguel said he could not envision a life without Louis, but he also could not stop thinking about who Louis might be sleeping with. He could not give up on Louis—or the desire for a monogamous relationship. We discussed what monogamy meant to Miguel. He had dreamed since he was a child of having a close, intimate, monogamous marital relationship with another man. He had rejected several men to whom he was attracted because they wanted an open relationship. Now he found himself in an open relationship and was depressed. He made an appointment to see me again the following week.

Exactly 24 hours before the second appointment, I received a cancellation call from Miguel. (Miguel had been told that he would be financially responsible for an appointment canceled with less than 24 hours notice.) He said he had given our conversation a lot of thought and then decided to end his relationship with Louis. When he made that decision, he felt great—for about 15 minutes. Then he thought about not wanting to lose Louis and changed his mind. When he did that, his depression returned. Again, he vowed to break up with Louis and felt great for another 15 minutes. When he changed his mind yet again, his depression returned.

After going back and forth between wanting to break up and wanting to stay together, he noticed the pattern. Breaking up felt better than staying with Louis, despite the ambivalence attached to both decisions. He thanked me for the conversation we'd had, and said he was going to break up with Louis that night and would not need my help any more. The following Christmas I received a card and note from Miguel thanking me again for helping him see what he already knew inside—that staying with Louis would only cause him to continue to be depressed. Miguel's one session caused him to have a flight into health.

The Relationship or the Content?

Psychotherapist do not agree as to what really makes therapy an effective tool. The most obvious explanation is that the client discusses various problems, gains insight into either the causes of the problems or what the client needs to do to alleviate them, and then implements changes and leads a happier life.

There are, however, some psychotherapists who contend that clients would benefit equally as much if the client and psychotherapist discussed sports or music or current events instead of focusing on the client's life. They believe the factor that changes people in positive ways is the *relationship* between the client and psychotherapist, not the content of their conversations.

Psychotherapists are trained to make psychotherapy a positive experience, in which the client feels respected. Psychotherapists work hard at this and usually succeed. If a client winds up in long-term psychotherapy, the client often feels known and supported by the psychotherapist. Most psychotherapists, whether they feel it is the counseling relationship or the work done during sessions that helps clients most, believe that psychotherapy is in itself a corrective emotional experience.

Feelings About Your Therapist

In the course of therapy, it is likely that you will have many different feelings toward and regarding your therapist. In all likelihood, you will be able to identify many of these feelings. Some will be positive and will help you be close to your therapist. Others may frighten you. Some of the common feelings experienced by clients are discussed below.

Being Sexually Attracted to Your Therapist

A client who is sexually attracted to his or her therapist is almost a cliché. Movies, plays, books, and television have all used this as a theme. Like most clichés, though, it has an element of truth. Clients do sometimes become sexually attracted to their therapists.

Therapy is intimate. The client talks about his or her feelings, including those not often discussed outside of therapy, such as feelings of sexual attraction. And therapists, in general, are warm, supportive, and accepting. Under such circumstances, feelings of sexual attraction are likely to occur.

There is an ongoing debate within the mental health community about the nature of the sexual attraction clients often feel for their therapists. Some argue that such feelings are true and genuine: Clients do become sexually attracted to their therapists. Others argue that this attraction is a defense against other feelings. Clients become sexually attracted to their therapist in order to suppress their other less pleasant feelings.

Regardless of how these feelings are interpreted, one thing is certain. From the standpoint of the client, these feelings are real. Furthermore, this sexual attraction is not limited by sexual orientation. Those who are attracted to members of their own sex sometimes find they are sexually attracted to therapists of the opposite sex. It is perhaps more unsettling when a heterosexual finds him or herself sexually attracted to a therapist of the same sex.

I will use my own experience as a client as an example. I am your basic gay man. While I do have mild feelings of sexual attraction for females, most of my sexual energy is and has always been directed toward men. Yet during my first therapy experience, I remember laying in bed one night in a highly aroused sexual state thinking of my female therapist. I was scared and confused. I had been dealing in therapy with my attraction to members of my own sex, and suddenly the most powerful feelings of sexual attraction I had ever had were directed toward someone of the opposite sex. I could not figure out why this was happening.

I talked about these sexual feelings with my therapist and felt relieved when she told me they are common. She was also wise enough to tell me they did not mean I was a repressed heterosexual or that I should pursue my heterosexual feelings. She understood that sexual feelings can be aimed in many directions and that my feelings toward her were more about my relationship with her than my attraction to women.

Talking about my feelings helped me calm down and understand myself a little better. Therein lies the lesson. If you find yourself sexually attracted to your therapist, do not immediately jump to any conclusions. Simply note the feelings of attraction, talk about them in therapy, and learn whatever you can by beginning to understand them.

FEELING DEPENDENT ON YOUR THERAPIST

Many clients find themselves feeling dependent on their therapist. This can be scary for a number of reasons. If the client is the independent type and now feels dependent, he or she may not be comfortable with the situation. Or a client may be afraid to make decisions without consulting his or her therapist. Feeling dependent on a therapist is typically more difficult for men than for women.

Most clients, in reality, do not fear becoming dependent on their therapists. What does become scary, however, is when the therapist is not available. When a therapist goes on vacation, a client sometimes may become upset and wonder how to get along temporarily without regular therapy sessions.

If you are scared of your dependency, or scared when your dependency needs are not met, try to understand these feelings. Talk about them in the therapy hour. They are likely to resemble feelings of dependency you harbor toward individuals besides your therapist, particularly those with whom you are intimate. Mining this vein in therapy can be extremely productive.

BEING ANGRY WITH YOUR THERAPIST

Everyone gets angry at least occasionally. Even the Dalai Lama, one of the more together people in this world, has said that he sometimes feels anger when he does not get his way. What is important, he believes, is not the anger itself but how he deals with it. He meditates to achieve mindfulness regarding the anger. Once he understands the anger, it dissipates.

Many things can trigger anger in a therapy relationship. One client got angry every time she saw her therapist glancing at the clock. Another client got angry whenever his therapist started their sessions a few minutes late. Still another was angry over his perception that his therapist did not take the client's income into account when raising the fee. Most people get angry when they believe someone is not treating them in the manner they feel they should be treated. Anger can be triggered by most anything, whether it is being cut off in traffic or your therapist telling you he or she is not available for telephone check-ins between appointments.

Anger is a subject therapists talk about at length amongst themselves. They try to understand the nature of anger and how to best work with a client who expresses (or does not express) it. Some schools of psychotherapy believe that people express anger once they reach the final straw in a long succession of "being wronged." These therapists believe that an expression of anger represents just the tip of the iceberg; the entire force of the long-repressed anger is often misdirected toward the last person to cause hurt. Other schools believe that most anger is related to parents and gets acted out later in life. Still other schools take anger at face value, considering it an emotion that arises from time to time in much the same way as other emotions.

Generally, anger is expressed in one of two ways, aggressive or passive. It is expressed aggressively, for example, by yelling or being sarcastic. As for passively expressed anger, consider this scenario: Your therapist tells you he or she is going on vacation for a month, which makes you angry. Somehow, you "forget" to mail a check to your therapist to pay for services rendered.

The most effective way to deal with anger is to discuss it. Herein is one of the beauties of therapy. Therapists are taught not to overreact to anger or take it personally. Instead, they have learned that when a client expresses anger, they should listen to what is being said and respond in a nonpunitive manner.

Trusting Your Therapist

Being able to trust your psychotherapist will benefit you as a client. The more you are able to trust your psychotherapist, the easier it will be to talk about parts of yourself that could be considered mean, sneaky, self-centered, dishonest, perverted, or otherwise shameful—stuff that hardly anyone talks about, yet very real and important. You'll have to deal with it if you want to make changes in your life. Without showing your therapist some honesty and trust, you cannot tackle things that make you feel uncomfortable.

Trust, however, is never easy, automatic, or complete. Trust takes time, and is always earned. The more violations of trust you have experienced in your life, the more difficult it is to trust your therapist or anyone else. My experience has been that it usually takes at least a year for a client to fully believe that he or she can trust me. Once a client trusts the therapist, work proceeds at a much faster pace. The client is finally able to put sensitive, deep issues on the table and thrash them out, as hard as that may be.

If you are currently in therapy, think about all the things you feel you cannot say to your psychotherapist. Those things indicate how much you still do not trust your therapist. Then ask yourself why. Has your therapist been unreliable? Has he or she not listened carefully to what you have said? Has your therapist engaged in an activity that is illegal or unethical? If you answer yes to any of the above, you should tell your therapist how that inhibits you.

If, however, your therapist has done nothing to indicate he or she is less than trustworthy, then your withholding facts about yourself is a topic for discussion, especially if you have been in therapy for a year or more. Bringing up your lack of trust with your therapist just may help you stretch yourself emotionally. You may then feel able to begin talking about things you had previously left unmentioned—things that almost always factor crucially in whatever changes you are trying to make.

Paul

A good example of a client overcoming trust issues is Paul, who initially sought therapy for two reasons. First, he had been injured on his job and was on long-term disability. The effect on his self-esteem was devastating, but there was little he could do since his injury was debilitating and caused chronic pain. Second, it was early in the AIDS epidemic, and several of Paul's close friends had died, leaving him feeling bewildered and helpless. He had no idea how to deal with those feelings.

Over the course of his time in psychotherapy, Paul's injury responded to treatment, enabling him to contemplate returning to work. But friends kept becoming ill and dying, and Paul decided to stay in therapy for support.

About two years into therapy, Paul said he wanted to tell me something that he had never told anyone: the great family secret concerning his father. He always described his father in the most glowing of terms, a great man who died young of a heart attack. All that Paul told me was true, but there was more. The hospital where his father died was not an acute care medical facility but a mental hospital for veterans. Paul's father was a veteran of the Korean War and suffered from post-traumatic stress syndrome. He had been periodically hospitalized but never fully recovered.

I asked Paul why he had never mentioned this, and he responded that he had always dutifully kept his family's secret. Paul's mother had been so embarrassed over the circumstances of her husband's death that the family moved to another city. She always admonished Paul and his siblings to never tell anyone their family secret. I then asked Paul why he was now able to tell me, and he said that he felt he had finally found someone to whom he could entrust this secret.

Paul was a high-functioning man and knew that what he said in the therapy room stayed in the therapy room. But he also said he needed to learn that was true for himself. It took him two years of being in therapy to learn that.

The following year, Paul decided to return to school for job retraining. The school to which he applied required that he write an autobiographical essay for the admissions committee to review along with his college grades. Paul wrote his essay about his father. From never having told anyone the secret, he gradually became able to first tell his psychotherapist and then complete strangers.

The Third Session Dilemma

The first and second sessions are often easy for clients. Most come to the first session either with a prepared story, or a willingness to answer questions posed by the psychotherapist as to why they are there. The second session is often devoted to telling the therapist everything that was left out of the first session. The therapist will often be quite active in the first two meetings, asking questions, clarifying issues, making comments. Consequently, the first two hours with the therapist pass quickly. And then comes the third session. The client has no idea as what to talk about.

The same thing happens in group therapy. Group members usually spend the first session introducing themselves and saying why they want to be in the group. The theme of the second meeting is often "What a nice group of people we are." Once these introductory stages are past, the group members need to get down to work. But what does that mean? That is the third-session dilemma.

Rest assured that if you experience the third-session dilemma, you are not alone. Psychotherapists see this all the time. If you find yourself in the third—or any other—session not knowing what to say, simply make being at a loss for words the conversation topic and ask your therapist how you might proceed.

CONFIDENTIALITY

Your psychotherapist is supposed to hold all conversations with clients confidential. The basic rule is that you may talk about therapy with whomever you wish, but a psychotherapist may not say anything about you as a client without your permission, except in the following circumstances.

While the laws in each state differ, most states require a psychotherapist to break confidentiality when there is evidence of child abuse or a client has become a danger to him or herself or others. Some states have laws requiring psychotherapists to break confidentiality at other times as well: California, for instance, requires psychotherapists to report incidents of elder abuse.

If you convince a psychotherapist you are going to attempt to kill yourself, the psychotherapist is obligated to attempt to stop you. In practice that means calling the police and asking them to seek you out and assess whether they too believe you are a danger to yourself. If they determine you are, they will take you to a mental health facility where you can be detained for up to 72 hours or longer, depending on legal proceedings.

If you convince your psychotherapist that you are going to hurt someone else—if, for instance, you say that you are planning to kill your unfaithful lover—the psychotherapist is required to inform both the police, and, if possible, your intended victim.

If you tell a psychotherapist that you have been involved in behavior considered to be child abuse (such as any sexual contact with a child), the psychotherapist is required to notify the local office of child protective services. Child protective services will then investigate this report and take appropriate action.

So be forewarned. Under certain circumstances, a psychotherapist is obligated to break confidentiality. If this is a concern to you, ask your psychotherapist what the law in your state requires.

Disagreeing With Your Therapist

At some point, you and your therapist will see things differently. Occasionally, these differences will be important, possibly about strongly held beliefs either of you have. In all but the most extreme cases, the way *not* to handle these differences is to end therapy because inevitably you will disagree with any person on some point. Taken to the extreme, that would mean there is no therapist with whom you can work.

And that is the point. Disagreements are unavoidable. Psychotherapy gives you an opportunity to discuss the differences of opinion in a clean way and reach some resolution, even if that means agreeing to disagree.

In a minority of cases, you and your therapist will see the impasse as unsolvable. This is most likely to occur when a therapist believes a client's alcohol or drug use is problematic. The therapist may believe the client needs to take certain actions such as stopping the substance use, joining a 12-step program, or entering an inpatient treatment program for substance abuse. The client will sometimes vehemently disagree, and both parties may then agree it is best to end the relationship.

Dealing With the Power Imbalance

There is a seeming imbalance of power in therapy. The client comes to therapy with a problem, seeking the help of a professional. That immediately puts the client in a one-down position. The client wants something from the therapist, and the therapist may or may not give the client what he or she is asking for.

I call this a *seeming* imbalance of power because the imbalance is actually illusory. The client is the consumer, who in almost all cases is seeing the therapist voluntarily and therefore has greater power. The client may or may not choose to come to therapy, and the therapist cannot do anything about that. The therapist can only be more powerful if the client agrees to come to therapy. Therefore, therapy is an equal relationship, with each individual bringing to the session what they have to offer.

My experience has shown, however, that it takes many clients a long time to understand that they are in fact equal to the therapist. In some ways, when that happens, it is a sign that the client has grown and perhaps therapy is nearing an end.

When a client does feel that he or she lacks power in the psychotherapeutic relationship, the best thing to do is talk about it. It is a great opportunity for the client to discuss feelings about feeling at a disadvantage as well as reactions to various authority figures (including his or her parents and other family members). Hopefully, the client will begin to take back power by truly recognizing that relationships are about differences, not power or authority. That reclamation of power—as well as the new insight into human relationships—can be a primary benefit of therapy for many clients. A perceived power imbalance is rarely the surface issue that brings clients into therapy, yet it is often one of the underlying reasons why they seek help at all.

WANTING TO SEE MORE THAN ONE THERAPIST AT A TIME

It can be controversial when a client wants to see more than one therapist at a time. Psychoanalytic psychotherapists usually refuse to see any client who wishes to consult or work with another therapist simultaneously. They contend this practice waters down feelings that arise during therapy sessions, thereby diluting the process of transference.

Other therapists do not share these concerns. They see themselves as consultants who let the client decide whether he or she is getting all that he or she needs from the relationship. They may go so far as to encourage clients to seek elsewhere what they are not getting out of therapy.

If you have thoughts about seeing more than one therapist at a time, discuss with your therapist how he or she feels about the idea. And listen carefully to his or her answer. The answer may make sense to you, or you might disagree, in which case more discussion may be necessary. Keep in mind, though, that some therapists will not work with a client who is also seeing someone else, and that no amount of discussion will change their mind.

When a Therapist is Over the Line—Reporting

Psychotherapists are human beings. As such, a small number of them will at times, either intentionally or unintentionally, go beyond what is acceptable in a psychotherapeutic relationship. In those situations, a psychotherapist should be reported to the state licensing board and perhaps to his or her professional associations.

But how is a client who is not a mental health professional to understand what is acceptable in a psychotherapeutic relationship?

Two obvious violations are sexual contact between a client and psychotherapist, and a client going into business with his or her psychotherapist. The line, however, is not always so clearly defined. When this is the case, the best course of action is to get a second (or third or fourth) opinion.

The best person from whom to seek such an opinion is another psychotherapist. Psychotherapists do not like it when one of their colleagues crosses the line. It is a black eye for the entire profession. All you need to do is call another psychotherapist and ask his or her opinion of the questionable professional behavior (without naming the offending psychotherapist). The second psychotherapist should be able to tell you whether the actions constitute a clear violation, lie in a gray area, or are actually acceptable professional behavior.

If there are other people whose judgment you respect, you might consult them, provided that they can keep the discussion confidential. You could also post an anonymous query on the Internet. Detectable patterns to any responses you receive might help guide the decision you reach about your therapist. Remember, though, that just as it is possible for you to post an anonymous query and not assume direct personal accountability, the same holds true for those who respond to you online.

WHEN TO END THERAPY

Whether by choice or circumstances beyond our control, there is an end to everything. The structure of psychotherapy allows for multiple endings. Virtually every time you see your psychotherapist there is an unnatural ending regulated by the clock. But you terminate your working relationship with your psychotherapist, though, because it is the right time to end. Trying to figure out what is the right time for therapy to end is not a clear-cut matter.

Ideally, the therapist and the client will mutually decide when to terminate. Either can raise the issue, and it works best when both come to the same conclusion. Therapy can also be phased out, especially when someone has been in long-term therapy. The client begins to see the therapist less and less until termination is complete.

For many, the end point of therapy occurs when the goals of therapy have been met. You may have begun seeing a psychotherapist because you felt depressed, and now you no longer feel depressed. Or you and your partner may have started couples psychotherapy because you were having problems, and the two of you have either worked it out or decided to split up. In either situation, you no longer have the same needs as when you began therapy.

Danielle

Danielle began therapy after breaking up with her lover. They had been together less than a year, but Danielle took it hard. She wanted a house with a white picket fence; her lover wanted excitement, travel, adventures, and anything but settling down. Danielle had the mistaken notion that she could still reap the benefits of her lover's intense energy and willingness to live on the edge, while at the same time taming her excesses. Danielle's lover, after their umpteenth argument over whether they should buy a house, flatly told Danielle that she never wanted to be tied down by real estate. She also told Danielle that she had met another woman who also wanted to travel, and the two of them would be leaving soon for places unknown.

Danielle went into a depression. She found it hard to sleep and hard to stop eating. Her consumption of alcohol greatly increased on the sleepless nights. She would drink before she went to sleep and occasionally when she awoke in the middle of the night. She had been a social drinker before the breakup but clearly became a problem drinker after the breakup. Only this was not clear to Danielle.

Danielle had her wake-up call when she was driving to work one morning. A police officer noticed her erratic driving and pulled her over. To Danielle's great shock, she failed a sobriety test. It had never occurred to her that the alcohol she consumed at night could leave her too drunk to drive in the morning.

Danielle did three things: She hired a lawyer; she stopped drinking completely; and she started therapy.

As soon as Danielle stopped drinking, her depression worsened. She could not sleep at all, and her food consumption increased even more. Just talking about her problems was not enough. She was referred to a psychiatrist who prescribed both an antidepressant and sedatives for nights when she could not sleep. But those still were not enough.

What finally made the difference for Danielle was joining a psychotherapy group for lesbians who were going through breakups. The members of this group affectionately called it "The Old Wives Club," since several members had been abandoned by their partners for younger lovers. Danielle continued with the individual and group psychotherapy for about a year. During that year, she learned much about herself. Most importantly, she learned to rely on herself for what she had been trying to get from her ex-lovers—an exciting life. She learned to have the stability she wanted, and to also go out and have adventures. She joined the local Sierra Club chapter for queer people, met many other lesbians with similar interests, and came to enjoy her life. At that point, she decided her life was working for her, so she stopped both group and individual therapy.

There are, of course, other reasons to end therapy. One possible reason is that you feel you are not getting much from your current work. You may find yourself going to therapy and telling the story of the week because you cannot think of anything more pressing to discuss. Or you may find yourself stagnating, going over the same material repeatedly, not making progress, and seemingly spinning your wheels.

This is not meant to cover a short period of stagnation. That always happens in therapy. In fact, a normal course of therapy will have many periods of seeming stagnation separated by small break-throughs when the work progresses much faster. All clients plateau until their next growth spurt.

When the stagnation continues over a long period of time, though, the possibility of ending the therapy relationship and look-ing at alternatives—finding a new therapist, stopping therapy alto-gether—should be considered.

When it is time to discuss an ending with your therapist, I sug-gest you also discuss your therapist's practices regarding former clients returning to therapy. Many therapists see their role as simi-lar to that of a primary care physician. They have many clients on their caseload but only see a certain percentage of them at any given time. If you have an infection, for instance, you may call your primary care physician for an appointment and treatment, and then not see that doctor again until another clear need arises. Many psy-chotherapists work off the same model: They build a long-term relationship with their clients, even though they may not be seeing many of those clients at any given time.

Because ending therapy mirrors so many other endings in our lives, it is wise to discuss the issue with your therapist over a period of time, rather than simply announcing one day that this will be your final session. Such a gradual discussion will give you the opportunity to work through the process of closure and what feel-ings and reactions it brings up.

CHAPTER 14
DIAGNOSIS

Regardless of whether you see a psychotherapist who subscribes to the growth model or the medical model, chances are that he or she will be asked to diagnose you using the medical model. This will certainly happen if you use your medical insurance plan to pay for psychotherapy. It is also very likely if you are seen in a publicly run clinic or a large counseling center. On the other hand, your therapist might never record your diagnosis if he or she subscribes to the growth model and if you are paying for therapy on you own and never request information about you to be released to a third party. Otherwise, at some point your psychotherapist will likely issue a diagnosis.

That diagnosis may or may not be shared with you. My experience is that even a high-functioning adult can have an emotional reaction upon learning his or her psychological diagnosis. Clients often interpret being diagnosed as meaning that something is seriously wrong inside their heads. If you have a diagnosis, I strongly encourage you to discuss it with your psychotherapist. Ask what the diagnosis is and exactly what it means.

Psychotherapists who subscribe to the medical model believe that they are ethically responsible for the assessment, diagnosis, and treatment of the client (patient) and that the client will comply with the entire process. During the assessment phase, the psychotherapist asks the client about behavior patterns, thoughts, feelings, and experiences. Using the answers to these questions, along with other information such as psychological test results, the psychotherapist arrives at a diagnosis. This diagnosis is important to a medical-model psychotherapist since it determines the proper and ethical course for treating the client.

In the United States, psychological diagnoses are based on criteria published in the most recent edition of the *Diagnostic and Statistical Manual of Mental Disorders* (*DSM* for short), published by the American Psychiatric Association.

Caution: Read the Following Paragraph Carefully!

You should exercise caution while reading the remainder of this chapter. Information concerning a particular diagnosis could leave you feeling seriously distressed, possibly thinking that you have a diagnosable mental disorder. Studies have shown that it is not uncommon for psychology graduate students to identify with many of the disorders listed below, so it is likely that to some degree you will too. *That does not mean you have a diagnosable mental disorder.* It merely means you share some symptoms or traits with people who *might* have a diagnosable mental disorder.

Please remember that everyone shows signs of almost all of the symptoms the *DSM* uses to describe diagnoses. Everyone has some symptoms of anxiety, some symptoms of depression, and traits similar to many of the personality disorders. It is not a matter of whether these symptoms are present but the degree to which they are present and affect on your life. Mental health diagnoses are difficult even for experienced clinicians. *Do not attempt to diagnose yourself. You will likely be incorrect.* The information is included here to facilitate discussing your diagnosis with a mental health professional.

The Five Axes of a Psychological Diagnosis

Psychological diagnoses are not as simple as most medical diagnoses. To do a complete psychological diagnosis, a psychotherapist must assess five separate characteristics. These five characteristics are known as the five axes of the diagnosis. Understood as a whole, the psychotherapist's assessment of the five axes forms the diagnosis for a client.

Diagnosis is a difficult subject for clinicians. Psychotherapists regularly receive literature in the mail announcing continuing education classes designed to improve their diagnostic skills. Some psychotherapists specialize in determining the proper diagnosis. And even diagnostic specialists do not always come up with the same diagnosis. So it is reasonable to take with a grain of salt any diagnosis that has been recorded for you.

Consider the following before you put the weight of your emotions behind your psychological diagnosis. A psychological diagnosis does not become a diagnosis because it passes an objective test. Rather, a standing committee of the American Psychiatric Association reviews the diagnoses in the *DSM* and votes on which will continue to appear in the next edition and which will be eliminated. When the committee's work is complete, the new edition of the *DSM* is submitted to the members of the APA for another vote. After the old diagnoses are eliminated and the new ones approved, a new edition of the *DSM* is published.

With each edition of the *DSM*, a few older diagnoses are eliminated, and many more are added. Homosexuality was voted out in 1973. Its replacement, which permitted psychiatrists to treat people unhappy with their sexual orientation, has now been eliminated too. Groups of psychiatrists regularly lobby for the inclusion of new diagnoses and occasionally for the elimination of old ones. Political considerations therefore sometimes enter into the process of including and eliminating diagnoses in the *DSM*.

Once a diagnosis is official, it is assigned a number. Mild depression, for instance, might be recorded as dysthymia (DSM 300.4). Dysthymia is the psychological word for what most people would consider relatively mild but still troublesome depression; the number that follows it is the number of that diagnosis in the *DSM*. The number is used to code the diagnosis in order to electronically process insurance claims.

There are hundreds of diagnoses in the *DSM*, but only a few are commonly used. The following material discusses the more common diagnoses for each axis. Remember, *do not try to diagnose yourself*. (This information is primarily taken from the *Diagnostic and*

Statistical Manual of Mental Disorders, Fourth Edition. American Psychiatric Association. 1994. Washington, D.C.)

AXIS I—CLINICAL DISORDERS

On Axis I, the psychotherapist describes the clinical symptoms the client is experiencing. This is close to what most people think of when they think of psychological diagnosis—and very often it is the entire diagnosis. While formal diagnosis requires assessment along all five axes, many insurance companies and clinics are interested only in Axis I, which may be as far as a diagnosis goes. It may not be a complete formal diagnosis, but it may be all the client gets.

Axis I indicates to what extent the client is depressed, anxious, using alcohol or drugs to excess, experiencing sexual problems, living with an eating disorder, or showing any of hundreds of other possible symptoms. Generally, the symptoms described on Axis I can be observed and measured. The *DSM* lists the characteristics of each particular disorder, which help the clinician arrive at an Axis I diagnosis corresponding to the client's symptoms. If there is no diagnosis on Axis I, it is virtually impossible for an insurance company to reimburse the client for psychotherapy.

It is not unusual for someone to have more than one diagnosis on Axis I. For example, a person might be both depressed and agoraphobic (afraid to leave home). Each Axis I diagnosis would be separately listed.

As stated earlier, the numbers after the initials *DSM* represent particular disorders. Where the letter *x* appears, it means the *DSM* has more than one diagnosis in that category, and the therapist needs to specify the proper diagnosis in further detail.

COMMON AXIS I DIAGNOSES

ADJUSTMENT DISORDERS

Adjustment disorders are perhaps the most common diagnosis given to insurance companies to justify why it is medically necessary for a client to see a psychotherapist. Many therapists believe adjustment disorders are the "mildest" diagnosis in the *DSM* that insurance companies will accept. There is a yet milder class of diagnoses in the *DSM* identified by V codes, which designate conditions not attributable to a mental disorder. For example, grieving after a partner dies would be classified with a V code. Insurance companies do not cover treating clients with V code diagnoses. Insurance companies only reimburse for mental disorders.

An adjustment disorder diagnosis means that the client is exhibiting symptoms of a mild mental disorder while dealing with something difficult in his or her life. To arrive at this diagnosis, the therapist must determine two factors. First, some specific stressful event, known as a *stressor,* has happened to the client within the past three months. Second, the client is having trouble functioning or is experiencing symptoms such as anxiety or depression that are beyond what would normally occur in reaction to the stressor. These symptoms may not simply be an overreaction to the stressor; instead, they may indicate a pattern of trouble adjusting to life situations.

Stressors can be one-time events such as breaking up with a partner, getting fired from a job, losing a substantial sum of money on the stock market, or living through a natural disaster such as a hurricane or an earthquake. Stressors can also be regularly recurring events such as performance reviews at work or conflict over a queer couple attending annual holiday gatherings involving one or both of the partners' families of origin. Stressors can also be ongoing challenges such family trouble or an abusive partner. Specific stressors are listed later in the diagnosis on Axis IV.

Presumably, adjustment disorder symptoms will cease within six months after the stressor first appears. If symptoms persist thereafter, they are no longer indicate an adjustment disorder, and the therapist should determine a more appropriate diagnosis.

There are six adjustment disorders in the *DSM*. If you are ever diagnosed with an adjustment disorder, you may only see the number of the diagnosis and not understand what it represents. Therefore, I have listed the six adjustment disorders here.

Adjustment Disorder with Depressed Mood (DSM 309.0): The predominant feature is a depressed mood—a feeling of hopelessness, often characterized by crying all the time.

Adjustment Disorder with Anxiety (DSM 309. 24): As a result of the stressor, the client has become quite nervous, jittery, worrisome, or is experiencing similar symptoms.

Adjustment Disorder with Mixed Anxiety and Depression (DSM 309.28): The client is experiencing excessive symptoms of both anxiety and depression.

Adjustment Disorder with Disturbance of Conduct (DSM 309. 3): Because of stress, the client is acting in an inappropriate way. The client may be violating the rights of others, driving recklessly, fighting, or not fulfilling his or her legal responsibilities.

Adjustment Disorder with Mixed Disturbance of Emotion and Conduct (DSM 309. 4): The client is exhibiting both emotional symptoms (anxiety and/or depression) and disturbed conduct.

Adjustment Disorder, Unspecified (DSM 309. 9): This is the vaguest of the adjustment disorder diagnoses. It means that, as a result of the stressor, any of a number of things are happening that do not fit neatly into the other diagnostic categories. The client might feel isolated, find it difficult to go to work or school, or feel bad physically.

Psychotherapists like the vagueness of adjustment disorder diagnoses. Something is always stressing someone out, and symptoms such as anxiety and depression are present to some extent in everyone's life. Arguably, a psychotherapist could diagnose just about anyone at practically at any time as having an adjustment disorder. Likewise, it is relatively easy to justify such a diagnosis. So if you want to use your medical insurance to pay for sessions in which you discuss life issues, your psychotherapist might indicate on the claim papers that you have an adjustment disorder.

Depression

Depression is common and comes in many forms. It can be mild or severe. You may find yourself feeling blue, or you may be so depressed that you are unable to take care of yourself. There are many theories about what causes depression: chemical imbalances in the brain, experiences of loss, unexpressed anger. No one knows for sure what causes depression; it may have several causes.

Depression is characteristic of several disorders identified in the *DSM*. Two, however, typify what most people view as depression.

The milder form of depression is called **Dysthymic Disorder (DSM 300.4)**: To be diagnosed with dysthymic disorder, the client must have been suffering from a depressed mood more often than not for the past two years. The client's own account of his or her emotional state can confirm this diagnosis, as can also observation by friends, family members, coworkers, and others close to the client. At least two of the following symptoms must have been present: the client's appetite is poor, or he or she is overeating; the client's sleep patterns are characterized by either insomnia or sleeping too much; the client is experiencing low energy or fatigue; the client is feeling low self-esteem; the client is having difficulty concentrating or making decisions. At no point during the two-year period can the client have felt free of symptoms or the depressed mood for more than two months.

If by your nature you tend toward being depressed, it is not difficult for a clinician to diagnose you as having dysthymic disorder. The range of symptoms is broad enough that almost anyone can fit this diagnosis at least sometimes.

The more serious form of depression is known as **Major Depressive Disorder (DSM 296.3x)**. To be diagnosed with major depressive disorder, the client must have had a severely depressed mood and/or a loss of interest in pleasure for a two-week period. As with dysthymic disorder, the client often has problems with eating and sleeping, although significantly more severe. Feelings of worthlessness are often present, and suicidal thoughts are common.

Major depressive disorder differs from dysthymic disorder in terms of the duration and severity of episodes. The symptoms of dysthymic disorder are less severe but occur over a longer time (at least two years), whereas individuals with a major depressive disorder may feel fine most of the time but sometimes lapse into a deep emotional void for short periods lasting as little as two weeks.

Generalized Anxiety Disorder

Generalized Anxiety Disorder (DSM 300.02) means that the client has been worrying and experiencing excessive anxiety about events in his or her life for at least six months. The client finds it difficult not to worry. More often than not during those six months, the client has experienced at least three of the following six symptoms: feeling restless, keyed up, or on edge; becoming easily fatigued; difficulty concentrating; irritability; muscle tension; and difficulty falling asleep, staying asleep, or having fitful sleep.

If you are by nature an anxious person, it is easy to be diagnosed with generalized anxiety disorder. The symptoms are broad enough to include a fairly large segment of the population.

Panic Attacks

No one is diagnosed as merely having a panic attack. The clinician must also determine if the panic attack is or is not accompanied by agoraphobia. Many people understand agoraphobia as a fear of leaving home, but it is actually more than that. It is a fear of being in places from which the individual believes he or she cannot easily escape or where leaving might be embarrassing. Such places might be a restaurant, an airplane or bus, a crowded party, or any number of other locales.

Panic attacks generally include any or all of the following symptoms: a rapid or pounding heartbeat, sweating, trembling, breathing fast or hyperventilating, chest pains, fears that you are dying, numbness, and chills or hot flashes.

There are two panic attack diagnoses. One is **Panic Disorder Without Agoraphobia (DSM 300.01)**. In this diagnosis, the client is having the panic attacks, but the agoraphobic aspect is missing. The other is **Panic Attack With Agoraphobia (DSM 300.22)**, in which the client experiences agoraphobia in addition to the attack.

Phobias

Phobias are irrational and excessive fears that persist, even though the individual recognizes them as unreasonable. Sometimes a person's reaction to such fears is to freeze and be unable to function; other times the reaction is a full-blown panic attack. Phobias can control people's lives in significant ways through avoidance and anxiety. Some common phobias are fears of animals, insects, heights, storms, blood, tunnels, bridges, enclosed places, and flying on airplanes. These phobias are all diagnosed as **Specific Phobia (DSM 300.29)**. Another type of phobia is a fear of people or situations in which a person might feel embarrassed. This is diagnosed as **Social Phobia (DSM 300.23)**.

Post–Traumatic Stress Disorder

Post-Traumatic Stress Disorder (DSM 309.81) is a condition that affects clients who have experienced or witnessed situations that involved death and dying or were life-threatening or emotionally crippling, either to the client or someone else. Rape, war, an abusive childhood, a car crash, or having been the victim of a crime are examples of such experiences. Even though the event is in the past, it still haunts the person. The individual has recurrent and disturbing memories and/or dreams about the event and feels at those times as if the event were just happening. Symptoms include difficulty sleeping, irritability, hypervigilance, jumpiness, and difficulty concentrating.

Substance–Related Disorders

Substance-Related Disorders (DSM 291.xx, 292.xx, 303.xx, 304.xx, 305.xx) are too diverse and complicated in nature to be covered in depth in this chapter. Alcohol and amphetamines are the chief substances abused in the queer community. Caffeine, cannabis (marijuana), cocaine, hallucinogens (LSD, ecstasy, et al.), inhalants, nicotine, opiates, sedatives, painkillers, and prescription medication are other commonly abused substances. Abuse may involve dependence on or addiction to the substance. A substance-related disorder diagnosis may indicate whether the dependence or addiction is active or in remission and whether the client is still using the substance.

If your psychotherapist indicates on Axis I that you have a substance-related disorder, he or she should explain to you exactly what it says. You will also want to know if your psychotherapist feels you need additional help besides psychotherapy. Substance abuse treatment or 12-step programs such as Alcoholics Anonymous or Narcotics Anonymous are often recommended.

Transgender-Related "Disorders"

To the ongoing shame of the American Psychiatric Association and the mental health profession in general, three diagnoses still officially classify transgendered children and adults as mentally ill. These diagnoses are listed below to help you—especially if you are transgender—understand precisely what they say.

Gender Identity Disorder of Adults (DSM 302.85) indicates that an individual strongly identifies as a member of the opposite sex. The person wants to dress, act, and live as a member of that sex, and feels and reacts as do members of that sex. The person no longer want to dress, act, or look like a member of the sex identified by his or her genetics or genitals. The individual may have a desire to take hormones to change his or her appearance, and may also want sexual reassignment surgery. This diagnosis was once called transsexualism.

Gender Identity Disorder of Children (DSM 302.6) covers the same basic criteria as gender identity disorder of adults, except the person being diagnosed is a child. The child either desires to be or insists that he or she is a member of the opposite sex. The child wishes to dress, act, and play as a member of the opposite sex. The child also wishes to primarily have friends of the opposite sex.

Transvestic Fetishism (DSM 302.3) is limited to heterosexual males who meet two criteria: They have an intense desire to dress in the clothes of women for sexual purposes, and this urge has caused them significant distress or impairment in their social functioning. Transvestic fetishism is sometimes accompanied by gender identity disorder of adults.

Kink-Related "Disorders"

As with transgender issues, the mental health profession has much to learn about human sexuality. Several specific disorders can be used to diagnose individuals who happen to engage in kinky sexual behaviors. Three of the more common disorders are listed below.

Fetishism (DSM 302.4): This "disorder" is recorded when an individual has, over a period of at least six months, experienced recurrent and intense behaviors and feelings of sexual arousal related to nonliving objects. The person must also feel distress about these feelings or believe they interfere with his or her social or work-related activities.

Sexual Masochism (DSM 302.83): This "disorder" is recorded when an individual has experienced over a period of at least six recurrent and intense fantasies, behaviors, or feelings of sexual arousal related to real (not simulated) humiliation, and/or being beaten, bound, or otherwise made to suffer. The individual or the clinician recording the diagnosis must also feel that these feelings or behaviors are causing difficulty socially or at work.

Sexual Sadism (DSM 302.84): This "disorder" is recorded when an individual has, over a period of at least six months, experienced recurrent and intense fantasies, behaviors, or feelings of sexual arousal related to the real (not simulated) physical or psychological humiliation or suffering of another person. The individual or the clinician recording the diagnosis must also feel that these feelings or behaviors are causing difficulty socially or at work.

The reason why transgender and kink-related diagnoses are usually inappropriate hinges on the individual's feelings of distress over his or her feelings or behaviors. Such feelings of distress are not, in my opinion, representative of a clinical disorder. What those feelings of distress *actually* indicate is that the individual has learned from others to feel shame over his or her transgender or kinky feelings. In a similar way, we are taught to feel shame about our homosexuality, though both society and the mental health community have generally progressed on this issue. The work of therapy in most cases *should* be to help the individual understand how misunderstood his or her feelings and experiences are, and how that training has caused the client to feel bad.

Axis II—Personality Disorders

Axis II describes personality disorders (and mental retardation). **Personality Disorders (DSM 301.xx)** differ from the clinical symptoms described on Axis I. Clinical symptoms describe behavior and moods that are in some way observable or measurable and thus are more or less based on objective information. Personality disorders are subjective evaluations by mental health professionals describing a client's traits.

A personality disorder diagnosis indicates that part of the foundation of an individual's personality is not what it should be. Personality disorders are general descriptions of maladaptive patterns of behavior, which tend to be enduring characteristics.

If someone has a personality disorder, the goal is usually to manage the disorder to minimize its effect on daily living. Very few mental health professionals claim they can "cure" someone of a personality disorder.

Personality disorders are controversial. They are difficult to research because there is widespread disagreement as to exactly what symptoms constitute them. Consequently, diagnosis is difficult, and no one really knows how prevalent such disorders are. Clinicians often disagree about whether an individual has a personality disorder and, if so, which one or ones. That there is great overlap between some of the personality disorders only confuses diagnoses more.

Rather than actually diagnosing a client as having a personality disorder, some clinicians indicate that an individual has traits similar to those of people with a particular personality disorder. This is a way of saying a client's symptoms and behavior lean toward a certain diagnosis but do not fully meet the criteria. Other clinicians might claim that an individual generally has the traits of a particular personality disorder, and that when faced with great stress, the individual shifts into the diagnosable category for that disorder.

A word of caution and hopefully comfort: You are not to blame for having a personality disorder if you actually do have one. You did nothing to cause it, nor is there anything you could have done to get rid of it. You do not have a personality disorder because you are not making a big enough effort to eliminate it.

The following paragraphs cover some of the more common personality disorders. This is not a complete list, nor have I included all of the diagnostic criteria for each personality disorder. This information is provided to give you a sense of what characterizes these disorders.

Borderline Personality Disorder

Borderline Personality Disorder (DSM 301.83) is somewhat misnamed. It is not on the borderline between any two diagnoses, nor does it mean someone is about to slip over a borderline. All personality disorders, including borderline personality disorder, are stable personality features and change little over time. More women than men are diagnosed with borderline personality disorders.

A borderline personality disorder diagnosis means the clinician has detected a general pattern of instability and impulsiveness in the client's life. This pattern is especially evident in interpersonal relationships, self-image, and affect. Abandonment is a constantly recurring theme in the client's life, and he or she generally makes frenzied efforts to avoid feeling abandoned. The client's relationships are often characterized by the extremes of idealization—whether putting a person on a pedestal or denigrating that person. At times, the client might find him or herself rapidly alternating between idolization and denigration. Impulsiveness often manifests itself as substance abuse, compulsive spending, or sexual compulsion. The client is frequently and inappropriately angry.

People with borderline personality disorders tend to be intense high-maintenance individuals. They do not step lightly in the world. You know they are there, because if you ignore them, you activate their feelings of abandonment, which in turn activate their rage. Eventually, someone will be the target of their anger.

People with borderline personality disorders are difficult clients. As a rule of thumb, many psychotherapists have no more than one or two clients with borderline personality disorders on their active caseload at any given time. Several therapists I know will only schedule someone with a borderline personality disorder as their last client of the day. These individuals are often very good at verbally assaulting people, including their therapist. Scheduling them at the end of a day gives the psychotherapist time to recover, if necessary, before meeting with other clients.

Narcissistic Personality Disorder

A Narcissistic Personality Disorder (DSM 301.81) diagnosis indicates the client has a grandiose sense of self-importance. The client thinks and acts as if he or she is the center of the world, or should be. He or she expects to be treated as special without necessarily having done anything to warrant such treatment. The individual has feelings of entitlement and expects special treatment and that his or her wishes will be satisfied. This person often takes advantage of others and lacks empathy.

Paranoid Personality Disorder

A **Paranoid Personality Disorder (DSM 301.0)** diagnosis indicates that the client has a pervasive mistrust of others. He or she is highly suspicious of others' motives, often believing those motives are malevolent. Without reasonable cause, the client suspects that others are deceitful, exploitative, or intending to cause him or her personal harm. Loyalty and trustworthiness preoccupy the client's thoughts. For example, he or she might continually entertain groundless suspicions about the sexual fidelity of his or her partner.

Obsessive-Compulsive Personality Disorder

An **Obsessive-Compulsive Personality Disorder (DSM 301.4)** diagnosis means the client's life is all about orderliness, perfectionism, and control—to the point where flexibility and openness to new or other ideas is lost. The client is preoccupied with rules, details, and schedules. His or her need for things to be perfect makes it hard to ever finish anything. Nevertheless, it is hard for obsessive-compulsive person to let anyone help, because then everything might not get done exactly as he or she ideally would like. People often view an obsessive-compulsive as miserly. Time and money are also big issues for this person. He or she can be quite rigid and stubborn too.

Dependent Personality Disorder

A **Dependent Personality Disorder (DSM 301.6)** diagnosis means that the client often feels a great and encompassing need to be taken care of by one or more people. This manifests itself as clinging behavior and a fear of separation. The client has difficulty making decisions without a lot of advice and reassurance.

Consequently, it is difficult for the individual to assume responsibility for his or her life. Fearing negative reactions, he or she often does not tell others about personal disagreements with them. The person lacks self-confidence. He or she may go to extremes to get nurturing and support. Being alone is difficult, since there is no one to tell the person what to do. And if a personal relationship ends, he or she will immediately start to look for another partner out of fear over being unable to take care of him or herself.

Antisocial Personality Disorder

An **Antisocial Personality Disorder (DSM 301.7)** diagnosis means the person feels the rules and laws that everyone else is supposed to follow do not apply to him or her. The individual will lie, cheat, scam, and misrepresent him or herself for his or her own profit or gain. This person is often impulsive, and probably has a history of being aggressive or fighting with others. He or she has been irresponsible, failed to follow through on promises, and may have lost many jobs. Most importantly, there is a lack of remorse for what the individual has done. He or she is indifferent to the suffering of others and has rationalized everything he or she has done as being all right. By most people's standards, this person lacks a conscience.

By nature, people with an antisocial personality disorder do not voluntarily seek psychotherapy. If they do find themselves involved in psychotherapy, it is usually because they have been coerced into being there, perhaps by a court order. As such, it is unlikely that anyone reading this book would be diagnosed with this disorder. You will, however, inevitably come into contact with people who exhibit these traits, and you should understand that they are playing by a different set of rules.

You should also be aware that it is common for someone with a personality disorder to find him or herself in a relationship with someone else who also has a personality disorder. Many people with other personality disorders will see antisocial personality disorder traits in their current or previous partners. In such situations, the first individual has almost certainly been victimized by the person with the antisocial personality disorder.

Histrionic Personality Disorder

An individual diagnosed as having a **Histrionic Personality Disorder (DSM 301.50)** is often seen by others as overly dramatic, with exaggerated expressions of emotion. Such a person is often called "theatrical." He or she is excessively emotional and wants to be the center of attention. Early on, this person learned to be sexually seductive to garner attention, and he or she consequently takes great care of his or her appearance. This person is easily influenced by events and other people—behavior that many view as shallow. Nevertheless, people diagnosed as having a histrionic personality disorder will sometimes surprise casual friends or acquaintances by confiding in all candidness that they believe their relationship to be special or even intimate.

Schizoid Personality Disorder

A person diagnosed as having a **Schizoid Personality Disorder (DSM 301.20)** lives in a bubble. In other words, this person has a general pattern of being disconnected from others. He or she has a narrow range of emotional expression that is particularly evident in relationships. Others see this person as cold, detached, or just flat.

Often labeled a loner by his or her peers, this person feels most comfortable with solitude. It is also often true that he or she may not actively desire sexual relationships, preferring instead to masturbate alone. He or she may not be especially interested in being part of a family and chooses to do things alone rather than with others. This person does not feel pleasure easily or often, staying a steady emotional course. He or she has few close friends and is reluctant to confide in other people, making only a few exceptions. In theory, this person may want a relationship, but in reality it is very hard for this person to let someone in. Psychotherapy is a safe place for this person to practice letting someone in.

AXIS III—GENERAL MEDICAL CONDITIONS

On Axis III, the clinician is asked to list all significant medical conditions that the client is experiencing. This is to help someone working with the client understand the "big picture" of his or her life. Sometimes what is put on Axis III is related to what appears on

Axis I. For instance, depression listed on Axis I may be caused by a diagnosis of AIDS, listed on Axis III.

AXIS IV—PSYCHOSOCIAL AND ENVIRONMENTAL PROBLEMS

On Axis IV, the clinician is asked to list all psychosocial and environmental problems that may have an impact on what appears on Axis I or II. What is listed on Axis IV may be the cause of the Axis I diagnosis, or it may affect how an individual is treated. Information listed on Axis IV is often related to situations at work, school, and in the client's social environment, or to issues of money, housing, medical care, legal proceedings, family, and relationships.

AXIS V—GLOBAL ASSESSMENT OF FUNCTIONING

On Axis V, the clinician is asked to make a judgement concerning how well the client is doing. The clinician is given a scale from 0 to 100, and descriptions for what those numbers indicate. A score between 51 and 60 indicates the psychotherapist believes the client is experiencing moderate symptoms, such as occasional panic attacks, or is having moderate difficulty socially, on the job, or at school such as having few friends or arguing with coworkers. A score from 61-70 indicates the client is having mild symptoms, such as occasional difficulty sleeping, but in general the person is functioning well. Scores higher than 70 indicate even better functioning. Scores less than 50, however, indicate serious problems.

With this assessment, the clinician is asked to give two numbers: one for how the client is doing right now, another to indicate the highest score the client would have had in the last year.

The score on Axis V is often critical to getting psychotherapy services approved by your HMO. Many HMOs will not authorize services for someone who scores higher than 60, saying such services are not *medically necessary.* Additionally, some HMOs feel their responsibility ends when the client has reattained a score equal to his or her highest level of functioning in the past year. HMOs seem to believe their job is to help you get back to where you were, rather than to achieve general mental health.

Chapter 15
Psychopharmacology

A popular advertising slogan in the recent past was "Better Living Through Chemistry." Several major drug manufacturers could easily reuse this slogan today. These companies advertise using actors to portray people whose lives have been completely changed by taking a certain drug, usually an antidepressant or antianxiety medication. It all seems so wonderful. But there is another side to the story.

Whether you should consider using psychoactive medication (medication that affects how you feel, think, and behave) is ultimately a personal question. There is no right answer for everyone, and that includes people who are experiencing similar symptoms. The determining factor is you. You will be the one taking the medication and dealing with the desired and undesired effects.

Medication does work, to some degree. To some extent, medication can cause you to feel, think, and act differently. There are benefits and costs to this. The question to ask is: Do the benefits outweigh the costs? The decision is yours. (It is rare for someone to be forced to take psychoactive medication against his or her will.) To make an informed decision requires an understanding of the role and effects of psychoactive medication.

America is obsessed with substances, legal or illegal, that alter the way we think, feel, and behave. This chapter will focus primarily on medications that are legal. Most require a prescription. Today, over 160 psychoactive drugs are approved by the Food and Drug Administration. More medications are in the research-and-development stage or are already being tested in clinical trials. Eventually, some will be approved and marketed. In short, psychoactive medication is big business, with revenues running into billions of dollars.

Besides prescription medications, there are nonprescription substances that have psychoactive effects, or so many claim. Some are sold as herbal remedies for anxiety, depression, sexual dysfunction, or other ailments. The most widely used over-the-counter psychoactive drug is one people rarely think of as a medication, but it is without doubt the mother of all substances that alter mind, mood, and behavior: alcohol. If alcohol could be turned into a pill that had the same effect on the mind and body as liquid alcohol, that pill would immediately be put on a restricted list. In addition, there are a number of illegal drugs that some people claim have therapeutic benefits.

We have been taught to both revere and fear the different medications our doctors can prescribe for us. When we have something physically wrong with ourselves, such as an infection, we turn to drugs as "miracle" cures. And in fact they sometimes are. Antibiotic drugs have saved millions of people from dying at a young age and generally have a positive reputation, though some will note their negative effects as well. For instance, it is believed that the overuse of antibiotics leads to mutations (and therefore stronger strains) of bacteria.

In the same way that we have been conditioned to believe antibiotics drugs make us physically strong, we have been taught that psychoactive drugs are needed by the morally or emotionally weak. Many drugs are revered. Psychoactive drugs are generally feared.

Only a physician—someone who has gone through medical school—may prescribe psychoactive drugs. Under the best of circumstances, the physician will be a psychiatrist—a physician specifically trained in psychopharmacology. Many psychoactive drugs are similar but differ in small ways. Psychiatrists are the people most knowledgeable about these differences. So while one's primary care physician can write a prescription for the same medications, the professional most qualified to do so is nearly always a psychiatrist. The majority of psychotherapists are not psychiatrists, so obtaining a prescription for a psychoactive drug often requires the services of a second clinician.

The Placebo Effect

Psychoactive drugs that have gone through the FDA approval process do work, and they tend to work well. If they are supposed to make us sleepy, they will do just that, if taken in the proper doses. If they are supposed to make us feel less depressed, that is usually the result.

To understand just how effective psychoactive medications are, you must first understand the placebo effect. If a group of people are helping to test a new drug during clinical trials, perhaps an antidepressant, half will take the drug, and half will take a placebo, a sugar pill that looks like the drug but has no psychotherapeutic effect. When researchers ask questions of the people who took placebo, usually between 30% and 50% report that they feel better and the "antidepressant" is working. Scientists know the change was not because they took an antidepressant but because they *believed* they took an antidepressant. Consequently, for a drug undergoing clinical trials to be approved from the FDA, much more than 30% to 50% of the study participants who actually received the drug must report that they feel better.

Intended and Unintended Effects

Now it is time to look at "the other side of the story." Rarely does any medication change us only in the way the scientists hoped. Medications often have unintended side effects, which are sometimes beneficial (and sometimes not). For example, Minoxidil became the standard prescription treatment for male pattern baldness after clinicians had noticed hair growth as a side effect when administering the drug to regulate high blood pressure.

Tricyclic antidepressants (discussed in detail later in this chapter) provide another instance of positive drug side effects. Besides treating depression, tricyclic drugs also help relieve symptoms of peripheral neuropathy. Many HIV-positive people take medications that cause peripheral neuropathy as an unintended side effect. When this happens, a tricyclic drug may be prescribed to treat the neuropathy.

But the success stories of Minoxidil and the tricyclics are far from the usual scenario. While some medications have side effects that are minor and easily tolerated or ignored, others can cause marked deterioration in the quality of a person's life. In such cases, that person cannot continue with the medication despite its benefits. A more likely situation occurs when a depressed person goes on an antidepressant such as Prozac, Paxil, or Zoloft, all of which belong to a class of antidepressants known as SSRIs (discussed in more detail later in this chapter). SSRIs do a good job of relieving depression but can have a major nasty side effect: For some people, SSRIs affect sexual functioning.

A significant number of the men who take SSRIs report feeling better, but they have a new difficulty regarding sex. Some have problems getting or maintaining erections. Others can get and maintain erections but are unable to have an orgasm. The drug might have made them less depressed, and for some that may mean being interested in sex for the first time in quite a while. Feeling sexual but having a sexual dysfunction can be so frustrating that some men elect to stop taking the SSRI antidepressant.

A good rule of thumb is that, unless there is an emergency, get a complete medical checkup before deciding to go on psychoactive medication. Some emotional problems have physical causes. A malfunctioning thyroid gland, for instance, can lead to the symptoms of depression. The cure for this is to treat the thyroid, not to take an antidepressant. So a medical checkup might prevent the wrong treatment from occurring. You should always discuss the possible use of psychoactive drugs with your primary therapist, especially if that individual is not the one prescribing the drugs.

Psychoactive Medications

Antidepressants

No antidepressant or class of antidepressants is any better at relieving the symptoms of depression than any other. There is no standout drug. The reasons for choosing one antidepressant over another have more to do with a drug's other therapeutic effects and unintended side effects than with its efficacy in relieving depression.

Expense sometimes factors into the equation. Insurance companies sometimes limit which prescription drugs they cover and often do not permit doctors to prescribe more expensive drugs. Two similar antidepressants can have a cost difference of over 500 percent.

Most of the antidepressants discussed below were originally developed to treat major depression. However, once a medication is approved by the FDA, physicians can use it to treat other conditions. Most of the people taking antidepressants are not taking them to treat major depression but to treat the milder forms of depression known as dysthymia. Some antidepressants are also used to treat various anxiety disorders.

If you decide to start treatment with an antidepressant, be prepared to stay on the medication for at least six months, at which time you should reevaluate whether to continue. Antidepressant medication generally takes several weeks to begin having a therapeutic effect, and often the therapeutic effectiveness slowly increases over a number of months. Discuss with the prescribing physician any disturbing unintended side effects you experience while taking the medication. He or she might want you to switch to another medication.

Selective Serotonin Reuptake Inhibitors (SSRIs)

SSRIs are among the most highly prescribed medication of any kind. SSRIs work in an area between the neurons of the brain called the synapse. SSRIs increases the amount of serotonin, a neurotransmitter, in the synapse. For reasons not fully understood, this relieves symptoms of depression for many people. Many SSRIs are also effective in treating anxiety, and one, Paxil, has been approved by the FDA for the treatment of panic disorders. Among the more common SSRIs are Celexa, Luvox, Paxil, Prozac, and Zoloft.

Of great concern to men and women who take SSRIs is the drug's adverse effect on sexual functioning. Early studies of the drug underreported sexual side effects. Recent studies suggest that about 50% of the men and women taking SSRIs will have some sexual dysfunction. Usually that turns out to be delayed orgasm. But erectile dysfunction and decreased libido, while less common, are also a concern.

A note of caution: These side effects usually occur at middle and higher level dosages. Lowering the dose can often decrease the sexual side effects. For some, the sexual side effects remit spontaneously. Other medications can sometimes lessen the side effects, and taking brief drug holidays can be helpful too.

Never stop taking an SSRI without consulting the physician who prescribed it. Otherwise, discontinuation syndrome might result, symptoms of which include headache, dizziness, tingling, and "electric shock sensations." While not life-threatening, they can be quite unsettling, and the prescribing physician should be able to address them effectively.

Tricyclic Antidepressants (TCAs)

TCAs are the oldest class of antidepressants, and for some people they remain the antidepressant of choice. They were discovered by accident. While TCAs were being tested as a medication that might cure tuberculosis, researchers noted that although the patients were not cured of tuberculosis, they became less depressed. Researchers later found that TCAs reduce depression by blocking the reuptake of the neurotransmitter norepinephrine. People taking TCAs often experience dry mouth. Constipation is another occasional unintended side effect. Weight gain is also common. Among the more common TCAs are Anafranil, Elavil, Norpramine, Pamelor, Sinequan, Surmontil, Tofranil, and Vivactil.

While most side effects are unwanted, occasionally they can be useful. As mentioned earlier, TCAs are used to treat people with peripheral neuropathy as a result of HIV medication. TCAs also tend to be constipating, which can help people suffering from diarrhea.

Monoamine Oxidase Inhibitors (MAOIs)

MAOIs first appeared in the 1950s. They work by preventing the breakdown of the neurotransmitter norepinephrine. Though once popular, MAOIs are rarely prescribed today. The biggest drawback to taking MAOIs pertains to the accompanying dietary restrictions. Foods that contain a high level of tyramine, such as wine and cheese, cannot be eaten. That is enough for many queer folk to reject MAOIs. Some common MAOIs are Nardil and Parnate.

Other Antidepressants

Wellbutrin: Wellbutrin is a popular antidepressant that prevents the reuptake of the neurotransmitter dopamine. Wellbutrin is also marketed under the name Zyban as an aide to stop smoking. The two drugs are identical and often prescribed in the same dosages. Wellbutrin is a popular antidepressant because it does not cause any sexual dysfunction, except in rare cases.

Effexor: Effexor is another new and increasing popular antidepressant that acts by inhibiting norepinephrine, serotonin, and dopamine reuptake.

Remeron: A new antidepressant, Remeron is usually prescribed when a person does not respond well to other antidepressants. It does not cause any sexual dysfunction; however, it does cause drowsiness. For individuals with a problem sleeping, this may be welcome. But the drowsiness may also occur during the day, making this medication problematic. Some people taking Remeron experience increased carbohydrate cravings leading to weight gains of five to 15 pounds. Remeron is less likely to interact with protease inhibitors than many other antidepressants—an advantage to HIV-positive people.

Desyrel: Also known by the generic name trazodone, Desyrel is another antidepressant that can be used as a sleep medication. An undesired side effect, although somewhat rare, is priapism: a condition in which a man gets an erection and cannot lose it. While that may seem like some men's ultimate fantasy, long-term damage to the penis can occur if priapism is not treated. Anyone who experiences priapism while taking Desyrel should immediately seek medical advice.

Serzone: A close cousin of Desyrel, Serzone increases REM (random eye movement) sleep and may be prescribed for that as well as its antidepressant properties. Serzone has no known effect on sexual functioning or weight changes.

Saint-John's-wort: A nonprescription medication often sold in health food stores, Saint-John's-wort does not have FDA approval to be marketed as an antidepressant. Many swear it works wonders, although just as many claim the opposite. HIV-positive people taking antiviral medication should not take Saint-John's-wort without first discussing it with their physician. Saint-John's-wort increases liver activity and, as a result, some antiviral HIV medications are processed out of the body more quickly, thus diminishing their effectiveness.

ANTIANXIETY MEDICATIONS

Antianxiety medications can be highly addictive. Therefore, all medications in this class should be taken only as needed, with the possible exceptions of azaspirones, certain medications for panic disorders, and L-Tryptophane.

Benzodiazepines

The class of medications known as benzodiazepines contains some of the most commonly prescribed medications. If you peeked inside peoples' medicine cabinets and looked at their prescriptions, you would find that more people have a benzodiazepine than any other class of psychoactive medication. Indeed, many people who rarely take any psychoactive medication like to keep a benzodiazepine on hand, just in case. The "just in case" usually means either anxiety or sleeplessness. Benzodiazepines are fast acting, so if you take a pill, you are likely to feel different within a short period of time.

Some people use benzodiazepines on a regular basis. If you are significantly anxious most of the time, or if you experience disabling anxiety in certain situations, you may want to consider benzodiazepines as a supplement to your psychotherapy program.

There are two problems with using benzodiazepines on a regular basis. The first is the sedation. If you are taking a benzodiazepine in order to function better, the sedative aspect will be unwelcome. The second and bigger danger is that benzodiazepines are potentially habit-forming. Some people become dependent even on low regular doses. When they stop or reduce the dosage, they experience withdrawal symptoms that are relieved only by taking additional amounts of benzodiazepine. If you have been taking a benzodiazepine on a regular basis and wish to stop or decrease the amount you are taking, consult your physician about how to gradually reduce the dosage and wean you off the medication.

A word of caution: Mixing a benzodiazepine and alcohol is dangerous and potentially lethal. Memory and functioning quickly become impaired. One beer may feel like four. Other effects include difficulty walking and slurred speech. Some people, particularly the elderly, experience memory impairment relating to the events that occur shortly after the benzodiazepine takes effect.

Short-acting benzodiazepines include Halcion, Serax, Versed, and Xanax. Mid-acting benzodiazepines include Ativan, Proscan, and Restoril. Long-acting benzodiazepines include Dalmane, Dizac, Librium, Traxene, and Valium.

Azaspirones

Azaspirones is the name for another class of medications commonly prescribed for anxiety. The most frequently prescribed medication is BuSpar, which interacts with the neurotransmitter serotonin. In contrast with the benzodiazepines, BuSpar is slow acting, nonsedative, and not considered habit-forming. For BuSpar to be effective, it needs to be taken regularly over a period of time. It is less sedative than benzodiazepines.

Nonprescription Medications

L-Tryptophane: A precursor of the neurotransmitter serotonin, L-Tryptophane naturally occurs in such foods as milk and turkey. Some people believe the presence of L-Tryptophane is why warm milk and Thanksgiving dinner are generally considered sleep-inducing. L-Tryptophane is sold in health food and drug stores. Though it does not have FDA approval, it has a devoted following who value it as a medication for anxiety and sleep.

MOOD STABILIZERS

Mood stabilizers are medications intended to help people diagnosed with bipolar disorder (formerly known as manic depression). They control the manic phase of this disorder but do not effect depression. Like other psychoactive drugs, they must be taken on a regular basis. Most people on these medications will be taking them indefinitely. People diagnosed as bipolar need to have an expert—a psychiatrist rather than a primary care physician—managing their medication. Some who experience bipolar mood swings may need both a mood stabilizer and an antidepressant. An antidepressant alone might send that person into a manic episode. Anyone diagnosed as bipolar must be very careful about which medications he or she is taking and when the dosages are consumed.

Mood stabilizers also help some people who appear to experience only depression and are already taking an antidepressant. The mood stabilizer gives a boost to an antidepressant that may not be working fully. Mood stabilizers can also be helpful in treating some of the subtler forms of bipolar disorder. The most commonly prescribed mood stabilizers are Lithium, Tegretol, and Depakote.

SEDATIVES

In virtually every culture, people for centuries have known that ingesting certain substances causes sedation. There are references to sleeping potions in Shakespeare's plays and other literary works from hundreds of years ago. A rule of thumb for any sedative is that it should be taken as little as possible.

The pharmaceutical industry has produced a wide variety of sleep-inducing medications. Some have serious and dangerous unintended side effects; others are relatively safe. But no sleep-inducing medication is free from unwanted effects.

Barbiturates are a class of medications that enable people to fall asleep and stay asleep. These drugs work spectacularly well but cause many complications. Seconal is perhaps the best-known drug in this class. If you swallow a Seconal, it is likely that soon afterward you will become very tired and fall asleep for a number of hours.

Foremost among the problems associated with barbiturates is that they are seriously habit-forming. And barbiturate addiction is difficult to treat. *No one who has been taking barbiturates regularly should stop cold turkey.* Doing so can cause seizures or even be fatal. A person dependent on barbiturates must be weaned off them under the care of a physician, preferably in a 24/7 detox program.

Another problem with barbiturates is how powerful they are. If one night you take a barbiturate to help you sleep, you are likely to feel tired or washed-out the next day. Enough of the drug stays in your system to affect you for a long time. Even worse, barbiturates can be fatal all by themselves. Many people have killed themselves, intentionally or unintentionally, by taking barbiturates. As such, physicians are reluctant to prescribe these medications to people who are depressed and cannot sleep. It is too easy for a depressed person to use barbiturates to commit suicide.

Barbiturates are also potentially deadly when combined with other psychoactive substances, particularly alcohol. Relatively small amounts of alcohol combined with equally small amounts of barbiturates are a fatal combination. This is known as *potentiation,* a process wherein one chemical multiplies the effect of another. Barbiturates potentiate with numerous medications. Because of the danger, barbiturates are rarely prescribed unless all other sedative choices have been exhausted. Some common barbiturates are Nembutal, Seconal, and Tuinal.

Many nonbarbiturate sleep-inducing medications are available. But again, once you get used to taking them, it becomes difficult to sleep without them. If you do stop taking them, it sometimes becomes necessary to take other medications to counteract insomnia induced by drug withdrawal.

Nonbarbiturate sedatives all differ in some ways. Some stay in your system longer than others—a desired or undesired effect, depending on your needs. Some common nonbarbiturate sleep medications are Ambien, Soma, and two benzodiazepines, Halcion and Restoril.

ANTIPSYCHOTICS

Psychosis is a condition of being disconnected from reality as most people perceive it. Signs of psychosis include hallucinations, either visual or auditory, delusions or extremely abnormal personal affect, such as a flat zombie-like attitude or inappropriate silliness or giggling. Such symptoms can be brought on by drugs such as methamphetamine, cocaine, or PCP. Most people who show these symptoms, though, experience them as a result of schizophrenia or some other serious emotional condition.

Most antipsychotic medications work by blocking the action of the neurotransmitter dopamine. Medications commonly prescribed for psychosis are Haldol, Loxitane, Mellaril, Moban, Navane, Orap,

Prolixin, Serentil, Stelazine, Thorazine, Trilafon, and Zyprexa.

Antipsychotic medications have many side effects, which often need to be counteracted by taking other medications. Some people, particularly younger men, initially react to these medications with muscles spasms in the head and neck. Their tongues may stick out, and they also may drool. Other medications quickly relieve these symptoms and are usually prescribed along with the antipsychotic. As many as one third of all people taking antipsychotic medications will develop symptoms similar to Parkinson's Disease, including shaking and trembling. Three quarters of those who regularly take antipsychotic medications develop akathisia, a condition character-ized by feeling restless, agitated, jumpy, and unable to sit still. Others develop akinesia, which resembles depression. And, after being on antipsychotic medication for several years, some people develop tardive dyskinesia, which involves involuntary movements.

For many people, the decision of whether to take antipsychotic medication is a choice between the lesser of two evils: living with the side effects or living with psychosis. Many people begin taking antipsychotic medication, stop when the side effects become too difficult to live with, and then find themselves back in an intolera-ble psychotic state. At that point, they must choose which set of symptoms is easiest to endure.

OTHER DRUGS AND TREATMENTS

Viagra: Viagra is the first FDA-approved medication for men who experience erectile dysfunction, or inability to get or maintain an erection. It increases blood flow into the penis, making it easier to maintain an erection. Viagra does nothing to increase sexual desire, but it does make sexual functioning easier.

Viagra was initially marketed for men who had physical problems that caused erectile dysfunction, such as diabetes. At the same time, it was made known that Viagra also works for men who experienced erectile dysfunction because of anxiety, stress, or other emotional problems. Viagra is also prescribed for men experiencing erectile dysfunction as a result of taking an SSRI antidepressant. Some men with no erectile difficulty occasionally take Viagra for pleasure.

Viagra interacts negatively with nitrites, a class of medications given to people with heart problems. Combining the two can be fatal. Two forms of nitrites, amyl nitrite and butyl nitrite, more commonly known as poppers, are used by many people, especially gay men, as a sexual stimulant. Combining poppers and Viagra is contraindicated. Viagra and nitrites should *never* be used within 24 hours of each other.

Marijuana: Marijuana has been an illegal drug for about 70 years. In recent years, though, a number of states have legalized marijuana for medical purposes. The legality of these measures remains controversial because there are still federal laws against growing, selling, and possessing marijuana. Various disputes over the legalization of marijuana are now working their way through the legal and political system.

Despite medicinal marijuana's uncertain legal status, there are places where it is sold openly with a doctor's prescription. The usual reason for the prescription is medical: pain, sleeplessness, decreased appetite resulting from a medical condition such as AIDS, cancer, arthritis, glaucoma, or other illnesses. Some physicians, especially if they subscribe to the medical model, are willing to prescribe marijuana for emotional conditions,

Because marijuana has been illegal for so long and has not undergone the FDA approval process, relatively little credible scientific research exists about its effects or its efficacy in treating various ailments. Most of what is known is anecdotal. Because of the controversy surrounding the legalization of medicinal marijuana, only certain physicians are willing to prescribe it and monitor an individual while he or she is taking it.

Ecstasy: Ecstasy is an illegal drug that some claim has a positive therapeutic effect. It is a mild hallucinogen related to amphetamines. If you obtain it on the black market, there is no way to know if you are getting the drug in its pure state or a bastardized form, let alone what the strength of the drug is. There are no scientific studies of the effectiveness of ecstasy in treating emotional conditions. All stories of its therapeutic benefits are anecdotal.

Electroconvulsive Treatment: Electroconvulsive Treatment (ECT) is an extremely controversial treatment for debilitating depression that involves sending electrical shocks to the brain. It is not a psychoactive medication, but I have chosen to include it in this chapter because it is a psychoactive treatment. ECT involves the administration of various sedative medications, some of which are psychoactive, in addition to the electroconvulsive treatment. ECT must be administered by physicians in a hospital setting. It is a treatment only used for severe and intractable cases of major depression, and even then, only after all alternatives have failed.

ECT has a bad reputation, dating back to the 1950s, when ECT was last popular. At that time, people were not given muscle relaxing medications before the procedure, and high dosages of electrical shocks were administered. Patients often had severe convulsions as a result. Since they were strapped to an operating table, the convulsions would sometimes break people's bones. Thus, the popularity of ECT waned.

Today, however, ECT is back. Smaller amounts of electricity are used, and the patient is given muscle relaxants and anesthesia. Most people do not remember the procedure. In fact, one of the unintended effects of ECT is short-term memory loss. It is not unusual for someone undergoing ECT to not remember several days before and after the treatment. ECT treatment may involve six to 12 sessions over the course of a month, so it is possible for an entire month to be wiped clean from a person's memory.

Clearly, this is a high price to pay. Consequently, ECT is used only as a last resort, when the only other option is living in a long-term vegetative state, unable to function. In those circumstances, the gains from ECT outweigh the losses. Many people who have undergone ECT have made public testimonials to its effectiveness.

It is difficult for someone with a major depression to make an informed decision regarding ETC. Quite simply, that person is too depressed to consider the ramifications. If you are prone to major depressions, the time to contemplate ECT is *not* when you are in the throes of a severe depressive episode.

There are some people for whom ECT is contraindicated, particularly those suffering from heart disease or seizure disorders. Otherwise, it is a tool in the treatment arsenal—a powerful tool with many negative effects.

Chapter 16
Boundaries

Your psychotherapist may be friendly but is not your friend. Your psychotherapist should not act or treat you as a friend, nor should he or she expect you to act or treat him or her as a friend. Your psychotherapist is not your business partner, customer, banker, client, or lover. Psychotherapists are mental health professionals who are expected to treat you—and expect be treated by you—as someone with whom they have a working relationship.

The relationship between a therapist and a client is special. Few relationships resemble it. The client talks openly about thoughts, feelings, and experiences while the therapist shares little similar information. Because clients can and often do open up in therapy, they tend to be much more emotionally vulnerable than their psychotherapists. Psychotherapists are ethically bound not to abuse this vulnerability. Therefore, psychotherapists are expected to limit their relationships with clients to psychotherapist/client interactions. Any other kind of relationship is improper.

One reason why states license therapists is to ensure their professional behavior meets acceptable ethical standards. The state has an interest in seeing that its citizens are protected. States attempt, through the licensing process, to make sure all therapists are aware of the potential for harm they possess. Consequently, therapists have pondered at length the boundaries of the therapy relationship: what is acceptable, what is unacceptable, and where the boundary is unclear and needs to be further discussed.

A maxim of the medical and mental health professions is: First, do no harm. *All that is said or done by the therapist is supposed to be for the therapeutic benefit of the client.* As such, the therapist is restricted from saying or doing certain things with a client that might be acceptable with someone who is not a client.

A small example is going to dinner with a client. It is far from unethical for a music teacher, an accountant, or a plumber to go to dinner and share a bottle of wine with a client. However, it is inappropriate for a therapist to do so. The only exception is if the therapist is doing this specifically as part of a therapy program. For instance, a client who experiences agoraphobia, an irrational fear of leaving home, might be seeing a therapist who takes a behavioral approach. That therapist may try to help the client use relaxation techniques in certain situations and might even accompany the client to a restaurant as part of therapy.

It was not always this way. Sigmund Freud, the grandfather of modern psychotherapy, sometimes invited a patient to have dinner with his family and even accompany them on summer vacations. He would, on occasion, become quite involved in and controlling of aspects of a patient's life. This was considered acceptable behavior at the time.

One hundred years later, standards have changed because of greater knowledge of what is therapeutic for a client as well as what has been learned about therapists abusing their contact with clients. This awareness has led to the expectation that psychotherapists will maintain a reasonable boundary between themselves and clients. If a therapist today did as Freud did, inviting clients to dinner and on vacations, that therapist would likely be accused of unethical behavior.

No Dual Relationships

The basic rule that all psychotherapists have agreed to follow is this: There are to be no dual relationships between psychotherapists and their clients. The only relationship a psychotherapist is to have with a client is the therapy relationship. The two are not supposed to hang out together. No business partnerships are permitted. Psychotherapists are not allowed to borrow money from or lend money to a client. Psychotherapists and clients are not to behave sexually toward each other—ever!

The responsibility for maintaining ethical boundaries rests with the psychotherapist. The client can ask to go into business with the therapist or even sexually proposition the therapist. The therapist is expected to say "no." Inappropriate contact between psychotherapists and clients is the most common reason psychotherapists lose their license to practice.

The boundaries seem clear, but in real life there are a number of situations, some particular to the queer community, in which the boundaries are hazy. Here is where good judgment should prevail. It is inevitable that psychotherapists and clients will in the course of normal activity find themselves interacting in some way outside of the therapy hour. When that happens, the therapist and client need to determine if that interaction goes beyond the acceptable boundary of psychotherapist/client interaction.

This can be particularly problematic within the queer community. Queer people tend to interact with other queer people. A queer person who lives in a predominantly queer neighborhood might buy food from a queer grocer, receive medical treatment from a queer doctor, take dance classes restricted to same-sex couples, and attend a queer-friendly church. Queer people also tend to see queer psychotherapists. It would not be unusual for a queer person to see his or her psychotherapist in line at the grocers, sitting in a doctor's waiting room, in a dance class, or at church.

The first three examples can be easily handled. The client and therapist might say hello at the grocers, nod in acknowledgment at the doctor's office, or make sure not to dance with each other. The church situation could pose more of a challenge. What if they both wound up on the same church committee? What if they were elected officers of the church and needed to have frequent contact regarding church matters? Would the psychotherapist be expected to resign? The answers are not always clear.

WHETHER TO SAY HELLO OUTSIDE OF THERAPY

Regardless of the size of the city you live in and regardless of whether you and your psychotherapist move in some of the same social, economic, religious, or political circles, it is likely that sometimes you will run into each other outside the therapy setting. If you and your therapist are alone when this happens, it is easier to handle than when you are with others.

It may seem like a simple courtesy for you and your therapist to merely say hello, but it is not that easy. The issue of confidentiality interferes with your therapist being able to say hello to you. The fact that you are his or her client is as confidential as what you say during the therapy hour. The rule regarding confidentiality is this: You can say whatever you want about being in therapy, but your therapist may not say anything about it without your permission.

If you and your therapist are alone, it is OK to say hello, although your therapist may let you initiate contact. If you are not alone, your therapist should not initiate contact, although you may do so if you wish. The therapist will not initiate contact because he or she does not want to put you in the awkward position of explaining how you know him or her. If your therapist is not alone, the same rule applies: You may initiate contact, but your therapist should not. Keep in mind that if you do say hello, and the person with your therapist asks how he or she knows you, your therapist is boxed in by confidentiality and will be forced either to lie or answer evasively. You should also keep in mind that an evasive answer, such as "I can't say," is in reality far less evasive than either you or your therapist would prefer. It is easy to deduce from such an answer that you are a client of that therapist.

If you and your therapist are likely to cross paths, it might be wise to discuss the best way for the two of you to handle the situation. Reaching an understanding while in the office will help you avoid awkward situations outside the office.

Telephone Contact

One area that sometimes causes difficulty is telephone contact between clients and therapists. The question is not whether telephone contact is permissible. It is. The question is how much contact is permissible and under what circumstances.

Most therapists have little telephone contact with their clients.

If there is telephone contact, it is usually business related: Perhaps one of them is ill and cannot make it to the next session. A minority of psychotherapists encourage telephone contact for issues related to therapy.

Susan is a good example of a psychotherapist making proactive use of telephone contact. A directive therapist, she often gives clients homework assignments to complete between sessions. When a client comes to a session without having completed an assignment because it seemed too difficult, Susan's typical response is "Why didn't you call me?" The same is true when a client reports that his or her last session was so depressing that he or she went home and vegetated the entire week, hardly leaving the house.

Robert, a psychotherapist with a background and orientation similar to Susan's, takes a different approach. He is not available for phone contact unless there is a major emergency. The time for contact is during the therapy hour. If a client calls and says he or she is depressed and needs to talk—even just a little—Robert suggests making an additional appointment. From his perspective, if it is serious enough to call him, it is serious enough to warrant an extra appointment.

Susan tends to return her phone calls almost immediately. She checks her answering machine several times a day, even when she is not in the office. Robert checks his answering machine once a day when away from the office, and will only return a call immediately if the client indicates it is an emergency. Otherwise, Robert might not return a phone message received on Saturday until he returns to the office on Monday.

More therapists are like Robert than like Susan. Most therapists want to deal with their clients during the therapy hour, and generally do not encourage other contact. The only way to know for sure is to ask your therapist about his or her boundaries regarding telephone contact.

Sex With Therapists

Sex between a therapist and a client is a special boundary issue that has clear rules. It is never permissible for a therapist to have sexual contact with a client—no excuses, no exceptions. And sex is not restricted to sexual intercourse or even oral sex. Sex with a therapist can be touching the sexual organs, touching to arouse sexual feelings, or verbal contact designed to arouse sexual feelings. The no sex rule should be interpreted in the most conservative manner. If it seems even remotely like sexual contact, it is strictly off-limits.

That said, there are a number of situations, in the queer community especially, that require further discussion.

HUGS

Is a hug at the beginning or end of a therapy hour sexual? The answer can be yes or no. We have all given and received hugs that were nonsexual, and we have all experienced hugs that were sexual. Usually we can distinguish, but some hugs leave us wondering. And therein lies the problem.

Whether to hug a client is somewhat controversial in the world of queer psychotherapy. In the 1970s, in the early years of the queer liberation movement, hugs between clients and psychotherapists were common. But this is no longer the 1970s, and attitudes have changed. A more conservative attitude toward physical contact between psychotherapists and clients has taken root, encouraged by licensing and ethics boards. Since it is difficult to prove whether a hug was nonsexual, many therapists avoid hugging clients. Understandably, they are concerned they may lose their license if a client accuses them of making sexual advances in the form of hugs. The fact is, while a hug may seem innocent from the point of view of the therapist, the therapist does not know how the client is reacting inside, whether the client feels sexually taken advantage of or sexually aroused by the hug.

Furthermore, some schools of psychotherapy maintain that hugs between a therapist and a client are inappropriate. The psychoanalytic school, for instance, limits many forms of contact with clients. A psychoanalytic psychotherapist will almost never hug a client.

If you have issues with your therapist hugging or not hugging you, you should definitely discuss them in the therapy hour.

Sex Clubs, Bathhouses, Sex Parties, Cruising, and Cybersex

Of particular interest to the queer psychotherapy community is what to do if a client meets his or her psychotherapist at a sex club, bathhouse, sex party, cruising area, or on the Internet. The mental health community has not sufficiently dealt with this issue. There have been very few discussions of this subject. Indeed, when I polled my colleagues on this matter, I found widely different ideas as to what is acceptable and what is over the line. Until the boundaries become clearer, if you run into your psychotherapist in a sexual setting, you will have to deal with it individually with your psychotherapist. To show how confusing this can be for you, the client, consider the following.

Philip, a clinical social worker in private practice in a large city, told me about the last time he went to a sex club. "It was in the early 1980s, and we were just learning about HIV. I decided to go to a jerk-off party at a sex club where I could have a little quick and safe fun with other guys. Basically, I just wanted to get off and go home.

"I had my hard dick out and was stroking it when I looked up and saw that one of the guys who had come over and was watching was a client I had been seeing in individual therapy for quite a while. I quickly zipped my pants, nodded hello, and went home.

"Later that week, I had my next scheduled appointment with the client, and we talked about the meeting. It profoundly affected him. He said he couldn't get the image of me stroking my hard dick out of his mind. He said it was upsetting, like seeing your parents having sex. After talking about this for the next month, it became apparent that he needed to stop seeing me as a client. Seeing me in that situation was confusing and upsetting for him. That was the last time I ever went to a sex club. The negative cost to the client was too great. I didn't want anyone else to have to go through that."

This view is not shared by all queer psychotherapists. Mitchell, a psychologist in private practice who is also the part-time director of a substance abuse program, is an example. "I occasionally go to sex clubs," he told me. "I believe clients need to understand that therapists are people and have a life outside of the office. That includes being sexual. I'm not in a relationship, so I don't have a regular sex partner. I also like going out and meeting new guys and getting it on.

"I've never to my knowledge run into any of my clients, but I imagine it will happen eventually. If it does, we'll talk about it. If the client can't deal with it, it may mean the fit between us is not a good one. This is a part of my life that I need for my own mental health."

Leroy, a licensed marriage and family therapist in private practice, offered a third opinion. "I wouldn't go to a sex club in the city in which I practice. It is too likely that sooner or later I will run into a client, and I don't want to deal with the impact of that. I am also afraid that somehow it will come back to haunt me, that I will be reported to my licensing board, which would not understand what is normal in the gay community. I don't want to risk that. My life is stressful enough as is.

"But I have always liked bathhouses and sex clubs. When I go on vacation to a city at least 500 miles from where I practice, I feel it is OK to go to a bathhouse or sex club. In fact, it is usually one of the first things I do. I often plan my vacation around being able to go to a bathhouse or sex club. If it should happen that I see a client, I figure we will talk about it later in therapy."

There are other issues as well. What should a client do if he or she sees his or her therapist engaging in sexual acts in a sex club, and the therapist does not see the client? Or, what should the client do if he or she has some direct sexual contact with his or her therapist in a dark sex club before recognizing who his or her partner is? The answers are not clear.

It is also not uncommon in the queer community for there to be privately arranged sex parties. These parties also exist in the non-queer community. If a psychotherapist is invited to attend and does so, and later in the evening, while he or she is engaging in sex with another person at a party, a client comes in, how is such a situation to be handled?

The ethical rules that do exist say that it would be proper for the psychotherapist to stop engaging in sex, get dressed, and probably leave. The client is not obliged to leave. Such a situation, should it occur, should definitely be discussed at the next therapy session.

Local cruising areas present similar issues and should be handled in a similar fashion.

The development of the Internet and cybersex presents a whole new set of boundary issues. Cybersex, two people using the Internet type messages of a sexual nature for purposes of arousal, can be done anonymously. Usually, each person uses a pseudonym. Sometimes, though, the communication involves the sending of pictures, often in anticipation of meeting in person. Thus, a therapist can inadvertently have cybersex with a client. And if pictures are later exchanged, the result can be devastating.

This issue is so new that it has not yet been addressed by the organizations that set ethical standards for psychotherapists. It is clear, though, that a therapist should never knowingly have cybersex with a client or someone who may be a client.

If this happens to you, once again, it should be discussed at the first appropriate opportunity.

When Do the Boundaries End?

The boundaries between psychotherapists and their clients definitely apply while the client is seeing a psychotherapist. But if the client stops seeing a psychotherapist, does that mean the boundary disappears? If a client and a psychotherapist agree to end their therapy relationship on a Friday, are they free to date each other on Saturday? The answer is no.

Once again, the client/psychotherapist relationship is considered special. The relationship is considered to go beyond the last session. But all things do end, including the restrictions on client/psychotherapist contact. The question is how long you must wait before your therapist can become your friend, lover, or business partner.

There is no rule that covers all situations. But there is a guideline that may be of help: From the last official meeting with your psychotherapist, the psychotherapist should wait at least two years before beginning any other type of relationship with you. This two-year rule is a *minimum*. If you have been in long-term therapy with a particular therapist, you should wait longer. In certain situations, boundaries may remain in place for life.

Thus, if a psychotherapist proposes any nontherapeutic relationship with you less than two years after the last time the two of you had a psychotherapy session, the psychotherapist is being inappropriate. There are no exceptions to this. The only question is whether the two of you should wait longer than two years.

If you saw a therapist only once, perhaps as an intake worker at a clinic, and two years later the two of you meet on the Internet looking for dates, it *may* be OK for the therapist to date you, depending on how attached you felt to that therapist. If you saw a therapist for a short time 20 years ago, and now you find both of you are prospective partners in a business deal involving many people, it *may* be ethically appropriate for your former therapist to become your business partner.

However, if the two of you saw each other regularly for any significant length of time, it is never OK, in my opinion, for your therapist to become your friend, lover, or business partner. As said earlier, the two-year rule is only a minimum.

Chapter 17
Alternatives to Psychotherapy

Psychotherapy is not the answer to everything for everyone. And it is not the only way. Beware of anyone who tells you otherwise. Psychotherapy is a tool, but it is not the only tool. It is a tool to be used in conjunction with the rest of your life. If there is not much in the rest of your life, that is part of the problem.

If many of us gave the same thoughtful care to our lives and personal happiness as we give to our automobiles, we might have a better life. Most people take their cars to a mechanic for periodic maintenance. The same cannot always be said for our bodies and minds. Mechanics use a variety of tools to keep our cars in top shape. The same can be true for us. This chapter presents information about tools other than psychotherapy that may be of help.

Spiritual Practices

Many of the forms of psychotherapy described in this book have their origins in spiritual practices. The first professional psychotherapists were undoubtedly spiritual leaders. They combined their understanding of human nature, behavior, and interactions with their religious philosophies to come up with an approach to living that, at least in theory, helped people live happier and more meaningful lives.

Most spiritual practices today also combine an approach to theology with an approach to living. The approach to theology differs, of course, from one religion or spiritual practice to another. It is the approach to living, however, that is important for mental health.

Most of these approaches have been time-tested. They contain directives on how to treat yourself, your family, and others.

Some caution must be used with spiritual practices because many of the underlying theologies do not understand what it means to be queer. This is, however, changing. The progressive wings of the mainstream Protestant and Jewish religions, for instance, have radically altered their stances on queer people. But there is still progress to be made.

Relaxation Techniques

You cannot be tense and relaxed at the same time. These physical and emotional states are opposite sides ends of the spectrum. If you tend toward anxiety, anything you can do to relax will help you to have a better life. Relaxation techniques can also help those who tend toward depression, compulsive activity, and other symptoms of distress.

Meditation

Many religious and secular practices utilize meditation. The major Eastern and Western religions all have meditation practices going back hundreds, sometimes thousands of years. And new meditation techniques are being developed all the time, although most still are variations on established meditation practices.

In its most basic form, meditation is sitting still, breathing, and perhaps a little more. In some meditation practices, you concentrate on a mantra (a word or phrase). In others, you concentrate on your breathing. In still others, you try to clear your mind of conscious thought and then are mindful of what comes to you while meditating. Some people use the word *sitting* as a synonym for meditation.

If you are in a major city, you will find a number of different meditation practices nearby. If you are comfortable with the religion in which you were raised, that is perhaps a place to start to investigate meditation. If you are not comfortable with the religion of your birth, or if you were not raised with a religious orientation, then choose any style that appeals to you. All major bookstores carry books on meditation practices.

YOGA

Yoga involves meditation but also much more. It is an approach to life that includes physical exercise, proper nutrition, spiritual practices, and meditation. Many people are attracted to yoga for the physical exercise alone, but the effects of that exercise are not merely physical. Yoga exercises are also calming. It is rare for someone to exit a yoga class in a tense state.

There are several ways to become involved in yoga. Perhaps the best is to take classes for beginners. The instructor can teach you basic yoga techniques in a way that minimizes the risk of injury associated with doing the exercises incorrectly. Second best is to watch videotapes showing the proper positions. If both of those options are unavailable to you, there are books on yoga.

Once you learn yoga exercises, they can be done almost anywhere at any time. People who are near you may not even realize you are doing yoga exercises. Closely tied in with the physical exercises are breathing exercises that can also be done anywhere at anytime. The breathing exercises are calming in stressful situations.

ACUPUNCTURE AND ACUPRESSURE

Acupuncture and acupressure were developed in China over thousands of years. In the past quarter century, these practices have become popular in the West. Acupuncture involves the insertion of thin needles into specific parts of the body. Acupressure is a very specific massage technique, although this description oversimplifies it. Both acupuncture and acupressure are used to heal physical problems as well as relieve tension. For either treatment, you will need to go to a licensed or certified practitioner of these techniques.

MASSAGE

A good old-fashioned massage is another way to soothe the savage beast inside of you. The approach to psychotherapy known as bodywork is derived from massage. Massage techniques vary. Some involve lightly manipulating your muscles, while others are considerably more forceful. At the end of a massage, most people are in a state of relaxation that usually lasts at least several hours.

Self-Help Groups

Self-help groups are integral to the mental health programs of many people involved in psychotherapy. Such support groups can supplement individual therapy, or they may constitute the central focus of a client's program with psychotherapy as secondary. They may even be a client's entire mental health program.

Self-help groups are not led by mental health professionals. They are nonprofit groups of people with a common interest who come together to provide understanding, knowledge, support, and other forms of assistance. Self-help is based on two concepts. One is that the best—and sometimes the only—person who can effectively offer help is someone who shares a common experience (such as addiction) with the individual needing assistance. The other is that there is power in a group that can be used to help members individually.

12-Step Programs

The most widely known self-help programs are 12-step programs through which people dealing with addictions come together to help each other remain clean and sober. Alcoholics Anonymous and Narcotics Anonymous are well known, but there are also a huge number of lesser-known 12-step organizations that usually focus on one drug in particular, such as methamphetamine or cocaine. Many of these organizations have counterpart self-help groups for partners, family members, and friends of the addict. Al Anon, for partners, family members, and friends of alcoholics is the best-known of these counterpart groups.

Many other kinds of 12-step programs can help people with destructive personal behaviors. Overeaters Anonymous, Overspenders Anonymous, Sex and Love Addicts Anonymous, and Sexual Compulsives Anonymous are but a few. Again, counterpart organizations usually exist for partners, family members, and friends.

Twelve-step programs are often queer-friendly. They stay focused on the issue that brings their members together. They do not take political positions, nor do they endorse or ally themselves with other organizations. While AA has a distinct spiritual component, it is nondenominational. Being queer is not relevant. If you are an alcoholic and have a sincere desire to stop drinking, you are welcome at Alcoholics Anonymous.

An integral part of 12-step programs is sharing personal stories. More nonqueer people hear about the lives of queer people at 12-step programs than at any other venue.

Twelve-step programs support a healthy approach to life, and they can benefit queer people in other ways. For instance, 12-step meetings, especially those in queer neighborhoods, are good places to meet other queer people. People attending 12-step meetings might go out for coffee after the meetings or get together for weekend activities where they continue to give one another social and emotional support.

There is also a mentoring component to 12-step programs. One member asks another member to be his or her sponsor. Usually, the sponsor has been in the program longer than the member to be sponsored. Their relationship is not unlike the relationship between a psychotherapist and a client. The sponsor tries to help the other 12-stepper stay sober by being available to talk about needs, concerns, and feelings as well as offer a more seasoned perspective on recovery.

If a program member needs help, sponsors and other members of the program are generally willing to be available at times when virtually no psychotherapist can be reached, such as in the middle of the night or dinnertime on Christmas Day.

The 12 steps refer to 12 ideas that were first developed by Alcoholics Anonymous and are now widely copied by other 12-step programs. The 12 steps involve a series of self-acknowledgments and actions based on those acknowledgments. It is not required that members accept or follow the 12 steps, but members are encouraged to keep an open mind regarding the accumulated wisdom the steps represent.

Agnes

Agnes is a good example of a lesbian with an alcohol problem whom 12-step groups helped. She was born into a family of heavy drinkers and could not remember an occasion—happy, sad, or otherwise—when the adults in the family did not drink. Agnes liked the smell, taste, and effect of alcohol. It made her feel liberated and powerful. When she drank, she became more aggressive in her flirting with women, and she liked that.

For 20 years Agnes drank heavily. She never lost a job because of her drinking, but she did lose several lovers. The turning point came when she reached 40. She drank heavily at her birthday party and had a blackout. After that, her blackouts became more frequent, and that scared her.

After thinking about it for a long time, Agnes called a friend who had become sober several years before. With her friend as a guide, Agnes began to attend AA meetings, found a sponsor, and had a relatively easy time starting to live a sober life. Her 12-step work helped her psychotherapy progress at a much faster pace. She became able to admit to herself the negative impact that alcohol had in her life.

Arnold

Arnold had a much more difficult time staying clean and sober. Alcohol was never a big factor in Arnold's life, so for years he never thought of himself as having a substance abuse problem.

In his 20s, Arnold had become attracted to the gay nightclub scene. On Friday or Saturday nights, Arnold went to dance clubs. Although he had been a moderate marijuana smoker in college, he generally shied away from other drugs. But Arnold soon found himself doing many different drugs, and one in particular, speed (also known as crystal or methamphetamine), was his favorite. He loved how it made him feel while dancing or having sex.

Arnold's use of speed increased over time. He became HIV-positive as a result of a night of unsafe sex and speed. He sought therapy to deal with the depression he believed was a result of becoming HIV-positive, but he was surprised when his therapist told him his depression was also related to his use of speed.

Arnold would not give up speed, but at his therapist's suggestion he did agree to take part in a harm-reduction program aimed at gay male users of speed. But he soon left the program, claiming it was for losers, and quit therapy at the same time.

Thereafter, Arnold repeatedly tried on his own to stop using speed—but with little success. After a couple of weeks of drug abstinence, he would find himself back at the clubs and using speed again. His speed usage increased, and he began to use needles to intravenously inject the drug. That too increased until he would sometimes injected himself ten times a day. This pattern continued until he became psychotic one night and was admitted to a psychiatric emergency room.

In the hospital, Arnold gave the name of his former therapist. When called by the hospital, the therapist said he would not see Arnold again unless Arnold agreed to attend 12-step meetings. Arnold agreed to give the meetings a try.

Success did not come easily for Arnold, who repeatedly began to use speed again, although each period of usage grew shorter in duration. During each relapse, he stopped going to therapy and 12-step meetings. But each time he eventually returned to both. Finally, the combination began to take hold, and words that Arnold had heard so many times before made sense as if for the first time. Though he has been clean and sober for over a year now, Arnold still feels fragile and believes he cannot maintain his sobriety without the 12-step meetings, which he attends daily.

MENTAL HEALTH SELF-HELP GROUPS

12-step programs are perhaps the best-known self-help organizations, but they are not the only ones. There are self-help organizations for practically every mental or physical affliction. AIDS, cancer, depression, or life events such as death and grieving have all spawned self-help groups. Sometimes professionals are hired to facilitate or lecture at specific events, but the organizations are usually member led and member run.

Alice

Alice benefited from attending a self-help group sponsored by the Depressive and Manic Depressive Association. Alice's mother is bipolar (formerly called manic depressive). When in a manic state, Alice's mother is psychotic and paranoid, a danger to herself and others. Once, she drove her car through the front door of a hospital, smashing into the lobby.

Alice felt she needed support for dealing with her mother's illness. She went to her first self-help meeting and actually found two meetings,: one for persons diagnosed as bipolar, the other for their families and friends. At the latter meeting, Alice found the support she needed to deal with the emotional issues that arose from trying to care for her mother.

Edgar

Edgar also benefited from attending a self-help group sponsored by the Depressive and Manic Depressive Association. He had, over the course of many years, experienced a number of manic episodes, but he did not acknowledge that he was bipolar until his late 40s.

Though outgoing, jovial, and impish, Edgar was shy about revealing his emotional inner self. For several months he said he wanted to attend the self-help meeting, but each time something came up that prevented him from going. Finally, he attended a meeting and sat in on the group for those with a bipolar diagnosis. Though he attended only that one meeting, it helped him to feel less ashamed of his diagnosis and to be more open with others in his life about his condition.

Appendices

Appendix A
American Psychological Association Guidelines
for Psychotherapy with Lesbian, Gay, and Bisexual Clients
(from www.apa.org/pi/lgbc/guidelines.html)

Attitudes Toward Homosexuality and Bisexuality

Guideline 1. Psychologists understand that homosexuality and bisexuality are not indicative of mental illness.

Guideline 2. Psychologists are encouraged to recognize how their attitudes and knowledge about lesbian, gay, and bisexual issues may be relevant to assessment and treatment, and to seek consultation or make appropriate referrals when indicated.

Guideline 3. Psychologists strive to understand the ways in which social stigmatization (i.e., prejudice, discrimination, and violence) poses risks to the mental health and well-being of lesbian, gay, and bisexual clients.

Guideline 4. Psychologists strive to understand how inaccurate or prejudicial views of homosexuality or bisexuality may affect the client's presentation in treatment and the therapeutic process.

Relationships and Families

Guideline 5. Psychologists strive to be knowledgeable about and respect the importance of lesbian, gay, and bisexual relationships.

Guideline 6. Psychologists strive to understand the particular circumstances and challenges facing lesbian, gay, and bisexual parents.

Guideline 7. Psychologists recognize that the families of lesbian, gay, and bisexual people may include people who are not legally or biologically related.

Guideline 8. Psychologists strive to understand how a person's homosexual or bisexual orientation may have an impact on his or her family of origin and the relationship to that family of origin.

Issues of Diversity

Guideline 9. Psychologists are encouraged to recognize the particular life issues or challenges experienced by lesbian, gay, and bisexual members of racial and ethnic minorities that are related to multiple and often conflicting cultural norms, values, and beliefs.

Guideline 10. Psychologists are encouraged to recognize the particular challenges experienced by bisexual individuals.

Guideline 11. Psychologists strive to understand the special problems and risks that exist for lesbian, gay, and bisexual youth.

Guideline 12. Psychologists consider generational differences within lesbian, gay, and bisexual populations, and the particular challenges that may be experienced by lesbian, gay, and bisexual older adults.

Guideline 13. Psychologists are encouraged to recognize the particular challenges experienced by lesbian, gay, and bisexual individuals with physical, sensory, and/or cognitive/emotional disabilities.

Education

Guideline 14. Psychologists support the provision of professional education and training on lesbian, gay, and bisexual issues.

Guideline 15. Psychologists are encouraged to increase their knowledge and understanding of homosexuality and bisexuality through continuing education, training, supervision, and consultation.

Guideline 16. Psychologists make reasonable efforts to familiarize themselves with relevant mental health, educational, and community resources for lesbian, gay, and bisexual people.

Appendix B
Psychotherapy Groups aimed at People Who Are Queer

The following lists contain names of some of the many queer-affirmative groups that psychotherapists are either conducting or trying to form. The sheer variety of groups will give you some idea of the possibilities for queer-affirmative group therapy and support groups. There are many more groups beyond those listed here.

Groups Aimed at Gay Men
A Long and Happy Life: A Therapy Group for Gay Men Who Are HIV-Positive
A Support Group for Gay Men with Disabilities
Bereavement Group for Gay Men Whose Partners Have Died
Coming-out Support Group for Gay Men of All Ages
Constructing the Gay Self: A Group for Younger Men
Formerly Married Gay Men
Foundations of Flirting: A Supportive, Enriching, and Exploratory Group for Gay Men
Gay Men's Grief Group (facilitated by a lesbian)
Gay Men at Midlife
Gay Men's Recovery Group
Gay Men's Incest Survivor Therapy Group
How to be Loved: Intimacy Classes for Gay Men
Joy, Inspiration, and Hope: A Retreat for Gay Men
Men, Intimacy, and Sexuality: A Psychotherapy Group
Men Over 40: Weekend Retreats for Gay Men 40 and Beyond
Midlife, Ready or Not: A Workshop for Gay Men

Positive Men Together: Gay Men's HIV Psychotherapy Group
Psyche and Spirit: A Psychotherapy Group for Gay Men
    Interested in a Spiritual Life
Relationship Workshops for Gay Men
Shy Guy: A Group for Shy Gay Men
The Spiritual Self: A Group for Gay Men
Therapy Group for Gay Men From Dysfunctional Families
"We Are Family" for Gay Men

Groups Aimed at Lesbians
12-Week Single Lesbians Relationship Group
A Support Group for Lesbians Who Have Been Abused
    by Their Partners
A Room of One's Own: Lesbian Therapy Group
Brick by Brick, Petal by Petal: Lesbian Support Group
Formerly Married Lesbians
Lesbian Working Mom's Group
Lesbians in Midlife Therapy Group
Relationship Breakup Group for Lesbians Whose Relationships
    Have Ended
Sexual Healing: A Lesbian Couples Group for Sexual Abuse
    Survivors and Their Partners
Single Lesbians Relationship Group
Supportive Therapy for Lesbians
What About My Needs? For Partners of Lesbians Healing
    From Sexual Abuse

Groups Aimed at Bisexuals
Support Group for Bisexual Men

Groups Aimed at Transgendered Individuals
Transgender Parenting Group
Transgendered People in Transition

Groups Aimed at Queer People
Bringing the Family Together: A Group for Families
    With a Gay Member

Gay and Lesbian Adult Children of Aging Parents' Support Group
Lambda Youth Group: A Support Group for Gay, Lesbian,
    Bisexual, and Questioning Youth
Living and Loving: A Weekend Group for Gay and Bisexual Men

Groups Aimed at Queer Couples
Lesbian and Gay Couples Group for Parents (who have children
    of all ages)
Lesbian Couple Support Group
Soul Mates, Playmates, or Stable Mates? A Group
    for Gay Male Couples
Talking to Your Partner: A Therapy Group for Male Couples
Therapy Group for Gay Male Couples

Appendix C
Sample Letter From a Psychotherapist to a Surgeon in Support of Sexual Reassignment Surgery

The following is an example of a letter that was sent to a surgeon by the psychotherapist of a female-to-male transgendered client before sexual reassignment surgery.

Dear _____:

I have evaluated _____ in terms of his emotional preparedness for sexual reassignment surgery and find that he is making this decision with clarity and a wealth of information. He is consistent and thoughtful about having his physical body brought into synchronicity with his identity and deep sense of self as a male. He has been "passing" overtly, is "out" in all parts of his life, and sees this surgery as the first of two whereby he can finally function with his body matching his heart, mind, and soul. He has asked himself and others difficult questions and is making this decision from a position of emotional strength.

Sincerely,

Appendix D
Exercise: Finding the Right Therapist for You

The following exercise will help you better understand the type of person with whom you are likely to have the needed chemistry.

Take a piece of paper and fold it down the middle. On the left side write the answers to the following questions. Each question should have its own line.

Which of your parents did you get along with better?
Which parent did you respect the most?
Which of your family members and acquaintances are you most comfortable with?
Which of your family members and acquaintances do you consider wise?
Which of your family members and acquaintances would you like to be more like?
Who has helped you in your life?
Who has understood you in your life?
Who has listened to you in your life?

Now, on the right side of the paper, write the answers to these questions.

With whom have you had an especially bad relationship?
Who, if anyone, has abused you emotionally, physically, or sexually?
Who has ever terrorized you, brutalized you, or violated you in any way?

Who, if anyone, in your life has been addicted to alcohol or drugs?
With whom in your life have you had significant conflict?
Which of your family members and acquaintances do you
    consider distant?
Which of your family members and acquaintances do you feel
    dislikes you?
Which teacher did you dislike in school?
Who has ever bullied or teased you?
Who in particular drives you crazy?
With whom do you not work well?
Which of your friends consistently lead you astray?

The next step is to keep this paper handy while going through the process of finding your psychotherapist. If you have had a particularly good relationship with someone (people in your left-hand column), the characteristics of that person might be characteristics that would be good to look for in seeking a therapist. If you have had a particularly poor relationship with someone (people in the right-hand column), you might consider avoiding therapists who remind you of that person.

Your list, however, is merely a suggestive guide reminding you of those with whom you have had good and bad relationships and, hopefully, some of the characteristics and styles of those people. Some people may want to begin therapy with someone who has the characteristics and styles of a person with whom they have had a poor relationship. Because of that one negative relationship, they may find themselves reacting poorly to everyone with a similar personality, and they may want to change that. Choosing a therapist who reminds them of a person, but who is not that person, may enable them to have a positive experience with and learn to accept people with similar personality characteristics.

The choice is yours. It should be based on what issues and personal qualities are important to you.

Appendix E
Questions to Ask a Therapist

Consider asking a prospective therapist some of the following questions.

Attitude Toward Queerness
Do you believe in love between two people of the same sex?
Do you believe that sexual orientation can or should be changed?
Do you believe an openly lesbian, gay, bisexual, or transgendered
    person can live a spiritually rich and satisfying life?
Do you know of any happy and successful long-term same-sex
    couples?
How do you generally work with gay or lesbian people?

Training
What has been your training?
What degrees have you been awarded?
Was there a particular emphasis your training?
What postgraduate training programs have you completed?

Experience
How long have you been practicing psychotherapy?
Where else have you worked besides your present position?
What jobs or careers have you had besides being a psychotherapist?
What nonprofessional experiences have you had that qualify you
    for the work you are now doing?

Credentials

Are you licensed by the state in which you practice?

What license(s) do you hold?

Have any complaints been filed against you with either a state licensing board or any other professional ethics organization?

What was the outcome of those complaints?

Are you a member of any professional organizations?
Which ones?

What is the criteria for membership?

Do you hold any certificates from any professional organizations indicating you have a special expertise?

Professional Orientation

How do you describe your professional orientation to psychotherapy?

Which of the major schools of psychotherapy are the most attractive to you?

Competence

Have you treated other people with problems similar to mine?

How do you determine how often we should meet?

Can you prescribe psychoactive medications if I need them?
If not, do you work with a physician or a psychiatrist who can evaluate me and prescribe medication?

Are you willing to consult with other mental health or medical professionals with whom I have worked?

Do you consult with other professionals regarding individuals on your caseload? How do you guard my right to confidentiality in those situations?

Are you willing or able to see my family members or life partner if that should seem necessary? If so, can or should I be present? Will you ever meet with them without my being present?

Have you ever been sued for malpractice? What was the outcome of that lawsuit?

Business Practices

What is your fee?

Is there a sliding scale? If there is a sliding scale, how does it work?
Do you accept any medical insurance?
Do you participate in any managed care or PPO insurance plans
How do you handle the paperwork? Do you, or do I, have to fill out
   the paperwork?
What is your telephone availability? Do you encourage or
   discourage telephone contact between meetings?

Personal
Do you personally identify as queer, gay, lesbian, bisexual,
   transgendered, or questioning?
Do you identify as being clean and sober? If so, are you in recovery?
   Do you attend any 12-step groups?
What is your personal experience as a client in psychotherapy?
   How do you feel it benefited you?

**Comfort and Chemistry (Questions to Ask Yourself After the
Initial Meeting)**
Did you feel understood? Did the psychotherapist understand
   your reason for being there?
Did you feel liked by the psychotherapist?
Did you like the psychotherapist? Did you like his or her values?
Did you agree with them?
Did you have an initial feeling of trust in the psychotherapist?
Did the psychotherapist appear to be sensitive to your feelings?
Did you feel respected by the psychotherapist? Did you feel he or
   she was treating you as an equal?
Did you feel comfortable talking to this psychotherapist?
   Were you able to say what you wanted to say? Were you able
   to be yourself? Did you feel a need to hide anything?
   Were you honest?
Did the therapist convey a feeling of personal warmth?
Did the therapist seem to have a sense of humor? Was he or she
   overly serious?
Did you get a feeling this person was wise? Knowledgeable?
   Was he or she able to go past theories and understand the
   nature of the world?

Did he or she convey an interest in you and your reason for being in his or her office?

Did the therapist make eye contact with you? Was that comfortable for you?

Did you get any feedback from the psychotherapist? Was it helpful? Insightful? Did you come away with any greater understanding of yourself than you had before the first meeting?

Did you disagree with the psychotherapist at any point? How did that go? Was the therapist defensive? Could he or she disagree with you in a comfortable manner?

Do you look forward to talking with the psychotherapist again?

Appendix F
Sample Advertisements for Psychotherapy Services

The following ads were all taken from paid advertisements in queer newspapers.

Ad #1

(Name of referral service)
A nonprofit organization of psychotherapists provides free confidential referrals to licensed psychotherapists in the gay, lesbian, bisexual, and transgender communities. If you are looking for a qualified therapist in (name of area), call and we will provide timely referrals to meet your specific needs. Paid for by participating licensed psychotherapists.

(Name of referral service)
Therapist Referral Service
(Toll-free phone number)

Ad #2

John Doe, MFT
(License number)/Japanese spoken
Individual and Couples Therapy
Relationships/Grief and Loss
Abuse and Recovery Issues
Leather/SM and All Ethnic and Sexual Identities Welcome
(City), (Phone number)

AD #3

Psychotherapy Group for Gay Men
Beginning in May!
Intimacy
Sexuality
Relationships
Personal Growth

Individual Sessions Available

John Doe, Ph.D.
Licensed Psychologist, (License number)
(Phone number)
(E-mail address)

AD #4

Jane Doe, LCSW
18 years experience

Anger Management
Personal Growth
Breakup and Loss
Individuals and Couples
Transgender Issues

(City), (Phone number)

Resources

Reading Material

Relatively few books besides this one and its predecessor, *The Lavender Couch,* are aimed toward the queer consumer of psychotherapy. Most books about psychotherapy with queer people are compilations of articles written primarily with mental health professionals in mind. Nevertheless, the following annotated bibliography should be of help to anyone interested in pursuing further knowledge about aspects of queer mental health.

Alexander, Christopher J. (Ed.) (1996). *Gay and Lesbian Mental Health: A Sourcebook for Practitioners.* Binghamton, N.Y.: Haworth.

Alexander, Christopher J. (Ed.) (1998). *Working with Gay Men and Lesbians in Private Psychotherapy Practice.* Binghamton, N.Y.: Haworth. Most of the articles in this book focus on psychotherapy techniques for private practice clinicians who see queer clients.

American Psychiatric Association (1994). *Diagnostic and Statistical Manual of Mental Disorders, Fourth Edition.* Washington, DC: American Psychiatric Association. The bible of the American mental health profession, this book contains the diagnostic criteria used by most mental health professionals in the United States.

Cabaj, Robert P. and Terry S. Stein. (Eds.) (1996). *Textbook of Homosexuality.* Washington, DC: American Psychiatric Association. Although quite expensive, this is the most complete and extensive compilation of articles on issues related to queer mental health.

Davies, Dominic and Charles Neal. (Eds.) (1996). *Pink Therapy: A Guide for Counsellors and Therapists Working With Lesbian, Gay, and Bisexual Clients.* Buckingham, U.K.: Open University Press. Published in the United Kingdom, this selection of articles presents several distinctly British perspectives on psychotherapy with queer people.

Gonsiorek, John C. (Ed.) (1985). *A Guide to Psychotherapy with Gay and Lesbian Clients*. Binghamton, N.Y.: Harrington Park. This early compilation contains some classic articles on issues related to queer psychotherapy.

Hall, Marny. (1985). *The Lavender Couch: A Consumer's Guide to Psychotherapy for Lesbians and Gay Men*. Boston: Alyson. The book that inspired this book.

Laird, Joan and Green, Robert Jay (Eds.) (1996). *Lesbians and Gays in Couples and Families: A Handbook for Therapists*. San Francisco: Jossey-Bass. Therapists who work from a systems perspective write about issues faced by queer people. The book contains an article presenting my own research on gay male couples (chapter 8).

Mallon, Gerald P. (Ed) (1998). *Foundations of Social Work Practice with Lesbian and Gay Persons*. Binghamton, N.Y.: Haworth. A social work perspective on queer mental health is the focus of the articles in this collection.

Ross, Michael W. (Ed.) (1988). *Psychopathology and Psychotherapy in Homosexuality*. Binghamton, N.Y.: Haworth.

Shernoff, Michael (Ed.) (1996). *Human Services for Gay People: Clinical and Community Practice*. Binghamton, N.Y.: Haworth.

Shernoff, Michael (Ed.) (1999). *AIDS and Mental Health Practice: Clinical and Policy Issues*. Binghamton, N.Y.: Harrington Park. This grouping of articles related to AIDS and psychotherapy concentrates on the experiences of gay men. The book also includes my article on the psychological issues faced by persons with HIV/AIDS when they return to work (chapter 2).

Internet Resources

Main Queer Directories

Lavender Links: www.pacificcenter.org/lavlinks.html
The Lavender Pages: www.lavenderpages.com
Queer Resource Directory (QRD): www.qrd.org/qrd/
PlanetOut: www.planetout.com/pno/search/

Queer-affirmative Psychotherapy Sites

American Psychological Association Guidelines for
    Psychotherapy with Lesbian, Gay, & Bisexual Clients:
    www.apa.org/pi/lgbc/guidelines.html

Mental Health Sites

Behave.net includes *DSM IV* criteria for many disorders,
    but be aware of the behavioral psychology bias:
    www.behave.net.com
Internet Mental Health, a free Web encyclopedia of mental
    health information: www.mentalhealth.com
MADNESS: An online discussion site for users of mental health
    services. To subscribe, send an E-mail with the message
    "subscribe madnesss" to LISTSERV@maelstrom.stjohns.edu
    and then type in your first and last names.
Mental Health InfoSource: www.mhsource.com
Mental Health Net, Professional Resources Index is a good
    general site for both professionals and clients. It includes
    DSM codes and diagnostic criteria:
    http://mentalhelp.net/prof.htm
National Institute of Mental Health (NIMH):
    www.nimh.nih.gov/
Online Sexual Addiction:
    www.onlinesexaddict.com

Psych Central, Dr. John Grohol's Mental Health Page,
an index for psychology, support, and mental health
issues and resources: http://psychcentral.com
Web MD, a comprehensive health Web site that includes
mental health resources: http://my.webmd.com/index

GENERAL HEALTH SITES

ZapHeath.com is an easily navigated health Web site
with a youthful slant: www.zaphealth.com

PSYCHOPHARMACOLOGY INFORMATION SITES

Drugs, Brains and Behavior (an online clinicians' textbook
by C. Robin Timmons and Leonard W. Hamilton):
www.rci.rutgers.edu/~lwh/drugs/
Dr. Bob's Psychopharmacology Tips (Dr. Bob is actually
an assistant professor of clinical psychiatry at the
University of Chicago; despite his disclaimer he offers
only tips and not scientific study results, this site is
packed with useful medication information):
www.dr-bob.org/tips/

TRANSGENDER SITES

International Transgender Online Magazine:
www.internationaltg.com
National Transgender Advocacy Coalition:
www.ntac.org
St. Louis Gender Foundation:
http://hometown.aol.com/stlgf1/index.html
Transgendered Christian Resource:
http://home1.gte.net/kstampa/frontpage.htm
Transgender Resource Guide (books, videos, and magazines
for and about cross-dressers, transvestites, transsexuals,
and transgender issues):
http://209.140.229.98/gnu.html

Telephone Hotlines

AIDS Hotlines

CDC National AIDS Hotline:
(800) 342-AIDS (342-2437)
CDC National AIDS Hotline TTY Service:
(800) 243-7889
La Línea Nacional del SIDA de los CDC Servicio en Español:
(800) 344 SIDA (344-7432)
Project Inform HIV/AIDS Treatment Hotline:
(800) 822-7422

Child Abuse Hotlines

National Child Abuse Hotline:
(800) 4-A-CHILD
National Child Abuse TDD Service:
(800) 2-A-CHILD

Domestic Violence Hotlines

National Domestic Violence Hotline:
(800) 799-SAFE (799-7233)
National Domestic Violence TTY Service:
(800) 787-3224

Sexually Transmitted Diseases Hotlines

National STD Hotline: (800) 227-8922

Substance Abuse Hotlines

SAMHSA, Center for Substance Abuse Treatment (CSAT)
National Drug and Alcohol Treatment Hotline
(Assists consumers in finding substance abuse treatment
in their communities):
(800) 662-HELP

SAMHSA, Center for Substance Abuse Prevention (CSAP)
Workplace Helpline
(Confidential consultations to employers, unions, and
community-based substance abuse prevention organizations
on the development and implementation of workplace
prevention programs and other related initiatives):
(800) WORKPLACE

SUICIDE PREVENTION HOTLINES

San Francisco Suicide Prevention (SFSP)
www.sfsuicide.org
(415) 781-0500
The Samaritans (UK and Republic of Ireland)
E-mail: jo@samaritans.org
United Kingdom: 08457 90 90 90
Republic of Ireland: 1850 60 90 90
National Adolescent Suicide Hotline
(800) 621-4000
Suicide National Hotline
(800) SUICIDE (784-2433)

OTHER HOTLINES

National Youth Crisis Hotline: (800) HIT-HOME
Panic Disorder Information Line: (800) 64-PANIC

Mental Health Organizations

American Association of Suicidology
4201 Connecticut Ave. N.W., Suite 408
Washington, DC 20008
Phone: (202) 237-2280; Fax: (202) 237-2282
www.suicidology.org
E-mail: ajkulp@suicidology.org

Befrienders International Central Office
(This international organization based in the U.K. offers support
to people around the world who are in crisis or suicidal.
Check out Befrienders' multilingual Web site.)
26/27 Market Place
Kingston upon Thames
Surrey KT1 1JH
United Kingdom
Phone: +44(0) 20 8541 4949; Fax: +44(0) 20 8549 1544
www.befrienders.org

National Alliance for the Mentally Ill
Colonial Place Three
2107 Wilson Blvd., Suite 300
Arlington, VA 22201-3042
Toll-free Helplines: (800) 950-NAMI (950-6264)
Phone: (703) 524-7600; Fax: (703) 524-9094
TDD: (703) 516-7227
www.nami.org

National Depressive and Manic-Depressive Association
730 N. Franklin St., Suite 501
Chicago, IL 60610-7204
Phone: (800) 826-3632, (312) 642-0049; Fax: (312) 642-7243
www.ndmda.org
E-mail: arobinson@ndmda.org

National Mental Health Consumers Self-Help Clearinghouse
1211 Chestnut St., Suite 1207
Philadelphia, PA 19107
Phone: (800) 553-4539, (215) 751-1810;
Fax: (215) 636-6312
www. mhselfhelp.org; E-mail: info@mhselfhelp.org

National Self-Help Clearinghouse
CUNY Graduate School
365 Fifth Ave., Suite 3300
New York, NY 10016
Phone: (212) 817-1822
www.selfhelpweb.org

PROFESSIONAL ORGANIZATIONS

American Academy of Child and Adolescent Psychiatry
3615 Wisconsin Ave. N.W.
Washington, D.C. 20016-3007
Phone: (202) 966-7300; Fax: (202) 966-2891
www.aacap.org

American Art Therapy Association, Inc.
1202 Allanson Rd.
Mundelein, IL 60060-3808
Phone: (847) 949-6064, (888) 290-0878; Fax: (847) 566-4580
www.arttherapy.org
E-mail: arttherapy@ntr.net

American Association for Marriage and Family Therapy
1133 15th St. N.W., Suite 300
Washington, DC 20005-2710
Phone: (202) 452-0109; Fax: (202) 223-2329
www.aamft.org
E-mail: centraloffice@aamft.org

American Association of Pastoral Counselors
9504-A Lee Hwy.
Fairfax, VA 22031-2303
Phone: (703) 385-6967; Fax: (703) 352-7725
www.aapc.org
E-mail: info@aapc.org

American Association of Sex Educators, Counselors,
and Therapists (AASECT)
P.O. Box 5488
Richmond, VA 23220-0488
www.aasect.org
E-mail: AASECT@worldnet.att.net

American Dance Therapy Association
2000 Century Plaza, Suite 108
10632 Little Patuxent Pkwy.
Columbia, MD 21044
Phone: (410) 997-4040; Fax: (410) 997-4048
www.adta.org
E-mail: info@adta.org

American Medical Association
515 N. State St.
Chicago, IL 60610
Phone: (312) 464-5000
www.ama-assn.org

American Psychoanalytic Association
309 E. 49th St.
New York, New York 10017
Phone: (212) 752-0450; Fax: (212) 593-0571
www.apsa.org
E-mail: central.office@apsa.org

American Psychiatric Association
1400 K St. N.W.
Washington, DC 20005
Phone: (888) 357-7924; Fax: (202) 682-6850
www.psych.org
E-mail: apa@psych.org

American Psychological Association
750 First St. N.E.
Washington, DC 20002-4242
Phone: (800) 374-2721, (202) 336-5500
www.apa.org

American Society of Addiction Medicine
4601 N. Park Ave., Arcade Suite 101
Chevy Chase, MD 20815
Phone: (301) 656-3920; Fax: (301) 656-3815
www.asam.org
E-mail: Email@asam.org

Association for Transpersonal Psychology
P.O. Box 29030
San Francisco, California 94129-0030
Phone: (415) 561-3382: Fax: (415) 561-3383
www.atpweb.org
E-mail: atpweb@mindspring.com

California Association of Marriage and Family Therapists
7901 Raytheon Rd.
San Diego, CA 92111-1606
Phone: (858) 292-2638; TTY: (858) 292-2650
www.camft.org

Canadian Psychological Association
151 Slater St., Suite 205
Ottawa, Ontario, Canada K1P 5H3
Phone: (888) 472-0657; Fax: (613) 237-1674
www.cpa.ca
E-mail: cpamemb@cpa.ca

Gay and Lesbian Medical Association
459 Fulton St., Suite 107
San Francisco, CA 94102
Phone: (415) 255-4547; Fax: (415) 255-4784
www.glma.org
E-mail: info@glma.org

National Association for Music Therapy
8455 Colesville Rd., Suite 1000
Silver Spring, MD 20910
Phone: (301) 589-3300; Fax: (301) 589-5175
www.musictherapy.org
E-mail: info@musictherapy.org

National Association of Social Workers
750 First St. N.E., Suite 700
Washington, DC 20002-4241
Phone: (800) 638-8799; (202) 408-8600
www.naswdc.org
E-mail: website@naswdc.org

Sandplay Therapists of America/
International Society for Sandplay Therapy
P.O. Box 4847
Walnut Creek, CA 94596
Phone: (310) 607-8535
www.sandplay.org
E-mail: sta@sandplay.org

Society for the Scientific Study of Sexuality (SSSS)
P.O. Box 416
Allentown, PA 18105
Phone: (610) 530-2483; Fax: (610) 530-2485
www.ssc.wisc.edu/ssss/index.html
E-mail: thesociety@inetmail.att.net

Queer Organizations

National Gay and Lesbian Task Force
1700 Kalorama Rd. N.W.
Washington, DC 20009-2624
Phone: (202) 332-6483; Fax: (202) 332-0207
TTY: (202) 332-6219
www.ngltf.org
E-mail: ngltf@ngltf.org

GLAAD (Gay & Lesbian Alliance Against Defamation)
Offices in Atlanta, Kansas City, Los Angeles, New York,
San Francisco, and Washington, D.C.
Phone: (800) GAY-MEDIA
www.glaad.org
E-mail: glaad@glaad.org

Human Rights Campaign
919 18th St. N.W.
Washington, DC 20006
Phone: (202) 628-4160; Fax: (202) 347-5323
www.hrc.org
E-mail: hrc@hrc.org

The Institute for Gay and Lesbian Strategic Studies (IGLSS)
Main Office: P.O. Box 53036
Washington, D.C. 20009-3036
Research Office: P.O. Box 2603
Amherst, MA 01004-2603
Phone: (413) 577-0145
www.iglss.org

Substance Abuse Information

American Council for Drug Education,
An Affiliate of the Phoenix House Foundation
164 W. 74th St.
New York, NY 10023
Phone: (800) 488-DRUG (488-3784)
www.acde.org
E-mail: acde@phoenixhouse.org

Center for Substance Abuse Prevention, Substance Abuse and
Mental Health Services Administration (SAMHSA)
Workplace Helpline
Phone: (800) WORKPLACE

Center for Substance Abuse Treatment, Substance Abuse,
and Mental Health Services Administration (SAMHSA),
National Alcohol and Drug Treatment Hotline
Phone: (800) 662-HELP

National Association of State Alcohol and Drug Abuse
Directors, Inc. (NASADAD)
808 17th St. N.W., Suite 410
Washington, DC 20006
Phone: (202) 293-0090; Fax: (202) 293-1250
www.nasadad.org
E-mail: dcoffice@nasadad.org

National Council on Alcoholism and Drug Dependence (NCADD)
20 Exchange Pl., Suite 2902
New York, NY 10005
Phone: (212) 269-7797; Fax: (212) 269-7510
Hope Line: (800) NCA-CALL (24-hour affiliate referral)
www.ncadd.org
E-mail: national@ncadd.org

National Clearinghouse for Alcohol and Drug Information,
A Service of SAMHSA, the Substance Abuse and Mental Health
Services Administration
P.O. Box 2345
Rockville, MD 20847-2345
Phone: (800) 729-6686
www.health.org
E-mail: webmaster@health.org

National Inhalant Prevention Coalition
2904 Kerbey Lane
Austin, TX 78703
Phone: (800) 269-4237, (512) 480-8953; Fax: (512) 477-3932
www.inhalants.org
E-mail: nipc@io.com

12-STEP PROGRAMS

FOR ALCOHOLICS

Alcoholics Anonymous (AA) World Services, Inc.
475 Riverside Dr., 11th Floor
New York, NY 100115
Phone: (212) 870-3400
www.aa.org

Dual Recovery Anonymous, Central Service Office
P.O. Box 218232
Nashville, TN 37221-8232
Phone: (877) 883-2332, (888) 869-9230; Fax: (615) 742-1009
http://draonline.org

Moderation Management Network, Inc.
(A non-12-step program for people who want to quit drinking)
P.O. Box 3055
Point Pleasant, New Jersey 08742
Phone: (732) 295-0949
www.moderation.org
E-mail: moderation@moderation.org

Secular Organizations for Sobriety National Clearinghouse
The Center for Inquiry – West
(A non-12-step program for people who want to quit drinking)
5519 Grosvenor Blvd.
Los Angeles, CA 90066
Voice mail: (310) 821-8430; Fax: (310) 821-2610
www.secularhumanism.org/sos/
E-mail : jimc@secularsobriety.org

For Drug Addicts

Cocaine Anonymous (CA)
World Service Office
3740 Overland Ave., Suite C
Los Angeles, CA 90034-6337
Phone: (800) 347-8998, (310) 559-5833; Fax: (310) 559-2554
www.cocaineanonymous.org
E-mail: publicinfo@ca.org

Dual Recovery Anonymous
Central Service Office
P.O. Box 218232
Nashville, TN 37221-8232
Phone: (877) 883-2332, (888) 869-9230; Fax: (615) 742-1009
http://draonline.org

Marijuana Anonymous World Services
P. O. Box 2912
Van Nuys, CA 91404
Phone: (800) 766-6779
www.marijuana-anonymous.org
E-mail: office@marijuana-anonymous.org

Narcotics Anonymous (NA) World Services, Inc.
P.O. Box 9999
Van Nuys, CA 91409
Phone: (818) 773-9999; Fax: (818) 700-0700
www.na.org;
E-mail: fsmail@na.org

For Gambling Addicts

Gamblers Anonymous
International Service Office
P. O. Box 17173
Los Angeles, CA 90017
Phone: (213) 386-8789; Fax: (213) 386-0030
www.gamblersanonymous.org
E-mail: isomain@gamblersanonymous.org

For Sex Addicts

Sexaholics Anonymous (SA)
P.O. Box 111910
Nashville, TN 37222-1910
Phone: (615) 331-6230; Fax: (615) 331-6901
www.sa.org
E-mail: saico@sa.org

Sex and Love Addicts Anonymous (SLAA)
P.O. Box 338
Norwood, MA 02062-0338
Phone: (781) 255-8825
www.slaafws.org
E-mail: Generalinfo@slaafws.org

Sex Addicts Anonymous (SAA)
P.O. Box 70949
Houston, TX 77270
Phone: (800) 477-8191, (713) 869-4902
www.sexaa.org
E-mail: info@saa-recovery.org

Sexual Compulsives Anonymous (SCA)
Old Chelsea Station, P.O. Box 1585
New York, NY 10011
Phone: (800) 977-HEAL
www.sca-recovery.org
E-mail:info@sca-recovery.org

FOR SEXUAL TRAUMA SURVIVORS:

Survivors of Incest Anonymous (SIA)
World Service Office
P.O. Box 190
Benson, MD 21018
Phone: (410) 893-3322
www.siawso.org

Incest Survivors Anonymous (ISA)
P.O. Box 17245
Long Beach, CA 90807-7245
Phone: (562) 428-5599
www.cs.utk.edu/~bartley/other/ISA.html

Sexual Assault Recovery Anonymous (SARA, Sarateen)
P.O. Box 16
Surrey, BC V3T 4W4, Canada
Phone: (604) 584-2626; Fax: (604) 584-2888
www2.vpl.vancouver.bc.ca/dbs/cod/orgpgs/1/1043.html

FOR THE PARTNERS OR FAMILY MEMBERS OF ALCOHOLICS

Al-Anon/Alateen Family Group Headquarters, Inc.
1600 Corporate Landing Parkway
P.O. Box 862
Virginia Beach, VA. 23454-5617
Phone: (888) 4AL-ANON
www.al-anon.org
E-mail: WSO@al-anon.org

Children of Alcoholics Foundation
164 W. 74th St.
New York, NY 10023
Phone: (212) 595-5810 Ext. 7760
www.coaf.org
E-mail: coaf@phoenixhouse.org

CoAnon Family Groups
P.O. Box 12124
Tucson, AZ 85732-2124
Phone: (520) 513-5028
www.co-anon.org

National Association for Children of Alcoholics
11426 Rockville Pike, Suite 100
Rockville, MD 20852
Phone: (888) 554-COAS, (301) 468-0985; Fax: (301) 468-0987
www.nacoa.net
E-mail: nacoa@erols.com

Drug Addicts

CoAnon Family Groups
P.O. Box 12124
Tucson, AZ 85732-2124
Phone: (520) 513-5028
www.co-anon.org

Nar-Anon Family Groups
P.O. Box 2562
Palos Verdes Peninsula, CA 90274
Phone: (310) 547-5800
www.onlinerecovery.org/co/nfg

Sex Addicts

Codependents of Sex Addicts (COSA)
National Service Organization
P.O. Box 14537
Minneapolis, MN 55414
Phone: (763) 537-6904
www2.shore.net/~cosa/
E-mail: cosa@shore.net

S-Anon International Family Groups
P.O. Box 111242
Nashville, TN 37222-1242
Phone: (615) 833-3152
www.sanon.org
E-mail: sanon@sanon.org

Recovering Couples Anonymous (RCA)
P.O. Box 11029
Oakland, CA 94611
Phone: (510) 336-3300
www.recovering-couples.org
E-mail: RCAWSO@iname.com